"Dave Walsh is the kind of guy you wish lived down the block (or, perhaps, down the hall), so you could have ready access to his wise, compassionate advice. Having this book by your bedside is a close second. His clear, thoughtful, real-world suggestions for how parents can best set loving limits will forever change the way you think about discipline and will make a significant, positive difference in your family's quality of life."

—Ann Pleshette Murphy, *Good Morning America*'s parenting expert and author of *The 7 Stages of Motherhood: Loving Your Life Without Losing Your Mind*

"Dr. Walsh's new book arrives in the Land of Immediate Gratification just in time. In it, he discusses discipline and self-restraint from neurological, developmental, familial, and cultural points of view. Walsh is an excellent scientist and cultural observer who gives sage, sensitive, and practical advice. *No* should be required reading for every parent who walks out of a hospital with a newborn."

—Mary Pipher, PhD, author of *Reviving Ophelia*

"A comprehensive guide, it is not just about how to say No, but gives sound, practical advice that will help parents raise considerate, motivated children who will succeed in school, jobs, and life. The chapter on self-esteem alone is worth the price of the book. *No* will help today's parents avoid raising the next Generation Me."

—Jean Twenge, PhD, professor of psychology, San Diego State University, author of *Generation Me: Why Today's Young Americans Are More Confident, Assertive, Entitled—and More Miserable—Than Ever Before*

*f*P

Also by David Walsh, PhD

*Why Do They Act That Way? A Survival Guide to
the Adolescent Brain for You and Your Teen
Dr. Dave's Cyberhood
Selling Out America's Children
Designer Kids*

NO

Why Kids—of All Ages—
Need to Hear It
and Ways Parents Can Say It

David Walsh, PhD

FREE PRESS
New York London Toronto Sydney

FREE PRESS
A Division of Simon & Schuster, Inc.
1230 Avenue of the Americas
New York, NY 10020

First Free Press trade paperback edition September 2007

FREE PRESS and colophon are
trademarks of Simon & Schuster, Inc.

For information about special discounts for bulk purchases,
please contact Simon & Schuster Special Sales at
1-800-456-6798 or business@simonandschuster.com

Designed by Davina Mock

Manufactured in the United States of America

10 9 8 7 6 5 4

The Library of Congress has catalogued the hardcover edition
as follows:
Walsh, David Allen.
NO: why kids–of all ages–need to hear it and ways parents can say it /
David Walsh.
p. cm.
Includes bibliographical references and index.
1. Child rearing. 2. Parenting. 3. Parent and child. 4. Character. I. Title.
HQ769 .W195 2007
649'.7–dc22   2006046854

ISBN-13: 978-0-7432-8917-7
ISBN-10:   0-7432-8917-X
ISBN-13: 978-0-7432-8920-7 (pbk)
ISBN-10:   0-7432-8920-X (pbk)

To Josephine Donnelly
1946–2005
Brian's Godmother, a Gifted Teacher, and a Wonderful Friend

Contents

NO

ONE

No: Why Kids Need It

Not too long ago, I was standing in line in a Target store behind a man and his young son, whose age I would guess at about three. Everything was fine until the boy looked to the left and found himself staring at a row of candy bars.

"Daddy, can I have one?" he asked as he grabbed and held one up for his father to see.

"No, not now. We're going to have dinner as soon as we get home," the father replied. A look of concern flitted across the dad's face, and I soon discovered why.

At hearing *No,* the three-year-old began a seemingly well-rehearsed routine. The young boy pleaded and whined. The father hung tough for a few minutes, but his resolve crumbled when the young extortionist brought out the heavy artillery: a full-throated wail. "I want one," he screamed loud enough that everyone within fifty feet could hear.

The father held out for one more second and then caved in. "Oh, all right. You can choose one. Now stop screaming."

The boy defiantly picked out *two* candy bars and looked up to check out the response. The dad reminded his son that he had said *one,* and the wailing resumed. "Okay, okay, but no more," the father said in a loud whisper. Realizing he was on a roll, the kid grabbed a third candy bar. When the father reached down to take it away, the boy let out an ear-splitting shriek and started a Milky Way tug-of-war. The battle ended quickly, but the three-year-old was the clear victor: He left with three candy bars and his father left muttering and beaten. This boy not only won the candy bar skirmish, he learned an enduring lesson: *No* does not mean no. *No* signals that it's time to escalate.

Every parent is familiar with these battles. We console ourselves by thinking, It's only a candy bar, or, It's not worth having a meltdown. Unfortunately, the stakes get a lot higher as the years go by. I recently had a conversation with parents who gave their sixteen-year-old daughter permission to go on an unchaperoned trip to Mexico over spring break with a group of friends. They talked with me after attending one of my seminars on the teenage brain, which are based on my last book, *Why Do They Act That Way?*

The mother spoke first. "We're really worried about what might happen on this spring break trip after listening to you tonight. Do you think we made a mistake?"

"Were you comfortable with your decision before tonight?" I responded.

"Not really," she answered. "We never thought it was a good idea. But now we're really worried."

"Why did you say yes?" I asked.

After exchanging uneasy glances, the father spoke. "We said no at first, but our daughter was relentless. When we found out that all her friends were going we finally gave in. We made a deal with her that she has to call us every day and check in. We also laid down the law about drinking, drugs, and sex."

"It sounds like you weren't comfortable with your decision even before you came here tonight. Am I right about that?"

"Yes, you're right," the mother blurted. "I'm worried sick about what might happen. I'll be holding my breath until she gets home."

She looked at her husband. "I just hate being in this position. We either let her go with the other kids or she makes life miserable for months."

The spring break trip and the Milky Way battle have a lot in common. While the stakes are a lot higher for the parents of teenagers, the difficulty in saying no is the same. The importance of saying and sticking to No is the same as well.

No: A Small but Important Word

No is just one syllable. It's easy to spell. It's shorter than *Yes.* Still, it's a word that many children and teens don't understand or pretend not to understand. Yet, No is even more important for children and teens than Yes. No builds a foundation for self-discipline, self-respect and respect for others, integrity, perseverance, and a host of other character traits that lead to a happy, productive life. In spite of its importance, however, more and more parents have a hard time saying it. Time and time again, sometimes in inconsequential moments and sometimes at crucial crossroads, we aren't able to say no even when we know we should. That's too bad, because given the latest research and a mounting pile of newspaper headlines, today's youngsters need a heaping helping of No.

Why Could My Mother Say It?

When I was eight years old the most welcome sound on a summer day was the bell on the ice cream truck as it made its way through our neighborhood. At the first chime we would all take off running for our houses as fast as we could. When I got home I would search the house till I found my mother. Out of breath, I would still manage to ask, in as plaintive a tone as I could muster, "Mom, the ice cream man is coming. All the other kids are getting something; can I please have some money for ice cream?"

More often than not my mother would smile and answer calmly, "I don't think so. Not today, David." Her tone wasn't angry or mean. She just said no. I, of course, would usually raise the ante in whatever way I hoped would change her mind. Sometimes I attempted to charm; other times I tried to bargain. Thinking that money was the issue, I tried something like, "Aw, Mom, c'mon. I'll get the cheapest thing. He has Popsicles for ten cents; that's what I'll get."

"No, not today." Her expression didn't change.

"Ten cents? C'mon, Mom, can't you spare ten cents?"

I can still hear her response. "David, it has nothing to do with the money. Sure I can afford ten cents, but I want you to learn something important: You don't always get what you want." This made no sense to me at all at the age of eight. As I recall, I usually protested awhile longer, until I saw that my attempts to change her mind were futile. Then I left and complained to my friends as they ate their ice cream.

It's funny that years later I still remember those scenes. Now, however, I understand how wise she was and can appreciate the important lesson she was trying to teach me. The truth is, we don't always get what we want. Ironically, people who learn that lesson seem to be the most fulfilled. So we're not doing our kids any favors when we teach them that the world will always serve up whatever they want on a silver platter. But that's what most of us do day in and day out when we forget the important lessons of No.

Why do so many adults today have more trouble saying no to our kids than our parents and grandparents did? It's not hard to understand. It's because all of us, parents and kids together, swim in a culture that says *Yes.* As we'll explore further in chapter 2, popular culture brainwashes us into thinking that we all deserve whatever we want whenever we want it. For instance, an ad for a ski shop in this morning's newspaper screamed out a variation of what we see and hear every day. In bold print it read, "Delayed Gratification Stinks. Buy 'Em and Ski 'Em in the Same Day." As we all become infected with this inability to deny or delay, we parents find it more and more difficult to teach our children that they're better off without some of what they want.

Of course, parents should not always deny their children's

wishes. Skillful parenting means saying no when we ought to. Part of loving, caring for, and guiding our kids is helping them harness their powerful urges, wants, and desires. Otherwise their out-of-control emotions can overrun and control them rather than the other way around. Kids need the coping skills and the perspective they can only learn from the well-placed *No*. That's as true for the honor roll student as it is for the troubled teen.

Saying no isn't just using tough love or treating your child harshly in order to help him or her in the long run. In fact, saying no in the wrong way or in the wrong situation is just as bad as not saying it enough. It's important to know when and how to use No so that, instead of stunting your children's growth, No helps them bloom and become more vigorous, strong, and productive.

The Parent Tool Kit

In today's permissive society, many parents think they can't say no. They feel sometimes that they've lost their bearings on when no is appropriate and when it is heavy-handed or overprotective. Saying no is sometimes misconstrued as naysaying, of being someone with a negative attitude who simply opposes suggestions or denies permission in a reflexive, mean way. But that's not what I'm talking about when I suggest you say no to your children. I'm urging you to take a strong parental stance with your children because they depend on you to help them learn to manage their desires so that someday they can do it effectively for themselves.

To help you figure out when to say no, why you should but don't, or when you're on track with saying and sticking to No, I've included a Parent Tool Kit in many chapters. The tool kit contains the knowledge, attitudes, and skills you need for saying no and the many ways of saying it. The more items you have, the better prepared you'll be for this important parenting responsibility. A well-stocked kit also helps you build up your kids for what life will dish out to them and will help them develop the inner strength and emotional resiliency they'll need.

The Parent Tool Kits ask a set of questions. The more you answer yes, the better equipped you are. In each chapter, we'll talk about how to improve your ability to say no.

Here's the first set of questions:

PARENT TOOL KIT

What I Learned about *No* from My Parents

Yes	No		
☐	☐	1.	My parents expected me to do household chores when I was a child.
☐	☐	2.	My parents had clear rules that I was expected to follow.
☐	☐	3.	My parents consistently enforced the family rules.
☐	☐	4.	My parents modeled respectful attitudes and language and insisted on respect from us kids.
☐	☐	5.	My parents encouraged us to share.
☐	☐	6.	My parents consistently backed up my teachers.
☐	☐	7.	My parents taught me to consider other people's needs as well as my own.
☐	☐	8.	My parents made sure that we didn't always get what we wanted.
☐	☐	9.	My parents enforced rules about TV and other media.
☐	☐	10.	My parents expected me to do as well in school as I could.

If you found yourself agreeing with the statements in the tool kit, you already have a good foundation on which to build. If you found yourself answering no to some items, you may want to do things differently than your parents by the time you finish this book.

In the following pages, I will explain why kids need No now more than ever and how we can say it.

The Stakes Are High: A Culture of Disrespect

My good friend Josie had been a teacher for more than thirty years. Not long ago as she walked to her classroom she saw a boy running down the hall toward her. She had probably asked thousands of energetic ten-year-olds to slow down over the years so she instinctively did what all teachers do: She reminded him to walk in the hallway. She wasn't prepared for what happened next, however. Instead of slowing down or offering an apology, the boy launched into a barrage of profanity.

As she recounted the experience, I asked her how she felt. "Discouraged," was her response. "Sometimes it feels like, instead of teaching, I'm all alone swimming against a riptide of disrespect."

I've heard the same story dozens of times in one form or another. Adults, especially teachers, witness kids adopting R-rated language, rude attitudes, and less-than-subtle threats on an alarmingly regular basis. Another friend of mine, who teaches in Oakland, California, sent an e-mail not long ago saying that, for her and many colleagues, teaching has become mostly behavior management because students are so ill-equipped to pay attention that they constantly find new ways to disrupt the whole class. She spends 80 percent of her time trying to get her students to pay attention, and only 20 percent actually teaching. When I shared her e-mail during a teachers' workshop in Minnesota a week later, heads all over the room nodded in agreement.

Telling teachers just to foster a better atmosphere of respect is a classic case of easier said than done. Too many teachers aren't dealing with just a few unruly kids, they're contending with a culture of disrespect. One out of three teachers told Public Agenda pollsters in 2004 that they were so discouraged by student behavior that they were seriously considering abandoning their profession. Administrators now wear bulletproof vests in some of our high schools. Only 55 percent of high school students themselves say that they feel safe at school. More and more students enter their schools through metal detectors under the scrutiny of security guards or police officers.

In the spring of 2006, the New York City school system began to enforce the ban on students' bringing electronic devices into the public schools. The school chancellor announced the random placement of metal detectors in schools throughout the city, and as a result more than eight hundred cell phones were confiscated.

Jesse Scaccia, a film producer and a former schoolteacher, wrote perceptively in a *New York Times* op-ed piece (May 23, 2006) that "cellphones do not belong in the classroom. A student with a cellphone is an uninterested student, one with a short attention span who cares more about his social life than education."

Yet, what did parents do when the school system enforced the ban? They protested, saying that cell phones were equal to safety for their children. And they threatened to bring lawsuits. Why can't these parents say no to their children and support the authorities in banning cell phones from the classroom?

Scaccia poses several questions for parents: When was there a truly urgent need to call your child and why wouldn't phoning the school office in order to reach him be fast enough? Scaccia writes, "Do you know why your children really want to take cellphones to school?" The main reason is that cell phones are status symbols, they make the kids look cool, or even funny when the cell phone rings and makes the class laugh while the teacher is talking—trying to teach your children something. Scaccia concludes, "There are legitimate causes that parents should be taking on. Rally against crowding in the classroom. Fight against the oppressive and culturally biased . . . tests. But you're wrong on this cellphone issue. In this case, you are part of the problem, not the solution."

The data keeps rolling in. An Associated Press–Ipsos poll released in October 2005 found that nearly 70 percent of Americans said that children are ruder than they were twenty or thirty years ago. Millions watch the ABC program *Supernanny* to try to get their kids to behave civilly. Dr. Jean Twenge, social psychologist and author of *Generation Me,* released results of a study in April 2006 that showed that children today really are ruder than previous generations.

The Stakes Are High: Academic Achievement

A less civil school climate also affects academic performance in three ways: First, energy and attention devoted to classroom management detracts from energy devoted to learning. Second, the constant undertone of tension, anxiety, and chaos makes learning more difficult. Third, the academic expectations for all kids, even the well behaved, sink. Ask any teacher in any part of the country and he or she will share the unspoken deal commonly found in classrooms: "You'll get a decent grade if you don't give me trouble in class." When good behavior was taken for granted, excellent grades meant exceptional academic performance. Today, many students can do just fine as long as they behave better than the troublemakers. Yet, this is taking a big toll on what our kids actually learn.

This decline in learning and true academic achievement—not just good grades for good behavior—isn't new; it's been slipping for decades. For almost a century, we Americans prided ourselves on having the smartest kids and the best schools in the world. The industrial and technological strength that we had as a result made the decisive difference in World War II and for several decades afterward. But a wake-up call came in 1983, and it was a thunderclap. An eighteen-member National Commission on Excellence in Education published a thirty-six-page report, *A Nation at Risk,* which alerted the country to how dangerously far American education had slipped.

The commission reported that American kids were less accomplished when compared with students in other countries. Out of twenty-one countries in which a group of achievement tests was given for mathematics, the sciences, and other skills, U.S. students ranked dead last in seven of the nineteen categories and did not rank number one or two in any.

"The educational foundations of our society are presently being eroded by a rising tide of mediocrity," wrote the commission. "If an unfriendly foreign power had attempted to impose on America the mediocre educational performance that exists today, we might well have viewed it as an act of war. We have, in effect, been committing an unthinking, unilateral educational disarmament. History is not kind to ditherers."

That report shocked a lot of people with its message that our kids weren't at the top of the class compared to those in our peer nations. In fact, they were much farther down in the pack than anyone ever suspected. So for the last twenty years or more, we've had one initiative after another trying to get our kids back on track academically, but it's still hard to find good news. The latest international comparison was done in 2003, and American eighth graders ranked fourteenth in math and tied for ninth in science.

These numbers indicate a major problem in our schools and it stems partly from an erosion in children's self-discipline and in what used to be known as the work ethic. It is true that schools need to be funded better, teachers need to be paid better, and administrators need to be energized and mobilized with a new sense of mission. But we fool ourselves if we think that the problem can be solved while our kids lack the character tools they will need for real success in school and adult life. University of Pennsylvania psychologists Angela Duckworth and Martin Seligman published a study in December 2005, showing that self-discipline is twice as important as intelligence in predicting school success.

Katie teaches at a large California high school. Like many of her colleagues, she spends much of her energy managing class behavior and trying to motivate students to learn. During an American history class, a group of students seemed to be a lot more interested in talking and fooling around than they were in learning about the causes of the Civil War. Evaristo, a recent immigrant from Tanzania, became more and more frustrated with his classmates. "What is the matter with you?" he shouted as he turned to face them. "Don't you know that where I come from kids would die for the opportunity to go to a school like this? You have a good teacher working hard to get you to learn and all you can do is be lazy and fool around." Evaristo's outburst quieted them down—for about fifteen minutes.

Our children are failing to learn and we are failing our children.

We are not equipping them with the inner skills of self-discipline and self-management they need in order to learn. While federal and state governments make the academic-testing industry rich, the root cause of our academic stagnation is ignored: Too many of our kids assume that their lives should constantly be packed with experiences that are entertaining but also easy. Surveys indicate that half of all students spend less than four hours a week preparing for their classes, and yet four-fifths say they complete their assignments. If kids are asked to spend only four hours a week on their homework, they are not challenged. Another survey found that high school students say there is more emphasis on sports at their schools than on academics.

It's tempting to blame teachers for this state of affairs, but before we do that it might be a good idea for us parents to look in the mirror. The problem isn't restricted to inner-city schools, either. While the problem has a different flavor in affluent and poor communities, the underlying attitude of entitlement is the same. An English teacher in one of the most expensive, prestigious private schools in the Midwest shared this with me during a break in a teacher workshop I was leading on No.

"I realized that I don't give many C's or D's to my students anymore. If they turn in an assignment on time, they'll get an A or B."

"Why?" I asked, certain that I would hear about whining and complaining kids. I learned that, at least for her, the kids weren't the problem.

"I don't want to fight with the parents," she explained. "C's and D's bring angry phone calls from parents. An F brings some of them into the school for a face-to-face showdown. We're not talking basic skills here. These kids can read and write. My students are bright kids from affluent families. They'll get into the prestigious colleges all right, but they're not being challenged to excel."

"What's the parents' complaint?" I asked.

"Oh, they tell me that their son or daughter worked hard on the assignment and a C or D is discouraging. Sometimes there's a subtle threat when they remind me that smart kids avoid tough teachers because lower grades will bring their grade point averages and class rank down, thereby hurting their chances of getting into the 'right' college."

This drift to make assignments easy and fun is taking a toll. ACT®, the company that administers the widely recognized college entrance exam, issued a report in August 2005 showing that, not surprisingly, the problems with low academic achievement have become apparent in colleges, where hundreds of thousands of students show up inadequately prepared. About half of the ACT test takers lacked adequate reading comprehension skills. Only 51 percent had scores high enough to suggest that they could succeed in college-level social sciences classes. The situation in math and science was even more dismal. Only 41 percent were ready for college algebra and only 26 percent were ready to tackle college biology.

Colleges can't remedy these problems, which go far beyond their student populations. In December 2005, the National Assessment of Adult Literacy, the most important measure of how well American adults can read, assessed results of the test administered in 2003 by the U.S. Department of Education—the first since 1992. The report revealed a stunning decline in the reading skills of college graduates. Only 31 percent of college graduates entering the workforce could read at a proficient level. That's less than one out of three and a 22 percent decline in a little over a decade. Mark Schneider, commissioner of the National Center for Education Statistics, an arm of the U.S. Department of Education, said in an understatement, "These are big shifts."

The Stakes Are High: Character Capital

Dave and Carol came to see me for marriage counseling some years back. They had been together for several years and Carol had twin sixteen-year-old daughters from a previous marriage. While there were a number of stresses on the relationship, disagreement about how to parent Stephanie and Linda was at the top of the list. Carol insisted that the twins' growing defiance and disrespect were normal for teenagers, while Dave was convinced that things were getting out of hand.

"I know you need to cut teens some slack," Dave said during one of our sessions. "But don't you think that when Carol and I agree on a curfew we should stick with it?"

"Yes, I do," I replied. "The two of you should make sure you're on the same page ahead of time. Once you are, then you should enforce the consequences together if the girls don't comply."

"Well, that isn't what happens. We're together until the girls get to Carol when I'm not around. Then she either renegotiates the curfew or backs down on the consequences."

We worked on issues like handling curfew and lack of respect over the course of several sessions. Dave and Carol made some good progress. That progress counted for naught, however, when the big crisis hit. Here's what happened:

Dave and Carol decided to join some friends for an overnight bike trip on a scenic trail more than one hundred miles away from home. Dave argued that Stephanie and Linda should either spend the weekend with an aunt they knew well or else ask the aunt if she would stay with them at their house. The girls lobbied Carol hard to be left home alone, convincing her that they were old enough and responsible enough to look after themselves. Once Carol agreed, Dave went along in spite of his uneasiness.

In the days leading up to the weekend, Stephanie and Linda spread the word around school that they would be home alone and started inviting friends over for a party. On Saturday night, friends and friends of friends arrived in droves. At midnight more than one hundred teens were all over the house. By the time the neighbors called the police, dozens of kids were drunk and the house had been trashed. A phone call shortly after midnight from the police station summoned Carol and Dave back to the city. During the long drive home, Carol and Dave agreed to remain calm and firm with the girls even though they were beside themselves with anger and disappointment. "We'll just deal with this one step at a time," David assured Carol. He thought to himself, This is not the time to say, "I told you so."

Stephanie and Linda were in tears when Carol and Dave arrived at the police station to pick them up. The sobbing continued as they drove home. David and Carol were stunned by the condition of the house, which they had left neat and tidy less than twenty-four hours earlier. Broken furniture was strewn about, carpets were stained, and there was trash in every room. "I'm too upset to talk now," said Carol. "We'll discuss this in the morning."

The family conference took place the next day. Carol spoke first. "I can't believe you girls did this. We specifically said no kids over at the house while we were gone. You promised us that we could trust you."

"Mom, I'm sorry," Linda sobbed. "We just had a couple of kids over. We didn't know everyone else would show up. It wasn't our fault."

Dave interrupted. "What do you mean it wasn't your fault? You didn't keep your word. Now you have to accept responsibility. In addition to cleaning up the mess, being grounded, and losing car privileges for a month, you're going to have to pay for part of the damage. We'll have to get a final estimate, but I'm sure it's going to cost more than ten thousand dollars. You'll have to figure out with your friends how you're going to help pay."

"What are you talking about?" Linda shouted. "We haven't got that kind of money, and we didn't do it in the first place. We made a mistake, but it's not the end of the world. We've learned our lesson. You can't punish us for other kids. That's not fair. Anyway, that's why you have insurance."

David and Carol recounted the entire episode to me in a session later that week. The final damage estimate exceeded thirteen thousand dollars. The hardest thing for both David and Carol to accept was the fact that their daughters felt put out by the punishments that they received. Carol told David that she finally saw what he'd been trying to tell her for many months. "It's amazing to me that the girls resent *us* for what happened. They really think that we should just pay for all the damage with insurance and move on."

Is this only an extreme example of kids gone wild, or is this story just one of many that are symptomatic of a growing tide of irresponsibility? All kids make mistakes, sometimes big ones. For mistakes to be learning experiences, however, kids do have to learn to take responsibility. That lesson begins with kids listening to No and accepting the consequences when they disregard the Nos they hear.

Stephanie and Linda, Evaristo's classmates, spoiled three-year-olds, and others like them make up the American workforce of the future. Traditionally, a country's economic fortune depends on an abundance of natural resources, a talented workforce, and access to capital. Another ingredient, however, may be more important than talent, and that is "character capital." Being a smart worker isn't good enough. Companies like Enron, Tyco, and WorldCom had plenty of smart people at the helm. What these companies lacked, however, was character capital. Executives blinded by greed and unable to accept responsibility ruined the lives of tens of thousands of employees, and they cost investors, taxpayers, and the country hundreds of billions of dollars. There were so many corporate scandals in the past ten years that *Forbes* magazine posted a "Corporate Scandal Sheet" keeping tally. What are our children learning from these disgraceful business practices? Can we parents and other adults who do believe in honesty and hard work wrest the headlines from deceitful executives and teach our children to climb out of this mess?

The Stakes Are High: Swollen Expectations

The 2005 ACT report on college freshmen's lack of preparation, cited earlier, contained another reason for concern: Three-fourths of high school students expect to complete a college degree, yet only 30 percent are on a college-preparatory track. This starkly reflects the kids' widespread attitude that they don't have to work to achieve; they expect it all to be handed to them. So many high school kids fall into the trap of thinking, Of course I'm going to get a college degree, but I don't have to put in any work now, because that will all just happen for me.

Our kids' financial expectations have swollen too. Ameriquest Mortgage Company asked a research firm to conduct a national poll of students. The results of this Smart Savings Survey showed that most of today's students expect a starting salary of more than fifty thousand dollars, expect to own their own home quickly, and to retire before they are sixty—unrealistic expectations, according to Ameriquest. But these expectations aren't surprising since children in 2005 spent 500 percent more than their parents did at the same age, adjusted for inflation. The discrepancy between what kids want and what they can afford is evident in the fact that the average college student now has four credit cards and more than three thousand dollars in credit card debt.

These outsized expectations start early. Michael Mann is in demand as a Santa Claus in the Twin Cities. His natural Santa appearance and jovial personality make him a popular holiday fixture at Nordstrom's department store at the Mall of America. He recently told me that he is stunned by how quickly the wish lists of three- and four-year-olds have escalated. "Ten years ago kids asked for toys in the fifty-dollar range. I thought that was high, but the Santa visitors this past year asked for laptops and Xbox 360s costing hundreds of dollars." Then Michael added something directly related to No. "I started telling the kids that Santa's elves aren't good at electronics and began to steer them toward less extravagant gifts." "How did the kids react?" I asked. "Oh, the kids were fine. And it was really interesting to see the looks of relief and appreciation on the faces of the parents. They were glad I was cooling off some of the kids' expectations. I understand that they appreciated me saying no in a nice way. But I was left wondering why they weren't doing it themselves."

The Stakes Are High: Our Economic Future in Peril

The world economy is changing. Two or three generations ago, the most important skills in the workplace were practical, hands-on abilities. The most common jobs entailed toiling in the fields, bringing a crop to harvest, and doing a shift in a mill or on an assembly line. That's ancient history now. Many of these tasks are now handled automatically by ever more sophisticated machinery and mechanical processes, not just in the United States but all over the world. Shift work has been increasingly exported to other countries where production costs are lower. All workers have entered a worldwide information economy.

The "worldwide economy" is the other big change. In the twentieth century, simply being born in the United States was an economic advantage. Coming into the world in Peoria rather than Shanghai cemented your chances of living a prosperous life. Not anymore. In a world knitted together with high-speed Internet connections, computers send CAT scans to technicians in Australia or the Philippines instead of Illinois, and IRS tax returns are completed in Israel and Asia as easily as Indiana—and a lot more cheaply. That's why four hundred thousand tax returns were done in India in 2005, and how radiologists in Australia or Switzerland can read and return a CAT scan in less than twenty minutes, twenty-four hours a day, seven days a week. Young people in developing countries will catch up and pass our kids in the next generation. Between 1997 and 2002, productivity in China increased by 17 percent annually, and they aim to have the best university system in the world within the next decade; they're paying top dollar to woo the leading science professors and researchers from Europe and America to China. The top foreign-language class now requested around the world is Mandarin. Twenty percent of scientists and engineers in the United States today are immigrants. Fifty-one percent of doctorates in engineering awarded by American universities are now earned by foreign students.

An executive with Cargill, one of the world's leading agribusinesses, confided during a recent interview that his company has difficulty finding its top scientists in the United States. "We have to hire the best and brightest for us to maintain our competitive advantage. For generations we found them in American graduate schools. That's no longer the case. More and more of our recent hires are in China and India."

Thomas L. Friedman, in his 2005 best seller *The World Is Flat,* summarizes the lessons of the global economy with this anecdote. Friedman recalls that when he was a boy his parents used to say: "Tom, finish your dinner—people in China and India are starving."

Now he tells his daughters: "Girls, finish your homework—people in China and India are starving for your job."

It is clear that the economic future will belong to hungry kids, not entitled kids. It will belong to kids who know how to work hard, delay gratification, make sacrifices, and discipline themselves. These are all the lessons of No. Our country's and our kids' economic future is at stake in our ability to say no.

Peering into Our Kids' Future

Before we go any further, I would like you to pause for a moment. Make yourself comfortable and sit quietly for a few minutes and imagine some years into the future, when your kids are grown and living on their own. The question I have for you is: What kind of adult do you hope your kids will become? What admirable traits do you hope they will have?

Please, really give it some thought. Many parents think about what they hope *will not* happen in their kids' lives. That is only natural, especially in a media culture that seems addicted to scaring people with exaggerated warnings about the latest danger lurking out there. We have all had friends or family members whose children have taken unpredictable turns, gotten into trouble, had emotional problems, or made unfortunate decisions. But forget about all these negative scenarios for now. Think good thoughts about what you'd like to see. What qualities of character do you hope your child will develop? Will he or she be kind, compassionate, competitive, driven, fair-minded, resilient? You might find it helpful to write down your answer.

_____

_____

_____

I ask a lot of parents this question and give them time to write down their answers. Most parents say they want their kids to grow up to be competent, responsible, and caring adults. These are the qualities they most often mention, which is understandable.

But the next question is more difficult:

How is my child going to get from here to there?

The answer is:

Only with a lot of guidance. Only by learning how to say no.

It's human nature for us to want to keep our kids smiling and cheerful. But you know what? If our kids never get mad at us, or get frustrated or become disappointed, that might be a warning sign that we aren't doing our job as parents. How will your kids learn to deal with frustration and disappointment if they never have any practice? How will your kids learn self-discipline if you don't teach them? It is your job to teach these important life lessons by saying no.

If not you, then who?

And if not now, then when?

Raising Kids

This book explores some very important parenting skills. You'll discover some aspects of your parenting style that you want to keep, others that you want to modify, and still others that you want to change. Once you've determined what you want to change, you can plan to take action according to these three steps:

1. Become aware of what you need to change.
2. Consciously choose how you want to act.
3. Repeat the action until it becomes comfortable.

Now, pause and think about these two questions found at the conclusion of most chapters:

- What do I want to continue about my parenting and my relationship with my child(ren)?
- What do I want to change?

Dos and Don'ts

These dos and don'ts are suggestions—they're good starting points for learning how to change from saying yes to saying no when it's important.

DO

- With your spouse or partner, or as a single parent, develop a list of desirable traits, qualities, and behaviors that you want your children to have.
- Model the type of behavior you want to see in your kids. You're the most powerful teacher they have.
- Learn as much as you can about your child's growth and development to gain realistic expectations of your child's behavior. Many communities offer child development and parenting classes. Read books that describe what to expect. Some include *What's Going On in There? How the Brain and Mind Develop in the First Five Years of Life,* by Lise Eliot (Bantam, 2000); *Touchpoints: The Essential Reference—Your Child's Emotional and Behavioral Development,* by T. Berry Brazelton (Da Capo Lifelong Books, 1992); and my own *Why Do They Act That Way? A Survival Guide to the Adolescent Brain for You and Your Teen* (Free Press, 2004).
- Get to know your children's teachers and let them know that you support them and will back them up in their expectations of behavior and classroom performance.

DON'T

- Don't do things for your kids that they should be able to do for themselves.
- Don't become a nonstop entertainment committee for your children.
- Don't give your children everything they want.
- Don't become a doormat for disrespectful behavior. Tolerance and patience are important parental traits, but you are

allowed to insist—and should insist—on courteous and responsible behavior by your children.

What do I want to continue?

_____

_____

_____

What do I want to change?

_____

_____

_____

Two

Saying *No* in a *Yes* Culture

In the early 1970s, government and business leaders in Mexico had a big problem on their hands. The world was shifting to an information economy, so the ability to read and write was more important than ever. Yet, rates of adult literacy remained stubbornly low in many Mexican workplaces. After several failed initiatives, Miguel Sabido, the producer of a very popular television program, decided to try an experiment. For a number of months in 1973 Sabido wove pro–adult literacy messages into the dialogue of the male lead in his top-rated program. In the twelve months that followed, adult-reading-class registrations across Mexico soared by an astounding 800 percent.

Media's power has only increased in recent years with the advancement of telecommunication technology. Today, for example, political candidates must finance media campaigns with enormous sums of money and put their faces and messages on the screens that now dominate our lives, or they have no chance of influencing voters. In fact, a campaign manager for a U.S. senator recently told National Public Radio that media plans have become more important than the candidates themselves. A research study I coauthored showed that beer companies' budgets for media campaigns not only predict teenagers' favorite brands, but that exposure to these ads also predicts which teens will start drinking.

Whoever Tells the Stories Defines the Culture

A multibillion-dollar worldwide advertising industry is built on media's ability to form attitudes and values and to change behavior. Media messages influence us to a great degree because they use stories and stories have traditionally shaped our attitudes, values, and behavior.

We human beings come from a long line of storytellers. For many centuries our ancestors sat around campfires spinning yarns. Though the kitchen table has replaced the campfire in modern times, the storytelling hasn't stopped. Some stories recount the news with a bit of drama, humor, or entertainment; others are intended as moral lessons. Some are forgotten in minutes while others survive for thousands of years.

Stories have meaning for both children and adults no matter what their age, although interpretations will differ. For example, a Bible story like the Good Samaritan can teach young children the importance of helping one another. In addition, an adult who knows that, historically, Samaritans were a despised lower class will be reminded of the harm done by prejudice.

Stories teach cultural norms and values that are critical to the health of a society. They communicate what is, and is not, important to a group. Stories identify our heroes and define their qualities. *Charlotte's Web* teaches millions of children the importance of bravery and honesty. *The Three Little Pigs* stresses the value of a job well done. Whether in children's books or adult novels, stories have the power to shape a culture.

But a monumental change in who tells our stories happened in the past sixty years. Since World War II, the mass media, especially movies, television, and, more recently, video games provide an ever larger number of the stories we hear. The way tales are told has also changed.

Teams of Hollywood scriptwriters, directors, and video game

producers have replaced parents, teachers, pastors, elders, authors, and sages as the primary storytellers. Multimillion-dollar electronic productions have replaced stories shared around campfires and tables, or stories read by flashlight under the covers late at night. Mass-media stories, delivered with dazzling special effects, are beamed to billions of people all over the world in a matter of seconds.

There are of course benefits to this new type of storytelling. The technology driving this change, for example, throws open cultural doors and new worlds around the globe very quickly. But the downside is that most mass-media storytelling exists to sell things, to "deliver eyeballs to advertisers," to move merchandise off the shelves. Traditional storytellers aimed to entertain, educate, and inspire. That shift is crucial. The media story that gains and holds our attention long enough to convey an advertiser's message, that succeeds in delivering eyeballs, proliferates. Selling is the primary goal; entertainment, education, and inspiration are secondary. An entertainment executive once summed it up: "It's all about bucks, baby. The rest is conversation."

We'll explore the effects of this shift further in chapter 13, but for now let's affirm that this generation of kids spends more time learning about life through electronic media than any other activity. The amount of time they spend in front of screens dwarfs how many hours they spend in the classroom or talking with their parents. Kids today are exposed to more stories that are more powerfully presented than at any time in history. Some are good. Too many are not. We, as parents, must choose our children's media stories carefully. Why? Because whoever tells the stories defines the culture.

Parent Tool Kit: *No* in a *Yes* Culture

Electronic media surround us, as pervasive as the air we breathe. This pervasiveness clouds our awareness of the media Yes culture and how saying no to our kids is made so much more difficult. Use the questions in this kit to figure out how aware you are of the cultural norms that constantly reinforce Yes.

PARENT TOOL KIT
No in a *Yes* Culture

Yes	No		
☐	☐	1.	We make sure that we read a lot to our children.
☐	☐	2.	We pick books that our kids like, that educate and entertain.
☐	☐	3.	We identify the subtle but powerful Yes messages in the media.
☐	☐	4.	We talk with our kids about the values the media promote.
☐	☐	5.	We pay attention to our kids' movies, TV programs, and video games.
☐	☐	6.	We believe that virtues like perseverance, patience, and generosity are critical.
☐	☐	7.	We discuss our parenting priorities from time to time.
☐	☐	8.	We try to make sure that we don't over-schedule ourselves or our kids.

If you can't answer yes to most of these questions, then you might be a lot more influenced by cultural pressure to always say yes than you think.

The Power of Advertising

At a parenting seminar in Texas some years ago, a young mother shared an example of the power of advertising. "During dinner one night my husband told me that he thought the movie we had just seen the night before might be his all-time favorite. My three-year-old daughter immediately chimed in that she had a favorite movie too. When I asked her what it was, she went on and on about how she loved *The Lion King*. She was absolutely convinced that it was her favorite and that's why we absolutely had to go to McDonald's so she could get the puzzles that came with the Lion King Happy Meal. "What was startling about this conversation, Dr. Dave," she added, "was that the movie hadn't even come out yet. The premiere was still a week away, but the advertising had already convinced my daughter that it was her all-time favorite."

If the mass-media stories our children hear and see teach them cultural norms and values, the ads embedded in those stories do, too. Advertising was born in the media, first the print media, then radio and of course television, then the Internet and video games. Advertisers always improve their techniques, but the gist of what they do is nothing new.

Before the industrial revolution, the dominant form of mass media was the newspaper. Publishers of newspapers made their money then by charging for the newspaper itself. There were no advertisements. The newspaper hired people to gather the news, write and edit the stories, and then a newspaper boy would sell it on the corner for a couple of pennies. The industrial revolution of the nineteenth century and its proliferation of manufactured goods generated a need to create markets for its products.

No one knew if a sales message would drive people to buy a product because it was mentioned in a newspaper. But the first advertisements did work. Other newspapers followed with more advertisements, transforming the whole business so that the pennies a reader paid for the newspaper became less and less important in the business model of newspaper publishers. Advertising has grown so much over the years that the average Sunday newspaper in the United States today is about 30 percent information and 70 percent advertisements. Once that advertising formula took hold in the newspaper business, it kept morphing and growing into other mass media as they developed.

There's nothing wrong with selling stuff, just as there is nothing wrong with buying stuff. But what has happened over time is that advertisers have become more sophisticated and more effective at bypassing the simple, straightforward type of message they used to deliver, which generally appealed to reason or common sense. Advertisers have learned that it is more effective to bypass the rational part of the brain and instead target the emotions, crafting messages that appeal to pleasure, or give you a feeling of need you never knew you had, or take advantage of your weakness for convenience and instant gratification. It all adds up to a constantly reinforced cultural Yes message—to you and your children—that all your needs and desires should be met instantly, exactly the way you want, so that you never have to wait for anything or deny yourself anything.

The Golden Rule of Influence

When you stop to think about it, an advertiser's basic job is to change our behavior, to persuade us to switch from brand X to brand Y, or to buy something new. While that goal might be simple, its execution is difficult, because the advertiser has to get inside our heads and make us *want* to change, to *motivate* us. The best way to do that is to target emotions that motivate behavior. It's no accident that our words *emotion* and *motivation* come from the same Latin word, *movere*, meaning "to move."

The savvy advertiser avoids the brain's thinking center, the cortex, and makes a beeline for the brain's limbic system, the seat of emotions. In other words, the most effective ads slip in underneath the brain's thinking radar, like a stealth missile. The last thing an advertiser wants is for us to be alert to how he is trying to influence us. That just wouldn't be as effective. The golden rule of influence decrees that the chance of success increases when the person being influenced doesn't know it. If it seems far-fetched to think that a commercial can wire you to have a positive impression of a product, a value, or an idea without your understanding that it is manipulating you, just ask yourself how often you see a new commercial and have absolutely no idea what is being advertised.

Advertisers work very hard to use their small piece of time to create an emotional state. That is why, increasingly, after seeing twenty-five seconds of a thirty-second ad for the first time, we ask ourselves, "What are they advertising anyway? Cars? Food? Vacations?" But the advertisers have their reasons for keeping us in the dark. They know their ad will work best if they can first evoke a particular emotion or mood and maximize that effect. Then, and only then, when they have us feeling the way they want us to feel, do they make the connection to their product or service. Here's an example.

Several years ago my daughter Erin and I were watching television during the holidays when an advertisement caught our attention. We saw images of a sleigh being drawn by horses through snow-covered woods. A house with a wreath on its door stood on a small hill. The next scene showed friendly faces exchanging gifts around a fireplace. Since we didn't yet know who the advertiser was, we began to guess based on the images we were seeing. I thought it was Hallmark; Erin guessed Budweiser. We were both wrong. In the final seconds of the ad, with the image of an airplane floating above billowing clouds, a soothing voice intoned, "American Airlines— bringing friends together for the holidays." It was beautiful! Now here's the key question: At the end of that ad, how do you think Erin and I *felt* about American Airlines? "What a wonderful company that would bring friends together for the holidays. God bless them!"

This very effective commercial did not appeal to the cerebral cortex, the thinking part of the brain, with information about the airline's safety record, the training requirements of personnel, or the specifications of its jet engines, but went straight for the heart.

A Million *Yes* Messages a Year

Unless you live in a cave, you and your children are exposed to more than a million advertisements every year on billboards, in newspapers and magazines, junk mail, on product packaging, and in the electronic mass media. The average child in the United States will see more than forty thousand ads each year on TV alone. Wherever advertisers can put an ad, they will.

All those ads target our emotions and form neural connections in our brains. We are unaware of this happening, but each time we see a commercial repeated, those neural connections are strengthened, as is the unconscious association between that product, service, or message and the emotional state it evokes. That connection is inactive until we see a reference to the product or service, which triggers the emotion that subtly pushes us to action, often without the slightest idea why. We might be able to resist the pull of that emotion in most cases, but since we often are unaware of where the emotional association came from, it's unlikely we can resist all the time.

Here's another ad I still remember from several years ago: It starts with a shot of an adorable little girl having a imaginary tea party with a friendly elephant. They laugh and skip around the yard, which is shrouded in a soft, dreamy light. Everything is just right, and the little girl is clearly having a wonderful time, but twenty-five seconds into the commercial I had no idea what was being advertised, although I didn't really care because the commercial was clearly plucking my parental heartstrings with thoughts of my own kids' innocent fantasy play.

"Maybe you can't give her everything she wants," a voiceover intones. As I recall, the commercial closes by saying, "But for all the rest, there's MasterCard."

Let's be honest here. The real message to the parent watching that commercial is: *Give your kid whatever she wants.* Of course, that was never spoken. It was all wrapped in very attractive, inviting emotional images that made me feel good.

Another commercial starts with a man leaving on a business trip. Before going out the door he gives his little girl a big hug and tells her that he will miss her. Later in the trip he is in a hotel room on the phone wishing her a happy birthday. In real life that little girl would probably be disappointed that her dad was not home to help her celebrate her birthday, but in this ad she is all smiles. The commercial, not surprisingly, was for a cell phone company. As happy endings go, this was pretty limited. A real happy ending would have had him rescheduling the trip so he could be there for his little girl's birthday, instead of giving her five minutes of phone time from a foreign country. The point is, however, that the commercial succeeds in evoking a warm, agreeable emotion.

Both commercials play off the same parental anxiety: the worry

that because we are so busy, and running around all the time, we are
not giving our children everything they need. Advertisers take advantage of our nagging worry that our busy lives prevent us from
giving everything we want to our children. But we can assuage that
guilt by buying something! Which brings us back to the difficulty of
saying no in a Yes culture.

The *Yes* Messages: More, Fast, Easy/Fun

Electronic media and advertising team up to form very potent
cultural norms and messages that influence every one of us.
Three overriding themes together create and reinforce the Yes
culture: *More, Fast, Easy/Fun.*

The messages we see and hear every day constantly remind us
that "more is better."

"Whoever has the most toys wins."

"Shop till you drop."

"The more we have the happier we'll be."

"Things are a measure of success in life."

Advertisers do not engage in a subversive, planned, thought-
control program to make it difficult to say no to our kids, but they
do use highly effective techniques and messages to motivate us consumers to change the way we feel and behave. T. Boone Pickens, the
Texas oilman and billionaire, actually put it into words: "Our job is
to make people unhappy with what they have."

He's absolutely right. A lot of talented people work very hard to
make a lot of money by selling us things we don't need. They bom-
bard us with messages geared to make us unhappy with what we
have or who we are, so that we will crave the new and improved
version of something, the bigger this or the faster that. Parents and
kids alike are pressured to buy into this. Michael Mann, Nordstrom's
Santa Claus, sees the "more" list grow with each passing Christmas;
teachers see their teenage students' work suffer because of long
hours spent during the school week working to earn extra money
for fast food, stylish clothing, and the latest high-tech gadgets. The
high school prom has ballooned from a dance into an extravagant

affair with stretch limos, lavish flowers, expensive clothes, and dinner parties at four- and five-star restaurants. An entire prom industry has blossomed in order to tap into the $4 billion high school
prom market. The average teen couple, or their parents, now pony
up an average of $800 for the night. Several private high schools in
the New York City area made national news in the fall of 2005,
when they announced the end of school-sponsored proms because
of the extravagance, drinking problems, and sex associated with the
dances. They decided that "more" had become too much.

Colleen realized that more had become too much when her
thirteen-year-old son Philip came in the door after school and told
her that he needed a new cell phone that recorded video, text mes-
saged, and played games. Somewhat taken aback by his casual statement that he *needed* an expensive cell phone, she asked him what he
meant. "All my friends have them," he answered. "They're awesome.
When can I get one?"

"I don't think the question is when, Philip," she answered. "The
question is if."

"Mom, *all* the kids have them," he protested. "I've got to get
one. Besides, it's a safety thing. You can't get in touch with me if I
don't have a cell phone."

"Philip, it's your job to let me know where you are so I *can* get in
touch with you. For the few times it really makes sense to carry a
phone, you can borrow mine. No, you can't have one."

Philip didn't give up. He kept pestering Colleen for a cell phone
whenever he got the chance. To Colleen's credit, however, she held
her ground. "You know, Dave," she said, "I really worry what these
kids are going to do when they wake up and discover that they can't
have everything they want."

"I know what you mean," I answered. "At least you're helping
Philip learn that lesson now."

Fast and Instant Gratification

Our culture is obsessed with anything fast. Products are constantly promoted as great new innovations because they are

"ready in seconds." *Do it now* is the message; we are told that it is foolish to wait for something if we don't have to. If you want to go on a vacation, just go. Don't worry about paying for it until next month's credit card statement arrives.

Instantaneous is the new cultural norm. We have fast lanes on the highway, express lanes at the supermarket, fast food, instant messaging and cell phone communication, one-minute management techniques, and one-minute bedtime stories for our kids. A heartburn remedy that brings relief in twenty seconds trumps the one that works in thirty.

In our attempts to have it all, speed is important because it enables us to pack in as much as possible so we can race on to the next thing. If something takes too long, we're not interested. And if fast is good, faster is better, so products are constantly redesigned to gain speed and save time. Theoretically, those saved hours and minutes should give us more time for relationships, families, and leisure. But in spite of all the time savings, we have less time than ever before. The percentage of Americans who said that they "never have enough time" grew by 50 percent in the past generation.

We also like things to be resolved or "fixed" quickly, and we want our efforts rewarded without delay: We have become a society obsessed with instant gratification. Children are by nature impetuous and impatient. They are already inclined to want their needs filled immediately. When this natural impatience is reinforced in a thousand different ways by our Yes culture, the drive toward instant gratification becomes overpowering.

In a culture that prizes fast, it's tempting to cave in to the demands our kids make. But, if they don't learn to wait, it will be very difficult for them to develop the life skills so important for maturity. Many goals and achievements in life take time and patience. Mastering complex concepts in school, for example, requires persistence over time. Learning to read a book or play a musical instrument requires dedication and practice over many years. Sometimes we have little in the way of immediate tangible rewards as we develop a skill, and progress toward our goals is slow.

Unfortunately, we are not only conditioned to get what we

want quickly; we are taught that difficult problems should be solved quickly. Television programs resolve complex personal dilemmas and even traumas for their characters in thirty minutes—actually twenty-two minutes not counting commercials. So not only do we have two-minute popcorn, we have twenty-two-minute solutions to tragedy. Problems, we are told, should be resolved quickly. There is no time to deal with complicated and sensitive interpersonal issues, so we look for a facile strategy—or worse, a medication—to put them behind us immediately.

Children can be conditioned to expect instant rewards either directly or indirectly. The direct message comes from the media, which tell kids that they should have what they want right now. All of us have heard "Don't delay, act now" a thousand times. Children also learn about instant gratification from the example that we adults set for them. They watch us as we try to get everything we want. They pick up from us that *wait* is a dirty word.

Teachers can attest to the impatience of today's children. When George Noble, one of my kids' grade school teachers, retired, I asked if he thought kids' attention spans and patience had shrunk over the course of his thirty-year career in the classroom. "Are you kidding?" he responded. "They've shrunk in the past ten years. If kids can't figure out a problem quickly, they want to give up. I thought maybe I was just getting old, but I hear the same complaints from the young teachers just starting out."

This predilection for speed, coupled with the racing images on television and video games, creates a constant state of stimulation and excitement for children, actually wiring their brains to prefer a hyper state and to maintain it. Some children do it with nonstop activities; many others turn to TV or video games. Anything that cannot measure up in terms of immediate sensory stimulation or excitement is condemned as boring by kids, and being boring is a mortal sin in our Yes culture.

Parents and teachers have to compete with this desire to rush. Solving complicated math problems or reading a book can seem boring compared to the latest Xbox 360 video game. If a class is not entertaining enough to occupy their attention, many students will entertain themselves or create their own excitement, often by acting out. I had a recent conversation with Dr. Ed Hallowell, an expert on attention deficit disorder and author of the best-selling book *Driven to Distraction*. "ADD and ADHD are brain-based disorders, all right," he told me. "But our instant-gratification, media-driven culture is creating a nation of attention-disordered kids."

Parents in Wayzata, an upper-middle-class Minneapolis suburb, realized that the frantic pace of daily life was taking a toll on their families. Racing from team practices, to music lessons, to Scout meetings, to choir rehearsals, to church activities left everyone with little time to breathe, let alone have a meal together. To get some perspective on the problem and what they could do about it, in 1998 a parents' group invited Professor Bill Doherty of the University of Minnesota to meet with them. Doherty had received media attention for his research on the harm that overscheduling has on children and families: lack of family time, high stress, loss of time for creativity and reflection, anxiety, and burnout. As a result, the Putting Family First movement began; it seeks to raise awareness about the importance of balance and the dangers of overscheduling, and urges youth organizations to adopt family-friendly schedules and policies.

But when Wayzata started Putting Family First, everyone wondered what would happen when Doherty presented the new approach to the community's youth-sports directors, since team sports are often the worst offenders in overscheduling kids. Yet, the first to speak up when Doherty finished speaking was David Gaither, the commissioner of the Wayzata-Plymouth Youth Football League. "Football will play," was all he said, meaning that he was all for the change. He realized that teams are valuable for kids but end up being counterproductive if they steal too much family time. Today, almost ten years later, the Wayzata-Plymouth Football League proudly bears a Putting Family First logo. Among its rules: no weekend practices; no practices during the dinner hour; no consequences for missing a game or a practice; and playing time for all kids. Despite the fact that they have abolished elite teams, Wayzata regularly comes out the winner.

Today, school boards, youth-serving organizations, communities of faith, and even youth athletic leagues in communities across the country support Putting Family First.

Easy/Fun

The Yes culture also feels that the pacing of activities should be fun as well as fast. Frustration, pain, and discomfort have no place in our culture, and children learn that pain, whether physical or psychological, is always bad and should be avoided at all costs. Kids are so sold on the notion that everything should be quick and easy that more and more of them think that everything should be fun. Kids who are programmed to think that everything will be easy and fun for them grow up with a deeply entrenched sense of entitlement.

Please don't think that I'm a puritan arguing in favor of pain for pain's sake. However, discomfort, disappointment, and distress are simply part of life, and children and adults need to deal with them. How do we teach our kids to cope with the pain of boredom, disappointment, and rejection if we do everything we can to shield them from it? Don't we want them to develop virtues like perseverance, patience, commitment, determination, and diligence? These virtues don't come automatically; kids have to learn them. And the lessons are not always easy or pleasant.

The Era of *Yes*

Of course, saying no to an insistent child is a lot more difficult than saying yes. Yes makes life quieter and more peaceful. What's more, our culture tells us that Yes will make our children be happier and love us more. But what's the real effect of Yes? Here are some life lessons that the Yes culture teaches our kids:

"Entertain me."

"Everything should be fun."

"Rewards without work."

"Instant gratification."

Saying yes too often creates a pattern for which there is no end. A yessed kid, in short, can't develop the skills to be successful in work or in relationships. Competence and relationship skills demand self-discipline, something that is not always fun or pleasurable to achieve. Hard work and persistence are part of the recipe for success. If our kids can't delay gratification, rein in their drive for pleasure, handle setbacks, put other people's needs on a par with their own, and manage their emotions, they reduce the likelihood of creating a happy, productive life for themselves.

In our permissive culture, adults and children constantly hear messages that we should do whatever we want: *Eat what you want, buy what you want, go where you want, be who you want to be.* From well-meaning self-help gurus to dollar-grubbing hucksters, we constantly hear that we should give in to our urges, even though our society has seen negative examples time and time again, from spoiled millionaire athletes to self-indulgent corporate executives, that highlight the danger in letting people do whatever they want. And yet there seems to be little sign of an end to the era of Yes.

That is why today saying no is harder than ever and why it's up to you to do it yourself. Helping children learn self-discipline often seems as if you're swimming against the tide—and you are. But that's exactly why it's so important for you to give your kids the gift of No. Eventually, despite what the media and cultural norms tell you, your kids are going to have to stare an immutable No in the face. And they'll be a lot better off if you've taught them what it looks like.

DO

- Read or tell stories that promote values. Two very good guides that help you find books for children and teens that celebrate virtues and values are *Books That Build Character: A Guide to Teaching Your Child Moral Values Through Stories,* by William Kilpatrick (Touchstone, 1994), which recommends more than three hundred award winners, and *Books to Grow By,* by Bob Keeshan (Fairview Press, 1996), which cross-references books with values such as self-discipline and generosity.

- Slow down and take time to listen to your children. Encourage them to communicate by paying attention to what they are saying. They'll be more likely to share if you say: "Tell me what you did in reading class today," instead of, "How was school today?"
- Limit your child's media diet to two hours a day or less—for children over two year of age. (Children under two should not watch TV or videos. Babies' brains need real-world activities.)
- Keep a list of what you buy for your child. Do you seem always to be buying more "stuff"?
- Teach your children patience. Make sure that periodically they have to wait for things.
- Evaluate whether you allow your child to face No.
- Make family meals a priority. Track how many evenings your family has dinner together each week. If it's not often, then add one meal, even if it means eating later. Then, try adding another one. Research shows that kids who regularly eat meals with their families are less likely to engage in high-risk behaviors.
- Create some family time. Schedule family activities together, whether it's going for a hike or a bike ride or learning a new card game.
- Decide if your kids are doing too much. If they're always on the go, it may be time to drop an activity.

DON'T

- Don't put a TV or video game system in your child's bedroom. Kids with media in their bedrooms spend five hours more a week in front of a screen, spend less time with the family, and watch more "gimme" messages. Chapter 13, "Raising MediaWise Kids" will explore media use.

- Don't give in to nagging in a store. See chapter 12, "Taming the Gimmes," for more discussion and strategies.
- Don't buy your child everything he or she sees advertised.

What do I want to continue?

_____

_____

_____

What do I want to change?

_____

_____

_____

THREE

No and the Brain

A few years ago my neighbor Emma, a close friend, was having some problems with her vision, so I would often drive her to the market or appointments. This time I took her to her eye doctor.

"I don't know what's going on, but I can't see as well as usual," Emma told her eye doctor. "My vision is getting cloudy."

The eye doctor examined her, asked a few questions, and did a quick series of tests.

"Emma," the doctor explained, "your vision is getting cloudy because you're developing a cataract."

"What do we do about that?" Emma asked the doctor.

"We wait," the doctor said. "We'll wait to let it get thicker so we can remove it more easily."

The way to correct a cataract is to surgically remove it, but there are risks associated with this type of surgery. To reduce the risk, ophthalmologists wait and let the cataract grow and thicken. The thicker the cataract, the lower the risk of the surgery, so Emma's eye doctor wanted to wait at least a few months and perhaps a couple of years.

That is the scenario for most adults; but if a child develops a cataract—a rare phenomenon that occurs in less than 1 percent of children, often as a complication of German measles or Down syndrome—the physician takes immediate action, scheduling the surgery to remove it as soon as possible. The treatments are different because so much growth is going on in the brain of a small child that any impairment in vision could lead to permanent loss of vision. An adult's brain and vision are fully developed and can adapt to the changes in vision that a cataract causes.

Think about the difference like this: When you push your hand into freshly poured cement, you leave a permanent imprint, but if you push your hand against hardened, cured cement, you might wipe away some dust, but that's about it. The brain of the adult *is* wired, whereas the brain of a young person is *being* wired. The young brain is under construction from before birth all the way into the early twenties.

Unlocking the Brain's Secrets

Until the late twentieth century, a living brain could be studied only by observing a person's behavior and developing theories of what must be going on inside. That changed with the development of powerful machines like MRI (magnetic resonance imaging); PET scans (positron emission tomography); fMRI (functional magnetic resonance imaging); and SPECT (single photon emission computerized tomography). This amazing technology allows scientists to peer inside a brain without harming it and watch this miraculously complex organ work. The new technology helps us understand how children's and teens' brains develop, and why No is so important to that development. In this and other chapters you'll learn more about childhood and adolescent brains than anyone knew just ten years ago.

The Parent Tool Kit: Brain Basics

The following facts give you some basics on the workings of children's and teens' brains.

PARENT TOOL KIT
Brain Basics

1. Experience plays a major role in the wiring of the brain.
2. The brain is more sensitive to experience during growth spurts.
3. Brain growth spurts continue all the way into the early twenties.
4. The brain's growth spurts are called "windows of opportunity and sensitivity."
5. A baby's brain triples in size in the first year.
6. The adolescent brain is still "under construction."
7. Strong drives are "hardwired" into the brain.
8. Scientists are now discovering circuits for the "moral brain."

The brain is basically an electrical system. In fact, right now your brain is, on average, generating enough equivalent power to light a twenty-five-watt light bulb. It turns out that the old cartoon image of a light bulb appearing over the head to signify an idea was a lot more accurate than anyone imagined at the time.

The basic unit or building block of the brain's electrical system is the brain cell, also called the neuron. Although neurons come in different shapes and sizes, they all share a common structure. Each has a cell body with a long cable extending outward. Electrical impulses travel down these cables (technically called "axons") to branches, or dendrites, where they pass out of the cell through the branches, jump across a tiny gap (which is called a "synapse"), and enter the branches of neighboring neurons.

A human baby is born with about one hundred billion neurons, and each of those hundred billion neurons has about ten thousand branches. One hundred billion neurons with ten thousand branches each make the possible number of connections about one quadrillion. It is impossible to calculate the number of ways to configure a quadrillion connections. We cannot even calculate how many songs could be composed by arranging the eighty-eight keys on a piano keyboard in different combinations and different sequences. The late Francis Crick, the codiscoverer of DNA, once said that the possible number of neural configurations in just one brain exceeds the number of atoms in the known universe.

Those numbers are pretty impressive and give you some idea of the massive job the brain has in organizing itself. When a baby is born, only 17 percent of the neurons are linked, which leaves the vast majority, 83 percent, to be wired together later. The process of wiring those billions and billions of neurons starts before birth and speeds forward in the days, weeks, months, years, and even—we now know—the decades that follow. At birth a baby's brain weighs only about three-quarters of a pound, but it grows fast as all those connections are being wired. In fact, the brain's normal rate of growth is to *triple* in size that first year. No wonder it is so important to wake up at all hours to feed your baby.

Just a few short years ago scientists thought that the wiring was finished by the age of ten to twelve because the brain typically reaches three pounds by then—the normal adult size. But important recent discoveries about the brain reveal that, although brain mass doesn't increase past the age of ten, a lot of construction is going on all the way into the early twenties.

The process of wiring together these neurons is driven by two powerful forces: genetics and experience. Genes provide the materials and rough blueprint needed to build a human brain and determine which neurons connect with others and when. This wiring process driven by genetics is a kind of "hard-wiring," complemented by the "soft-wiring" shaped by life experiences. Take language, for example. Babies come into the world with the genetic ability to make sounds, an example of hard-wiring, but which of the world's sixty-five hundred languages he learns to speak is shaped by the experiences he will have—by the customized soft-wiring.

For most of the last century, scientists debated whether genetics and natural inheritance or nurture and experience were more important in gaining skills, in learning quickly, and in succeeding in life. Recently it has become clear that, in nearly all cases, nature *and* nurture affect the brain's ability to interact with *and* respond to the environment.

The crucial role of experience in the brain is summed up in a favorite phrase of neuroscientists: "The neurons that fire together wire together." The more they fire together—pass on an electrical charge from one cell to another—the stronger the connections between the neurons become. This process continues throughout a child's life and is still at work every moment of a teenager's life. When a high school student is trying to remember new Spanish words, she'd be well advised to write them out, say them out loud, and use them with her friends so that eventually she remembers them. By repeatedly firing the neurons that do the work of thinking about those words until the connections became strong enough to hold, she wires the new Spanish terms into her brain.

Although experience is key to brain wiring, not all experiences are equal. Some have a much greater effect on brain wiring than others, and the experiences that have the greatest impact are those that occur during a brain's growth spurts.

Growth Spurts in the Brain

It turns out that the brain is modular, its neurons wired together into circuits that perform complex tasks. Some regulate heart rate and body temperature, and others enable us to write poetry or figure out Sudoku puzzles. Cordoned off into different regions of the brain, every circuit seems to have its own timetable. As a child grows, certain brain structures associated with particular functions have periods of intense activity and development, while others remain relatively quiet. Then the quiet structures awaken and begin to develop rapidly, while previously active structures end their growth spurts. In the middle of a growth spurt, the brain's various structures act like a room full of preschoolers: While two in one corner drift to sleep, three in another will act up. When those three go to sleep, others will wake up and fuss.

Neuroscientist Marian Diamond of the University of California at Berkeley found that at the onset of a growth spurt, the area of the brain ready for intense growth starts to overproduce dendrites, the branches at the end of the brain cells. During a growth spurt, these branches go through hypergrowth. This process is known as blossoming. As a result, the number of branches that grow greatly exceeds the number that will survive.

After this overproduction of dendrites, experience takes over. Remember: *The neurons that fire together wire together.* Experience causes certain neurons to fire, and as they fire, the branch connections that bridge one cell to another get stronger. The branches that don't fire begin to shrink, wither, and eventually disappear. This process is called pruning. Experience, therefore, prunes or sculpts the circuits of the brain.

These periods of blossoming and pruning are critical in brain development. Experiences during growth spurts, more than any other time, physically shape the brain's neural networks, or wiring. Take, for example, Albert Einstein's advice about child rearing: "If you want your children to be brilliant, read them fairy tales. If you want them to be more brilliant read them more fairy tales." As a three-year-old listens to a fairy tale while her brain is in the process of blossoming and pruning, she is developing her imagination. While an adult might enjoy a fairy tale, it is not going to build the neural networks for imagination because the blossoming and pruning of those circuits happened many years earlier.

Consistent with the brain's modular design, these developmental processes occur at certain times, and if neurons are not wired together during these windows of opportunity, the branches of these cells will start to be pruned away. With a piece of underripe fruit, if you buy it green, you can let it sit for a couple of days to get ripe, but if you let it sit too long, it will spoil. You have a window of opportunity for eating the fruit. When a window in the brain closes, it loses that opportunity for further development.

Windows of Opportunity, Windows of Sensitivity

The ramifications of blossoming and pruning illustrate how pivotally important the events in our children's and teens' lives can be. Put simply: *Experiences that a child has during the brain's growth spurts will have a much greater effect than at any other time in that child's life* on the development of cognitive abilities, skills, self-discipline, patience, perseverance, and generosity. This is why these growth spurts are also called windows of opportunity and windows of sensitivity.

That's why Emma could wait for her cataract surgery, whereas a young child with a cataract needs to have it removed right away. A cataract reduces the amount of information being processed by the optic nerve and sent to the brain traveling through those axons and dendrites, but Emma's optic nerve and visual circuits are fully wired, so the effect is minimal. In a child, the window of opportunity to wire vision is wide open, but it won't be open for long; if the dendrites are not used they will wither away. So every day counts as the doctor decides on treatment for a child.

Phonemic awareness, our ability to distinguish different sounds, is another example of how blossoming and pruning play a role in development. A newborn is a citizen of the world. She can learn any language. As she hears a B sound and an R sound, for instance, the circuits in the auditory cortex (the hearing center of the brain) wire together in response to these phonemes. With repetition—neurons firing together and wiring together—particular circuits fire in response to different sounds and enable the baby to recognize specific phonemes. Research shows that the window of opportunity for phonemic awareness is open widest in the first three years of life. It doesn't shut completely after that, but it is never again so wide open.

This window of opportunity also explains why one of the strongest predictors of a child's reading ability in school is the amount of one-to-one conversation between caregiver and child in the first three years of life. The ability to differentiate sounds is the first crucial step on the path to associating sounds with letters. Kids who don't learn to distinguish sounds during that time usually have trouble learning to read later on. Reading's first lessons don't happen in school: They happen in the crib during that important window of opportunity.

Many people understand this intuitively. That's why most people instinctively talk to newborns in a very special way, as in "Hel-LO ba-by, ba-by, ba-by!" Parents all over the world, communicating in countless different languages, all engage in some variation of this baby talk, a way of speaking that features constant repetition, over-pronunciation of consonants and vowels, delivered in an octave above normal speech. The reason we do this is to make it easier for a baby to pick out the individual sounds we are making so he can make sense of them. We instinctively know that the baby's little brain is in the process of wiring itself for language.

Beneficial experiences enable the brain to wire the appropriate circuits during the periods of blossoming and pruning. Experience determines which neural connections survive and which wither away. Adverse experiences during the blossoming and pruning periods have a greater negative effect than they might otherwise have, because, when bad things happen, the brain is especially vulnerable to them and can more easily be hurt. The same window of opportunity to wire the brain for a normal, healthy life is open for whatever happens, good or bad. On the other side of the window of opportunity is the window of sensitivity.

Here's an example of sensitivity at work: A series of ear infections in a two-year-old, if severe and frequent enough, can interfere with the wiring that will enable the baby to differentiate sounds and will impair his hearing permanently. The window of sensitivity for the wiring of the auditory cortex is open wide, which makes it particularly susceptible to interference. An adult's auditory cortex is already wired, so a few ear infections, as long as they heal eventually, won't impair his ability to distinguish the word *tad* from the word *dad*. A two-year-old's auditory cortex, however, is still under construction. Ear infections may put him in danger of missing out on prime time for learning sounds, because they occur during the window of sensitivity.

Vision and hearing are obvious brain functions, but the same wiring process is at work in domains that we might not automatically associate with the brain. For example, it's important for a third grader to learn to resolve differences with playmates and figure out how to get along with other children. If he doesn't develop the brain circuits for sharing and compromise while the window of opportunity is open, how will he know how to deal with workplace disagreements years later?

Nine-year-old Seth came into the kitchen with Jonah. "Mom, Jonah hit me. Tell him to go home," Seth sobbed.

"He wouldn't let me use his Game Boy, Mrs. Hanson," Jonah explained. "I don't want to go home yet."

Marjorie put down the book she was reading and motioned for the two to come closer. She crouched down to their eye level and spoke calmly. "So, are you two friends having some trouble getting along?"

"Mom, make him go home," Seth repeated.

"Mrs. Hanson, make Seth take turns," Jonah whined.

"I'm not making either of you do anything. I think you're getting old enough to figure this out for yourselves," Marjorie said as she reached out to take their hands. "Seth, do you know how to share and take turns? If not, maybe I need to put the Game Boy away for a while. Jonah, do you know how to get along with Seth without hitting? If not, maybe the two of you shouldn't play together for a while. Now, I want the two of you to go back into the family room and figure this out. Okay?"

She tousled each boy's hair and sent them on their way. Five minutes later she heard laughter coming from the family room.

Adolescents' developmental windows relate to the wiring of impulse control and anger management. That's why we need to pay attention when a teenager spends hours playing violent video games while this window of opportunity is open wide. It also makes sense to encourage kids to get involved in service projects and volunteer opportunities while major brain circuits related to social relationships are blossoming and pruning.

Rodney reminded his son Alex to mow the lawn before he went out with his friends. "Remember the deal you agreed to this morning, Alex."

"Aw, Dad, do I have to do it now? I'll do it tomorrow," Alex moaned.

"Alex, there are two reasons. First, the grass is too long. Second, you agreed this morning to mow before you got together with your friends. You've had hours to get the job done. So, no, you can't put it off till tomorrow."

Alex walked out of the room, slamming the door as an exclamation point, before his father had even finished. Rod remained calm as he called for his son to come back into the room. Seconds passed before Rod repeated his request loud enough to make sure Alex heard him. "Alex, I asked you to come back and finish this conversation."

Alex returned and glared at his father. Rod remained calm, but his voice was firm. "Alex, I'm angry that you walked away while I was talking and I will not tolerate you slamming doors in my face."

Alex started to escalate. "I didn't slam the door. I closed it," he yelled. "And why do you have such stupid rules anyway?"

Rod was getting frustrated, but still he kept his cool. "Alex, please listen to me. There are two issues I want to make clear. First, I understand that you're angry because you can't go out with your friends. But it's not okay to walk away while I'm talking and it's not okay to slam doors. You can be angry, but you need to deal with your anger without being disrespectful. Second, when you make a commitment, I expect you to keep it. Now, if you want to go out at all today, I suggest that you start managing your anger better and get the lawn mowed." Rod waited for a few seconds and then asked, "Okay?"

Alex wasn't happy but he did mow the lawn and he didn't slam any doors in the process.

The Hardwired Drives

We need to know something else about brains before we can connect the dots and understand the brain basis for No. In addition to all the things we learn, our brains come equipped with certain powerful drives that are hardwired from birth, like software already installed in a new computer.

- Fight/Flight
- Seek Pleasure/Avoid Pain

- Social Connection
- Seek Approval/Avoid Disapproval
- Empathy
- Guilt

Fight/Flight

One famous hardwired drive is our natural emergency switch, the fight-or-flight response, as it was dubbed in 1929 by the Harvard physiologist Walter Cannon. Confronted with danger, a person's body surges with adrenaline and other potent hormones, preparing either to clash with the physical threat directly (fight) or to seek escape (flight). This mechanism kicks in not only in the face of physical threats but sometimes with psychological stress. Let's say, for example, that an Iraq War veteran is walking down the street and hears a car backfiring. Immediately, that veteran's brain activates the fight-or-flight response, not because of real mortal danger but because the backfiring car made a sound that triggered a memory of gunfire. At that moment the Iraq War veteran has no control over this mental mechanism. It's automatic.

Seek Pleasure/Avoid Pain

Another innate drive is the seeking of pleasure and avoidance of pain. Sigmund Freud described this hardwired drive as the Pleasure Principle in his 1900 classic, *The Interpretation of Dreams.* Freud didn't know the biophysiological details of brain functioning; he just watched how people behaved and identified these tendencies. Today, we know that a "pleasure circuit" (sometimes called the "reward circuit") comprises a number of structures in the emotional centers of the brain that specialize in producing a feel-good chemical called dopamine. We are attracted to things and experiences that increase levels of dopamine. One of the reasons that drugs and alcohol are addictive is that they create surges of dopamine in the brain. The brain's memory center, the hippocampus, records memories of dopamine-generating events and links to the brain's CEO, the prefrontal cortex, to figure out how to get the pleasure again.

The fight-or-flight hair-trigger response and the urge to seek pleasure and avoid pain are only two of the hardwired instincts. Other drives include those for connection, approval, empathy, and guilt. All of these together form the basis of the moral brain. It is extremely important that children learn to manage these drives, and the best way to teach them is using No.

Connection

Eight-year-old Lucy came home from school in tears and went straight to her room. Megan, her mother, saw her dash through the kitchen and knew something was wrong. She waited a minute before knocking gently on Lucy's door. "Go away," came the muffled response.

Megan's question, "Lucy, honey, what's wrong?" brought silence.

Megan tried again. "Did something bad happen at school?"

This time, Lucy responded. "Yes, something bad happened. I don't have any friends. All the other kids hate me."

Megan opened the door, looked at her daughter's tear-stained face, and walked over to her and started to rub her back. Lucy turned over and reached to hug her mom. For the next ten minutes she told Megan, between sobs, how her friends wouldn't let her play with them during recess and that they didn't like her anymore. Megan mostly listened and tried to comfort Lucy.

A few minutes later Lucy's older brother Thad poked his head in the room to tell Lucy that her friend Sandra was on the phone. "Should I tell her you'll call her back?" Thad asked.

"No," said Lucy. "I'll talk to her."

After Lucy left to talk with Sandra, Thad asked his mom what had happened. Megan was explaining to Thad that Lucy had a bad day at school when Lucy came back into the room smiling from ear to ear. Oblivious to the fact that Thad was even there, Lucy excitedly told Megan that Sandra had called to say how sorry she and the other girls were for being mean. "She said they were all super-sorry and asked if I would play with them tomorrow."

Lucy had an emotional roller-coaster ride when her friends were alternately mean and nice to her, because of the brain's powerful drive for human connection. We see it in newborns, who pay special attention to human faces as soon as they can focus their eyes. It's obvious in preteens and teenagers who beg for more time with their friends. Brain scientists have identified hormones in the brain, oxytocin and vasopressin, that are involved in these interactions. I'll explain them further in chapter 5, but for now suffice it to say that we are hardwired to connect to other people. In fact, a lack of connection can cause a "failure to thrive," which can be fatal for babies and young children.

Seek Approval/Avoid Disapproval

The desire for connection also powers a related impulse, our innate desire for approval and natural fear of disapproval. The reason we are so sensitive to approval and disapproval is that we want to maintain connection. When we sense approval, we feel confident that a connection will be maintained. Conversely, our fear of disrupting a connection makes us worry about disapproval.

That's why parents can often correct a child without saying a word. They do it with "the look." My siblings and I knew what my father's look of disapproval meant. When we crossed a line, he had a way of turning his head, fixing his eyes, and changing his facial expression. We automatically knew that he was upset. Now I know that the discomfort "the look" caused stemmed from our brain-based reaction to his disapproval.

Seeking a parent's approval is one bedrock of connection and the foundation of conscience. Feelings of security or insecurity are associated with behaviors that a parent approves or disapproves of. Moral behavior is based on relationships, not rules. In chapter 5, I will spend more time explaining the secure connection that is the basis for discipline and for an effective No.

Empathy

The third of the moral drives is empathy, the ability to share in another person's emotional experience. If I am capable of empathy, when you are happy I experience that happiness myself, or if you are sad, I experience that sadness. Our capacity for empathy makes emotions contagious. The examples are all around us. We cry at movies as we vicariously experience the same emotions as the actors do on the screen. When one baby cries, other babies start to cry too.

Aristotle wrote about empathy in *Poetics* more than two thousand years ago, but we now understand that its roots are in the brain. Neuroscientists have identified the neurons that fire in response to the actions and emotions of other people, which they call "mirror neurons." What happens when you put a group of people in a room and someone starts to yawn? Other people start to yawn as well. For many years, this propensity was explained as an unconscious response to the power of suggestion, but we now know that mirror neurons fuel this reaction.

As with many important scientific discoveries, the discovery of mirror neurons involved some good luck. As a *New York Times* article explained, fifteen years ago in Parma, Italy, a graduate student returned from lunch to his research lab eating an ice cream cone. In the lab was a monkey whose brain was wired for a research project on how the brain plans and carries out movements. The grad student looked at the monkey while licking his ice cream cone. Each time he licked the cone, the machine that tracked activity in the monkey's brain came to life and sounded, even though the monkey remained motionless.

A research team led by the University of Parma neuroscientist Giacomo Rizzolatti studied this observation further and discovered that the same brain circuits fired in the monkey when it observed an action as when it actually performed the action. Recent studies reveal that human mirror neurons are far more numerous, complex, and sophisticated than those of any other species. "We are exquisitely social creatures," Dr. Rizzolatti told the *Times*. "Our survival depends on understanding the actions, intentions, and emotions of others. Mirror neurons allow us to grasp the minds of others not through conceptual reasoning but through direct simulation—by feeling, not by thinking."

Mirror neurons are key to the social and moral underpinnings of the brain. As we observe someone's actions or feelings, our mirror neurons fire in chain reactions and simulate the action or emotion in our own brains. These mirror cells, remarkably enough, are already active by the time we are born and play an important role in our ability to form connections with our caregivers. The University of Washington child psychologist Andrew Meltzoff has demonstrated that within one hour of birth, babies will imitate an adult sticking his tongue out.

Mirror neurons also allow us to feel empathy. Every time we observe another person experiencing an emotion, mirror cells activate the same emotional circuits in our own brains. That's why we get scared at movies. When we see someone being abused or attacked, we feel afraid because our mirror neurons are firing. Or we get angry when playing a violent video game. The implications of this research are sweeping. For example, a study in the January 2006 issue of *Media Psychology* found that when children watched violent television programs, mirror neurons activated the aggression centers of the brain, making them more likely to be aggressive in real life.

Guilt

Research on the moral brain indicates that we are also hardwired for guilt. It is built into us: When we do something we sense is wrong or bad, we feel tweaked by guilt. We might suppress or control this feeling, but it's still there somewhere, and that is a good thing, because guilt can motivate people to do the right thing.

The renowned psychologist Jerome Kagan says that our brains have evolved to have an innate sense of right and wrong. Although definitions of right and wrong vary from one social group to another, the notion of right and wrong is universal. As we will see in chapter 7, when children are about eighteen months old they develop a sense of what is right and what is wrong, based on the approval or disapproval of their parents. Even street gangs involved in illegal activities have a code of right and wrong, and even hardened criminals know when they have crossed the line and lie to cover up their transgressions.

Where *No* Comes In

The brain's circuits and drives are sometimes at odds with one another. They are all genetically encoded in our brains, but how we express them has a lot to do with our experience—that is to say, which drive gets reinforced.

Seven-year-old Martin has a powerful urge to fight with the boy who just pushed him on the school playground. As he prepares to throw a punch, however, he sees his favorite teacher out of the corner of his eye. He likes her and wants her approval. The drives compete, but a split second later, Martin shoves his fist into his pocket and walks away, his need for approval carrying the day.

Your challenge as a parent is to raise a child who can manage his competing urges. There is nothing wrong with seeking pleasure, but a child who never learns to manage his pleasure drive will be controlled by it. There is a time for assertiveness or even aggression, but a child who can't control the fight/flight response will be in constant trouble. Using No teaches your children the crucial skills of balancing competing drives.

I wrote in chapter 1 that most parents want their children to be competent, responsible, and caring. A child whose highest goal is to seek pleasure and satisfy his own desires will never be competent, responsible, and caring. He will acquire those three traits only if he learns to master, not eliminate, his hardwired fight/flight response and drive for pleasure. He cannot learn to do this on his own, however. It is your responsibility to teach him how to develop self-discipline by using No to influence his hardwired drives for connection, approval, empathy, and guilt.

In brain terms, our popular Yes culture is creating a generation of "dopamine addicts" by glorifying aggression and violence as a form of entertainment. This makes the parent's job of creating balance more difficult and more urgent than ever. If we want our children to enjoy pleasure but not be blindly controlled by it, we need to teach them No. If we want our child to respond to threats in an assertive, active way, but not turn into someone who seeks confrontation because of the adrenaline rush it gives him, we need to teach him No.

Experience plays a large role in determining which circuits get wired in a child's or teen's brain and which don't, so it is your responsibility to limit some experiences, provide others, and know when to say no.

DO

- Set clear rules and expectations for controlling aggression. For example, instead of saying, "I want you to get along with your sister," say, "You may not hit your sister, call her names, or use put-downs."
- Make your children your priority so that your bond of connection is secure. Spend time together, schedule family activities in advance, and have as many meals together as possible.
- Model the respectful and caring behavior you want your children and teens to emulate. For example, if your teenager starts to yell, calmly say, "I want to talk with you about this, but I am not going to get into a yelling match. Let's take five minutes, we'll both calm down, and we'll talk about this when you're ready to talk without yelling."
- Encourage children to "put themselves in another person's shoes" to develop empathy. For example, say to your six-year-old who is refusing to share, "How would you feel if your friends wouldn't share any of their toys with you?"
- Reinforce good behavior with approval, encouragement, and praise. For instance, "Jennifer, that was great the way you let your little brother have a turn."

- Show your disapproval of bad behavior. Begin statements with *I* rather than *you* and focus on the behavior. Instead of saying, "You're really rude," say, "I'm angry that you walked away while I was trying to talk with you."

DON'T

- Don't swear or use abusive language with your children or teens.
- Don't engage in name-calling or put-downs. They eat away at the bonds of connection.
- Don't rescue children or teens from the discomfort of guilt, which is a healthy and appropriate response when they have done something wrong. Rather than say, "I know you didn't intend to be mean to Heather," say, "When we're mean to somebody else like you were to Heather, it's important to apologize and try not to do it again."
- Don't let your children and teens spend hours watching TV programs or playing video games that promote aggression and disrespect of others.

What do I want to continue?

_____

_____

_____

What do I want to change?

_____

_____

_____

Four

Self-Esteem
Kids Need the Real Thing

S elf-esteem is the key to happiness." This mantra has emerged as an accepted truism of modern American culture. That's the reason you find raising children's self- esteem goals in the mission statements of school districts across the country. An entire industry has blossomed that guarantees "enhanced self-esteem" to those who sign up for courses, subscribe to newsletters, or enroll in weekend retreats. That goal wouldn't be a problem if only we defined *self-esteem* correctly. Most of what passes as self-esteem boosting, however, is feel-good chatter. The real deal *is* crucial to success and happiness, but real self-esteem is also more difficult to build and is directly tied to No.

Self-Esteem Quiz

Answer the following questions Yes or No, depending on whether you think these efforts will help Adam build positive self-esteem.

1. Yes   No   Adam's parents praise his performance regardless of the effort.

2. Yes   No   Adam's teacher never uses a "red pencil" because he doesn't want Adam to feel that his work is not good enough.

3. Yes   No   Adam learns songs and reads books that remind him how special he is.

4. Yes   No   Mom praises Adam for any effort on chores around the house.

5. Yes   No   Adam's parents steer him away from things that might frustrate or discourage him.

6. Yes   No   When Adam's teacher corrected him, his parents got upset and called the teacher to complain that she was hurting his self-esteem.

7. Yes   No   Adam's parents tell him not to pay attention to what other people think and that "the important thing is to please yourself."

8. Yes   No   Adam is learning that the most important goal is to "feel good about yourself."

9. Yes   No   Adam's parents don't want him to feel guilty because they're afraid that would hurt his self-esteem.

10. Yes   No   Adam learns that if he loves himself, he will be successful.

Scoring this quiz is simple. All the answers should be No because none of these actions will build Adam's real self-esteem, in spite of the fact that self-help gurus, talk show hosts, and pop psychologists tell us the opposite. Many parents have bought into three myths about self-esteem.

Self-Esteem Myth 1: Self-Esteem Comes First and Leads to Success

Second grader Cassie couldn't wait to show her family the list she made in school of all of the ways she is special. "Ms. Foster said that I should hang it in my bedroom and look at it every day so I remember how good I am," she beamed. Her mom and grandma looked at the beautifully colored sheet and read each item out loud.

"Cassie, this is great," her mother said. "And you really are fun, pretty, smart, helpful, and all the other things on your list. We'll put it up after dinner."

Her grandmother added, "You must feel good about yourself. Do you know how proud your mom and I are of you?"

Wonderful scenes like this one are helpful and are repeated millions of times a year in homes across America. After all, what's not to like about kids like Cassie feeling good about themselves? However, the implied promise is that you can build self-esteem with words alone and pave the way to classroom success, which is unfounded and unsupported by any scientific or academic studies. Spending time and energy trying to make kids feel better about themselves does not ensure their academic success. Over the past twenty-five years, self-esteem scores and academic grades have risen as SAT scores have dropped. Other studies involving tens of thousands of students demonstrate that self-esteem does not boost academic achievement. We have put the proverbial cart before the horse with the mistaken notion that self-esteem comes first and behavior follows.

Even if positive self-esteem does not lead to better classroom performance, it must surely lead to better relationships, right? Wrong again. Researchers could not find any connection between high self-esteem scores and popularity among high school students. Even more startling, a study at the University of Kentucky found that people with high self-esteem scores were actually more likely to have relationship problems.

Well, okay, even if teaching self-esteem doesn't improve academic performance or social relationships, doesn't it inoculate youngsters against the dangers of drug and alcohol abuse and violence? Sadly, once again, the answer is no. Teens who have high self-esteem are just as much at risk for substance abuse as their peers who have low self-esteem. And other research found that school bullies actually had higher scores on self-esteem measures than the kids they were beating up.

Nor does self-esteem pay off later in the workplace. There is no demonstrable link between positive self-esteem and career success.

True self-esteem comes from achievement. When a child or teen is successful, he feels satisfied and competent. He feels good about himself. What's more, if he knows how to get along with other people, he will have more friends, which, once again, will boost his self-esteem. In other words, personal successes and friendships engender self-esteem, not the other way around. Success, however, depends on self-discipline. I'll explain that connection after we explore more self-esteem myths.

Self-Esteem Myth 2: Self-Esteem = Feeling Good

Victor proudly tapes his spelling paper to the refrigerator. "What's that, Victor?" asks his father, Eduardo.

"It's my spelling test," answers Victor proudly. "I got seven out of ten words right, and Mrs. Reilly told me that I should be proud of myself. She also said that my printing was very good for a second grader."

"That's great, Victor," said Eduardo. "Wait till your mom gets home. She's going to be real proud."

Two days later Victor rips his arithmetic paper out of his backpack after school and throws it on the table. Eduardo looks at the paper and sees that almost all of his son's answers are wrong. "Mrs. Reilly says that you or mom should help with my adding and subtracting," announces Victor. "I'm so stupid in arithmetic that I got it all wrong."

"Don't talk like that, Victor. You're not stupid. We'll work on your adding after dinner. Why don't you go play now."

Later that evening Victor is in tears as he struggles with the concepts of "carrying" and "borrowing." His mother is trying to explain it, but Victor isn't even listening anymore. "I can't do this, Mama. I hate math," he sobs.

"Victor, honey, you're too tired," replies his mother. "I'll write Mrs. Reilly a note and ask her to give you some extra help. Why don't you get ready for bed and I'll come read you a story and give you a tuck-in."

As Victor trudges off to the bathroom to brush his teeth, his mother turns to her husband. "I don't think that they should be teaching second graders 'carrying' and 'borrowing.' It's too difficult. Victor gets so upset that I'm worried about his self-esteem."

When I taught high school French, Elena, one of my students, didn't have a knack for languages and worked hard to get C's. Her parents told me during parent conferences that they planned to ask the principal to let Elena drop my class. "How come?" I asked. "Elena studies hard, completes all her assignments, and is doing well. I enjoy having her in my class."

"And she likes you and the class," her father replied. "But in spite of her hard work, she's only getting a C. When the midterm grades arrived last week she was in tears. We're concerned this is hurting her self-esteem and could do long-term damage."

Fortunately, I persuaded Elena's parents not to let her drop French. She continued her hard work, and by year's end she had a solid—and legitimate—B. Elena's parents almost succumbed to another myth: that good self-esteem means feeling good.

As we saw in chapter 2, our popular culture constantly reminds us that we should always feel good. Misguided programs to improve self-esteem teach kids that "feeling good about yourself is more important than performance." Kids constantly hear, "Who you are is important, not what you do." Parents fall into the trap of thinking that we can increase children's self-esteem with praise and expressions of love. With our constant need to tell our kids that they are the best, most wonderful kids in the world, we begin to equate their smiles with positive self-esteem and their tears with negative.

Healthy self-esteem and feeling good are two different things.

By confusing the two we run the risk of protecting our kids from the very experiences that build true self-esteem. That leads us to the next myth.

Self-Esteem Myth 3: Stress, Challenge, and Disappointment Damage Self-Esteem

Any Cub Scout parent will remember the annual Pinewood Derby races. Each kid buys a kit that contains the basics for building his own car. The kit contains a block of pine wood, wheels, and axles, everything the kid needs to get the car going. All the kits are the same. Each Cub Scout is to use his own creativity to design his own car. Then all the scouts take their cars to a special gathering and race to see whose car has the best design. The boys look forward to this night all year long.

When my son Dan and I first heard about the Pinewood Derby, we bought the kit and I had a choice to make: How much should I help Dan design and build his car? I reminded myself: *Dave, this is Dan's car, not your car.* I helped Dan, but I did my best to limit how much. I made some suggestions and we discussed different options of what to do with the wheels to make them go faster. By and large, however, Dan's Pinewood Derby entry was truly his creation—not the best Pinewood racer ever designed, but it wasn't bad, and it was his. As we drove to the pack meeting, I looked over at Dan with his racer on his lap and very clearly saw his look of satisfaction. He felt pretty good about what he had created.

My heart sank when we got to the meeting and saw some of the aerodynamic masterpieces on display. They looked like they had been designed by NASA engineers and given hundreds of hours of testing time in a wind tunnel. You half expected rocket boosters to kick in at some point as they rolled down the big ramp they set up for the races.

Dan felt disappointed when his car came in dead last. He also was confused about why the other cars were so much better than his. By the time the pizzas arrived, Dan and his friends were comparing notes. The blue-ribbon winner was in our den, so Dan asked him how he had designed such a dynamite car. "My dad did it. Isn't it cool?" he answered. Dan discovered that most of the boys had received major help from their fathers or other adults. One boy told Dan that his father was so involved, the boy just sat back and watched his father design and build the entire car.

Dan was still disappointed on the ride home that night. Who wouldn't be? He wanted to be competitive and ended up with the slowest car in the derby. As we talked about it, I tried to help Dan understand that the value of the Pinewood Derby was not in coming in first place but that he had built that car himself. The blue-ribbon winner may have felt better than Dan that night, but I still think that Dan got the bigger, albeit more painful, lesson in self-esteem. He had learned how to build something and increased his skills.

The fear that disappointment is bad for our kids leads many parents to go to great lengths to protect them from life's bumps and bruises. Even though we do this with the best intentions, we are mistaken in thinking that stress and frustration will harm kids. Mild stress and challenges make kids learn and grow. But we end up hovering over them emotionally and physically, micromanaging our kids' activities in school, sports, clubs, and the Pinewood Derby.

Kids need to figure things out for themselves. When parents rush in and rescue them, thinking that we are helping them on the road to success, we are actually teaching them a kind of helplessness. Martin Seligman, author of *Authentic Happiness* and *Learned Optimism,* identified this trend toward learned helplessness almost twenty years ago, and he sees it as a major obstacle that prevents people of all ages from becoming competent, responsible, and happy. We do whatever it takes to give our kids an advantage, whether that means marching into our children's classrooms and battling teachers over grades, showing up for ball games to badger coaches about playing time rather than to cheer the team, or writing entrance essays for college-bound teens.

Ross constantly nagged the high school baseball coach to move his son, Paul, up in the batting order and let him pitch more innings. He wandered over to the coach after the team had just won an extra-inning squeaker. "Nice game, coach," Ross began. "Ya' know, Paul's arm is stronger all the time. I think you should've brought him in as the reliever in the seventh inning. Then we wouldn't have gone into extra innings."

Austin, a veteran coach, was as good with parents as he was with the kids. "Ross, I know you're really a team supporter," he replied calmly. "You're at all the games, so you know I give all the kids a lot of playing time."

"I know that, but Paul has talent that's not being used," Ross insisted.

Austin remained calm. "Ross, we're in first place and every kid on the team is seeing action. That's a pretty good season in my book."

"Yes, but Paul gets frustrated. Do you know how disappointed he is when you bring in a weaker pitcher in a crucial situation?"

"Learning how to deal with frustration and disappointment is all part of being on a team," was Austin's response.

Disappointment, discouragement, and frustration help build character and self-esteem. Life deals disappointments to everyone and at some point children have to stand on their own two feet. They have to learn how to handle setbacks and get through times of feeling discouraged. How will kids ever build the internal resources to cope with life's ups and downs if they never get any practice? When you shield your kids from everything that hurts, you are not doing them any favors.

The Connecticut Junior Soccer Association has a novel way to tone down overinvolved parents. Silent Sidelines Weekend is a semi-annual event where spectators are asked to limit their participation to applause and their talking to a conversational volume. Yelling is out for these silent weekends. Players, referees, and most parents like the result. It serves as a reminder that the games are for the kids, and, as one boy testified, kids like to play without being yelled at.

Parent Tool Kit: Building Positive Self-Esteem

Building your child's positive self-esteem *is* important, but you want to do it the right way. Use these questions to see how you're doing.

PARENT TOOL KIT
Building Positive Self-Esteem

Yes	No		
☐	☐	1.	Self-discipline is a building block for positive self-esteem.
☐	☐	2.	Children learn from disappointment and failure.
☐	☐	3.	Competency builds self-esteem.
☐	☐	4.	I use "honest praise" with my child. In other words, when she expends real effort, I praise her. When she makes only a half-hearted attempt, I let her know that she can do better.
☐	☐	5.	Children in our family are encouraged to express their opinions.
☐	☐	6.	I support my children's teachers.
☐	☐	7.	I encourage my child to gain new skills.
☐	☐	8.	I reward real effort.
☐	☐	9.	I expect my children to do chores.
☐	☐	10.	I support my children as they learn new skills and competencies, and I let them work things out on their own.

If you answered yes to the questions in this tool kit, you're less likely to be misled by the self-esteem myths. Now let's figure out what self-esteem really is and how we can help our kids accumulate enough of the right stuff.

What Is Self-Esteem?

Self-esteem is the set of all the opinions we have about ourselves. Although self-esteem didn't become a buzzword until the 1970s, the concept has been around for more than a century. The great

American psychologist William James wrote about it as far back as 1890 in *The Principles of Psychology*. As we grow up, we all develop opinions of ourselves. Every individual has many facets, so we end up with thousands of opinions about every aspect of ourselves, including, among others, height, weight, appearance, intelligence, athletic prowess, social skills, sense of humor, adaptability, willpower, and resilience. The sum total of these opinions is what we call self-esteem or self-concept, two terms that are often used interchangeably.

The way we envision our self-esteem is based on facts as well as our emotional responses to those facts. For example, Kyle struggles day after day to unlock the mysteries of reading as he stares at the confusing blots of ink on the page of his first-grade reader. While he remains stymied, his classmates are making good progress. Kyle realizes that he cannot read as well as the other boys and girls (the fact) and he feels frustrated, sad, and angry about it (the emotional response.) On the other hand, Loren is at the top of his reading group (fact) and he feels happy about that (emotional response).

The source of both Kyle's and Loren's opinions of their reading ability is their experience. But that's not the only factor at work. Praise or criticism plays a role as well. If Loren's teacher criticized and humiliated him for every little mistake he made in reading, his opinion would suffer despite the fact that he was the best reader in the class. Ridicule can so undermine confidence and distort an opinion that the underlying fact and a kid's appraisal are out of sync. An extreme example of the discrepancy between fact and feeling is the case of an eating disorder where an underweight girl is convinced that she is fat and needs to lose weight.

Kyle's opinions can change, but they won't change as a result of empty encouragement for effort that doesn't result in his learning letters and words. As the teacher diagnoses his difficulty and gives him reading assignments and exercises that help him get through his confusion, however, his skill and self-esteem will grow. When parents and teachers emphasize praise and positive feedback for no real achievement, they actually undermine real self-esteem. You can't boost real self-esteem with hollow praise. You foster it by encouraging and praising accomplishments.

Phil Ledermann, a veteran educator, shared this analogy with me: "Self-esteem needs to be reality based. Parents and teachers should serve as a mirror reflecting back to kids an accurate appraisal of how they're doing. Hollow praise acts like a 'funny mirror,' giving the kids a distorted picture. Kids who have always received reflections from a 'funny mirror' end up with a distorted image of themselves."

Linking self-esteem to competence leads us to the importance of No. Managing drives and emotions is a prerequisite for success. When a child can discipline himself, manage his emotions, and delay gratification, he is more likely to complete his homework assignments, learn skills, and get along successfully with other kids. Accomplishments and strong friendships will do more for self-esteem than a year's worth of self-esteem-building exercises. A child who takes on a challenge, perseveres, and eventually succeeds does not need to worry about self-esteem. He will end up with a well-deserved sense of pride in his abilities. He will know that he is capable not because of a self-esteem song he learned but because he was successful.

A child's achievements don't need to be big but they need to be real. They start small, as in, "Megan, thanks for picking up your toys and putting them into the box," or, "Megan, you made a good choice to wait." They get more substantive with, "Megan, I noticed that you stuck with that project even though it was hard. Way to go!" And eventually you end up with, "Megan, I was so proud to watch you walk across the stage and receive your degree."

Self-esteem doesn't always mean getting things right. In fact, mistakes can be great teachers. I used to catch my high school students off guard when I told them that G. K. Chesterton said, "If something is worth doing, it's worth doing badly." They got the point when I reminded them of another tried-and-true bit of advice: "If at first you don't succeed, then try, try again." Setbacks build self-esteem too, as long as a child learns to keep trying, from the twelve-month-old trying to stand to the seven-year-old struggling to learn scales on a piano. When a baby lets go of the couch for the first time, she has a look of surprise and then wonder on her face. The smile that shines next shows that she knows she has just done something spectacular. However, a setback usually follows as she plops to the floor. Her efforts to pull herself up again are eventually rewarded as she gets more and more steady on her feet. Within weeks she's likely to be tooling all over the house.

Self-Esteem and Muscles

Somehow, stress has gotten a bad reputation in our culture. That's why the marketplace is filled with "stress busters" and strategies to "eliminate stress forever." While extreme, prolonged stress is harmful, there is such a thing as good stress, and our kids need it. Good stress is energizing and motivating. We know this when it comes to muscles but we somehow forget when it comes to building self-esteem. Muscles grow more powerful when we use them. Each time they recover from stress, they get stronger and more responsive. If we don't continue to use them they get soft, flabby, and weak. Self-esteem works the same way. Kids need some stress to develop their psychological muscles of re-silience, stamina, determination, commitment, confidence, dili-gence, and perseverance. It's okay for kids to feel bad sometimes because it will enable them to feel good more often. Frustration, boredom, and disappointment are not particularly comfortable feelings, but kids need measured doses of them. If kids do not have negative experiences or stress, they do not build their psy-chological muscles, and they end up being emotionally flabby.

My mother didn't read parenting books and never talked about parenting techniques or styles with anyone, but she knew that some pain was good medicine. When I was six years old, a new boy, Jimmy Sutton, moved into our neighborhood. Our family had been among the first to move into our new development, so I watched the moving vans arrive, excited to see if the new families had any kids. When the Sutton family moved in, I saw that Jimmy was my age so I went over and tried to make friends. It did not go well. Before long we were arguing and I went home crying to my mother after Jimmy hauled off and hit me.

"Jimmy hit me!" I cried as I found my mother in the kitchen. I expected her to come to the rescue and was sure she would march over to the Suttons to get this straightened out. I didn't like what I heard next.

"Do you want to have friends to play with?" she asked me. She didn't really want my answer so she continued after taking a breath. "If you want friends, then you're going to have to learn how settle fights. You need to learn how to stand up to him and let him know that he can't get away with hitting you."

I was disappointed that she wouldn't solve my problem for me, but after a while I wandered back over to the Sutton house. I don't recall exactly how we settled that argument, but the two of us worked it out, and Jimmy Sutton ended up being one of my best friends throughout my grade-school years. My mother did not make it easy on me, but she made sure I learned the social skills I would need later in life.

I helped my kids learn this lesson when I had to deal with Dan and Brian arguing and fighting. When Dan was ten and Brian seven, they started screaming upstairs and soon raced into the kitchen as we were trying to get dinner ready for company. Each tried to outdo the other with shouts of "He hit me! Make him stop!"

I asked them to settle down and explain what had happened, but they were too angry. Each tried to convince Monica and me that he was innocent, and that our job was to punish the other one. The doorbell rang and I thought to myself, "Great. Our friends are at the door and we're in the kitchen trying to keep our sons from attacking each other."

Luckily our friends understood when I explained that we had a family emergency and could they relax while we tried to prevent World War III. In the kitchen, Monica already had each boy's attention. "I am not going to try to figure out what happened, and I'm certainly not going to solve it," Monica said. "I want the two of you to go sit in separate chairs in the family room. You're not to get out of those chairs until you've resolved this."

They both were really steamed, so it took a while for Monica's solution to work. We kept an eye on the boys until they were calm. Our friends patiently waited for at least a half hour. Eventually Dan and Brian settled down and worked out an agreement. They agreed to take fifteen-minute turns playing with the toy over which they were fighting. When I asked who would have the first turn, they agreed to flip a coin. They also promised that there would be no more fighting.

Resiliency

I used to compare parenting notes with my friend Michael when our kids were growing up. He would frequently joke that it's good for kids to have a "daily dose of pain." Although he said it tongue in cheek, his words contain an important nugget of truth. Pain is part of life and comes in a million different varieties, so it's very important for kids to learn how to deal with it. I'm not talking about physically harmful or psychically damaging pain, but the everyday stings of disappointment, discouragement, and frustration.

Overprotected kids become emotionally fragile and never learn to bounce back from adversity. A recent article in *Psychology Today* reported that a university counseling center had been inundated with first-year students before the fall semester was even half over. Many were struggling with heavy workloads, deadlines, and competition for the first time in their academic lives. A lot of these new students were collapsing under the same types of pressure that first-year college students have faced for generations. They were not prepared emotionally for their first real-life stresses.

All parents want their children to be able to handle adversity, to grow into individuals who can bounce back from tough times, disappointment, and even tragedy and trauma. Resiliency is the quality that enables them to do that. Yet, no matter how much we might want our kids to be resilient, they don't become that way automatically. Just as we have to teach children to be respectful, we also have to teach them to be resilient.

When our kids learn to deal with little setbacks as they grow up, they are better prepared to deal with bigger ones later on in life. We all learn how to cope through failure and mistakes. If a child never loses, she never learns how to deal with loss. If he is never disappointed, he never figures out how to deal with disappointment. If she is never frustrated, she never discovers how to overcome frustration. If he never has to struggle, he never develops the traits of persistence and determination. Sometimes, the most uncomfortable situations present the biggest opportunities for our kids—the crucible that forges the internal resources they need to succeed. Resilient kids will be willing to take on big challenges and take appropriate risks because they will be less afraid than kids who have never had that experience.

Bonnie Benard, one of the country's leading researchers on resilience, in her 2004 book, *Resiliency: What We Have Learned,* synthesizes decades of research and provides a blueprint for parents who want their kids to step up to challenges, recover from setbacks, and see things through to completion.

Resiliency: Ingredient 1, Support and Connection

Michael's mother, Mary, and stepfather, Jules, never miss parent conferences at school, volunteer to help with his youth group at church, and coach his soccer team. His friends enjoy coming over to his house to play because Mary and Jules talk and joke with them, and ask them about school.

Resilient kids are surrounded by people who encourage and support them, who believe in their ability to succeed. In chapter 5 I will explain that one of the basic building blocks for competent children is a sense of connection or attachment. That same factor shows up in the resiliency research as well. Ronald Feldman and his colleagues found that close relationships in the family are the best predictors for good behavioral outcomes. These kids feel emotionally connected to their parents and get time with their parents. They don't monopolize their parents' time, but they know that if they need their parents' support, their parents will be there. Along with that, they communicate with their parents. They know their parents will listen to them—Mom or Dad won't always take care of things for them, but they will listen to them and acknowledge their feelings. One of the key factors in creating resilient kids is that firm sense of connection with caring adults and the knowledge that parents or other significant adults are in their corner supporting them. Go to your child's choir recitals and games; offer to help them practice their lines for the school play; make time to help out with club activities.

Resiliency: Ingredient 2, High Expectations

Ethan, a high school junior, was discussing class selections for the next year with his friend Christopher in the school cafeteria. Christopher was telling Ethan that the coming year was going to be a breeze. "I have the most awesome schedule. I don't have any tough classes so I'm just going to enjoy the good life of being a senior," he announced.

"Are your parents going to let you get away with such a cushy schedule?" asked Ethan.

"They don't care as long as I get decent grades," replied Christopher.

"Man, my parents would never let me take all easy classes," Ethan said.

"Your parents need to lighten up," Christopher told Ethan.

"Aw, it's okay. I don't mind working hard. It'll get me ready for college," Ethan responded.

Resilient kids have parents, teachers, and other adults who believe in their ability to succeed, encourage and support them to do so, and have reasonable but high expectations. For instance, make it clear that you expect your child to attend school every day and complete all assignments. Every evening, check to make sure he's attended every class and has completed his work. Be specific about which chores need to be done and when and how he should do them. When your child makes a commitment, make sure he follows through.

Resiliency: Ingredient 3, Compassion

Ten-year-old Jasmine was upset as she told her grandfather what had happened at school. "The other girls were making fun of Miranda just because she wears old clothes," Jasmine said. "It's not fair, Grandpa. Miranda is really nice and her family doesn't have money for new clothes. How would those kids like it if their families suddenly couldn't get them new clothes?"

Her grandfather asked her what she could do to help Miranda. Jasmine had an immediate answer: "I'm going to make sure I sit with her in the lunchroom tomorrow. I know those other girls won't bother her if I'm there. Besides, I really like Miranda. Can I invite her over after school tomorrow to play?"

"Sure, honey, that's a great idea."

Resilient kids are not all wrapped up in themselves. They are interested in and look out for others. They get involved in service activities and volunteering in the community. The child who is all wrapped up in himself or herself makes a very small package. If we give our kids the message that the world revolves around them, we give them a false sense of importance. We want our kids to be compassionate, to be willing to help out, to know that other people are important too.

Natalie thought it was funny when some friends constructed a fake MySpace page on the Internet for a classmate they didn't like. Although Natalie hadn't taken an active role in it, she was talking and laughing on the phone about the obscene pictures and statements on the girl's page. Natalie's mother, Jan, overheard her. Jan signaled to Natalie to end the phone call. "Natalie," Jan began, "what were you and your friends laughing about?"

Natalie looked nervous and told her mother they were just joking.

Jan knew that Natalie wasn't telling the truth, and after some back-and-forth Natalie told her mother the full story. She finished with, "Mom, I didn't do anything myself."

"I hope that's true, Natalie," replied Jan, "but you knew about it and your laughing encouraged the others. The principal just sent a letter about cyberbullying and that's exactly what this is. I'm really disappointed in you."

"Mom, come on, it's not a big deal. It's just a joke."

"It may not be a big deal to you, but how do you think the other girl will feel when she sees it? Do you think she'll be laughing at your joke?"

Jan succeeded in helping Natalie imagine how painful this experience was for the girl who was object of their "joke." Before long Natalie was in tears and told her mother how guilty she felt for being so mean. Jan added, "I'm glad you're sorry, but I want to know what you're going to do about it." Jan ended up being proud of her daughter as Natalie, learning a lesson on compassion, called her friends and insisted they take down the MySpace page before anyone could see it. "Guys, this was really mean. I'd want to die if anyone did anything like that to me."

Resiliency: Ingredient 4, Autonomy and Resourcefulness

When our son Dan was in the sixth grade he decided to compete in the science fair with a chemistry project. His teacher signed off on Dan's choice and he came home excited to get started. It was an ambitious project and Monica and I were tempted to help Dan with the research, but we didn't. We let him track down the information and resources he needed. I'm still amazed at how he did it.

Dan figured that a good place to find answers to his chemistry questions would be the top-rated university chemistry department in the country, which just happened to be a mile from our house. On his own, he got the name and telephone number of a chemistry professor at the University of Minnesota, gave him a call, and caught him at his desk on his first attempt. Not only did the professor take the time to listen to Dan's questions, he invited him over for a visit. By the end of the week Dan had had lunch with the professor, taken a tour of the chemistry department, had answers to all his questions, and was well on his way to completing his project. The only help he got from us was the ride to and from campus.

Resilient kids are able to act independently and don't rely on others to do what they can do for themselves. Parents encourage their development when we support and assist them but avoid taking over and investing more in a project or activity than they do themselves.

Resilient kids set goals, work toward them, and learn from mistakes. They become aware of their strengths through experience. Success starts small, starts early, and grows. Little babies will work really hard at rolling over. Grade school kids learn to read. Middle schoolers finish a project. Teens put together a public service video. As children succeed in mastering different tasks, they experience their own competence.

Resiliency: Ingredient 5, Optimism

Resilient kids see the glass as half full rather than half empty and focus on strengths rather than weaknesses. They choose to look for the silver lining even when things go wrong.

A Yiddish folk tale told in a beautifully illustrated children's book, *It Could Always Be Worse,* by Margot Zemach, teaches this lesson in a delightful way. A poor, unfortunate man lived with his mother, his wife, and his six children in a one-room hut. The crowded conditions, quarreling children, and constant bickering between his mother and wife had him at his wit's end. Unable to stand it any longer, he ran to his rabbi for help. The rabbi heard his tale of woe, thought for a while, and then instructed the man to bring chickens, geese, and ducks into the hut. The man was puzzled but followed the rabbi's advice anyway, only to discover that adding the animals made things even more miserable. Each time he returned to complain, the rabbi instructed him to add yet more farm animals to the chaotic hut. Finally the man returned to the rabbi on the brink of despair. When the rabbi told him to release all the animals from the hut, the man was ecstatic to find the hut so peaceful and quiet. He had learned that "things could always be worse."

Optimism is a common trait in resilient youngsters, and parents can promote it by helping them regain perspective when they deal with setbacks and disappointments.

Resiliency: Ingredient 6, Determination

Both Dan and Erin attended the YMCA's Camp Widjiwagan in northern Minnesota each summer during their middle and high school years. They developed close friendships and learned respect for the environment and the importance of teamwork firsthand. They also learned the meaning of determination. Each year the counselors would lead them on longer and more challenging trips. The "Widji" experience culminated in a forty-two-day canoe trip in the Arctic wilderness the summer after high school graduation. The twenty-four-year-old counselor and five teenage "voyageurs" dealt with ice-covered lakes, raging rivers, lost gear, clouds of mosquitoes, subfreezing temperatures, gale-force winds, and paddling for twenty hours at a stretch. At the closing campfires, when parents and friends gathered to hear the "tales from the trail," the teenagers were asked, "Weren't you ever tempted to give up?" The campers would always answer proudly, "Never. No matter how hard it was we were determined to make it."

Kids don't have to go to the Arctic to discover that problems are nothing more than solutions waiting to be found. Parents can help them cultivate determination every time they hold back when they are tempted to jump in and rescue. Instead of saying, "This is how you do it," say, "Well, that didn't work, can you think of some other ways that might?" When your child asks for help with math, for instance, help her understand what she needs to do, but avoid just giving her the answer. When your teenager needs help with a chore, assist him, but don't do it for him.

Resiliency: Ingredient 7, Flexibility and Patience

Samantha, eleven, was struggling with her language arts homework. Mr. Holmes had circled the mistakes on her spelling and vocabulary quiz and told her to correct them for homework. "I hate doing this, Mom," she cried. "Mr. Holmes is so stupid. How am I supposed to know the right answer if he won't tell us? Will you help me?" she pleaded.

Joan sighed, put down her newspaper, and joined Samantha at the kitchen table. "All right," she said, "but we don't have much time. My favorite TV show starts in ten minutes. Let me take a look."

Joan looked at the page and started to tell Samantha the answers. Samantha dutifully corrected her paper according to her mother's directions. They were finished in time for Joan's show. "Thanks, Mom," Samantha said. "I really appreciate it."

Two blocks away, Samantha's friend Ashley was struggling with the same assignment. "Mom, can you help me with my paper? I have to correct all these mistakes by tomorrow." Terri asked her what she had to do. "I have to correct the wrong words," Ashley answered.

"Well, Ashley, how can you figure out the answers?" Terri asked.

"You could tell me. You know these words," Ashley declared.

"Yes, but then it would be my homework, not yours," Terri said. "What's another way to figure it out?"

"The dictionary, I guess," Ashley answered.

"Brilliant," laughed Terri.

"Mom, why don't you just tell me? It will be a lot quicker," Ashley tried again.

"Quicker but not better," Terri responded.

Ashley rolled her eyes, found the dictionary, and corrected her paper. When she finished thirty minutes later, Terri smiled at her and said, "Way to go, Ashley. Now don't you feel smarter?"

"No," replied Ashley, dragging out the word for dramatic effect. "It would have been a lot easier if you had just told me."

Samantha's evening was less work and less frustrating, but Ashley's was more work and more valuable.

For many of us it's easier to lower the bar than to raise the discomfort level. Too many of us step in too soon when there are disagreements, difficult problems, or disappointments. Sometimes, of course, parents need to intervene. Wise parents know, however, when to stay out, when to encourage, when to help, and how involved they should be. When you remember the true meaning of self-esteem and how it can help your child, making those decisions is easier.

DO

- Relax. If you're not having fun you may be pushing your kids too hard.
- Allow children time for free play. It's the natural way to learn self-regulation—how to control themselves—and social skills, including how to resolve disagreements. Social skills don't just happen, they are built through experience.
- Praise your child, but connect praise with real efforts, actions, or results, not half-hearted attempts.
- Provide care, support, and help, but don't always bail your child out of a difficult situation.
- Encourage, acknowledge when something is difficult, and have patience with your child's efforts.
- Turn failure and disappointment into learning experiences.
- Have high and clear expectations for your child's behavior.
- Help your children build social relationships by teaching them how to manage their own behavior.
- Let your child feel bad sometimes. He needs to experience both good and bad feelings and to know that feelings change and how to express both kinds. Feeling bad is sometimes appropriate. And it's not the end of the world.
- Expect children to do their chores and participate in the life and work of the family.
- Encourage them to volunteer and get involved in helping others.

DON'T

- Don't solve every problem or cut in and do a job or task for your child that he can do himself. Children learn perseverance by sticking with a difficult task and working through frustration. Help, but don't solve.
- Don't invest more in an outcome than your child does.

- Don't harass teachers or coaches on behalf of your children. If there is a serious problem, such as ridicule or put-downs, set up a one-on-one meeting to discuss your concerns.
- Don't overorganize kids.

What do I want to continue?

_____

_____

_____

What do I want to change?

_____

_____

_____

FIVE

Styles of Parenting

Unfortunately, children do not arrive in the world with an owner's manual, so we have to decide how we are going to deal with the thousands of situations and challenges we encounter as parents. The beliefs, attitudes, strategies, and tactics that we fall back on form our parenting style. As explored in chapter 2, parenting style is influenced by popular culture, as well as by how we ourselves were raised.

Peggy was the single parent of two "tweens," Ronald, eleven, and Rachel, nine. She came to see me for counseling at the suggestion of a neighbor whose family I had counseled. Peggy had divorced Walter two years earlier, after his third failed treatment for alcohol and marijuana addiction. Although Walter had promised to stay involved with the children, he had remarried and moved to another state within a year after the divorce. His contacts with Ronald and Rachel had become more sporadic with each passing month. Peggy realized that she was on her own in parenting and was worried because both of her kids were becoming harder for her to handle.

It didn't take long for me to get an idea of the problems Peggy was facing. Ronald and Rachel fought a lot, wouldn't help out around the house, swore, and disobeyed Peggy whenever they felt like it. "I feel like a doormat," she told me. When I asked her to describe her parenting style she told me that she didn't really have one. She explained that Walter had handled almost all of the discipline. "He kept the kids in line and now that he's gone, the kids won't mind me at all."

Then I asked her to tell me how things went when she and Walter were still together. She responded, "I had to return to work, so Ronald and Rachel were in day care from the time they were three months old. That meant that Walter and I were both with them in the evenings and on weekends. He had strong opinions on child rearing and since I was an only child, I figured he knew what he was doing."

"Did Walter come from a large family?" I asked.

"Four brothers and three sisters," Peggy answered. "He told me he knew how to discipline kids so I just let him take the lead."

I asked Peggy if she was comfortable with how Walter had disciplined them. "No way," she quickly responded. "He yelled a lot if the kids misbehaved. Sometimes he hit them when he got really mad or had been drinking. My parents never yelled at me and they certainly never hit me, so this was completely foreign to me. I hated the way he treated them, but I was afraid of him, too, so I didn't say much."

"What were his parents like?" I asked. "Were they strict, too?"

"Walter's just like his dad," Peggy said. "He always told me that his father ruled with an iron fist. I actually saw some of it firsthand. Walter's younger brothers were teenagers when we were dating, and Joe—that's Walter's dad—would yell at them just like Walter yelled at Ronny and Rachel. Scared the living daylights out of me a couple of times."

Next I asked Peggy to tell me how her parents had disciplined her. Peggy thought for a minute and then said, "Well, they actually didn't."

"What do you mean?" I asked.

"My parents and I were like friends. They pretty much let me do what I wanted. They were really easygoing. A lot of my friends were really jealous because my parents were so laid back."

"Didn't you have rules?" I asked.

"Not really. Like I said, I could pretty much do what I wanted. I didn't have any jobs around the house and they bought me whatever I wanted."

I asked Peggy if she thought that her parents had done a good job of raising her. After thinking for a while she answered, "Not really. Don't get me wrongI love my parents, but they never really gave me any direction. I got pretty wild when I was a teenager. I stayed out late, did lots of drinking and drugs, and they never did anything. That's how I got hooked up with Walter. We started partying together when I was a senior in high school. I got pregnant with Ronald the summer after we graduated so we decided to get married. I stopped the drinking and drugs as soon as I found out I was having a baby. Unfortunately, Walter never did."

Peggy and I had quite a few counseling sessions together and eventually included Ronald and Rachel. Peggy had realized that, since she didn't have any models for disciplining kids, she didn't know how to do it. Walter had kept the kids in line through fear and intimidation, and, once he was gone, there was nothing else to fall back on.

Peggy did learn to use many of the skills and strategies in this book. Like many parents, she used the parenting style she grew up with. We all have a tendency to resort to what's familiar when we're under pressure. "Your parents didn't put limits on you, so you don't have good ideas of how to put limits on your kids," I explained to her. I wanted her to know that she wasn't alone. "I don't know how many times I've said something to Dan, Brian, or Erin and realized that I was repeating something my parents used to say to me."

Countless messages and assumptions are wired into our minds and behavior based on how we were raised. That's not necessarily bad, of course. The way you were raised might have been wonderful. On the other hand, it might not have been wonderful. That's not really the point. The point is that parenting is too important for you just to go on autopilot. You can decide for yourself what kind of parent to be. The power and responsibility are yours, and you should make conscious parenting decisions and not fall into potentially bad habits just because they feel comfortable or familiar.

What Is Your Parenting Style?

Next, we'll examine different parenting styles and how each affects children and families. But first, reflect on your own style and the forces that helped shape it, beginning with how *you* were raised. Think back to your relationship with your parents:

- Who was in charge in your house?
- How much time did your parents spend with you?
- Were the rules clear or unclear in your family?
- Did your parents enforce the rules? If so, how?
- Were your parents easy to talk to?
- Did your parents take an interest in your activities, in and out of school?
- Were you expected to do chores or help around the house?
- Could you talk your way out of or into things?
- Were your parents lax, strict, or somewhere in between?
- Were your parents together on their parenting decisions?
- How did your parents handle discipline?
- Did either of your parents use physical punishment?
- Did your parents listen to you?
- Was it okay to make mistakes in your family?
- Did you usually have to deal with the consequences of your actions?
- Did your parents ever call you names or put you down?
- How did your parents handle disagreements?
- Did your parents give you too much freedom, too little, or just about the right amount?
- Did your parents get you whatever you wanted?

In answering these questions, did you realize anything or remember anything startling about how you were raised?

Now go back over these questions again, but this time answer them as if you are your son or daughter. How do the answers of your child compare with your own? What did you learn?

Finally, ask yourself these four questions:

- How is your parenting style like your parents'?
- How is it different?
- What parts of your parenting style would you like to keep?
- What would you like to change?

Parent Tool Kit: Choosing a Parenting Style

Use the following questions to see which parenting skills you need to add to your tool kit.

PARENT TOOL KIT
Choosing a Parenting Style

Yes	No		
☐	☐	1.	My partner and I agree on how to parent.
☐	☐	2.	Our family rules are clear and consistent.
☐	☐	3.	I follow through and enforce consequences when necessary.
☐	☐	4.	I have a good emotional connection with my children.
☐	☐	5.	I set age-appropriate limits and enforce them.
☐	☐	6.	I am able to listen to and have give-and-take with my children.
☐	☐	7.	I am consistent with limits and consequences.
☐	☐	8.	I make sure the consequences fit the behavior.
☐	☐	9.	I use No when appropriate.
☐	☐	10.	I stay out of verbal battles or endless negotiation.

Conversations about parenting styles are relatively new. Until the past couple of generations, we never really thought about them. For thousands of years parents just did what their parents had done and what their culture dictated. The assumptions that parents have about the best way to raise kids might be very different in a Tibetan village than in small-town USA. The way that parents in the Amish community raise their children is not the same as the style of parents in the military or a typical city or suburb.

As scientists learned more about child development, parents started to become more conscious of their parenting styles.

Child Psychology Is Born

Some people are surprised to discover that the field of child and developmental psychology began in the mid-twentieth century. Before then, children were not the focus of serious study. Many people assumed that children were unformed and incomplete and did not become people until they reached adulthood. Other commonly accepted views of children held that they were blank slates waiting to be filled in by adults, or that they were little savages needing to be tamed by adults.

That all changed thanks to the brilliant scientist Jean Piaget. Born in 1896 in Switzerland, Piaget first attracted notice when he began to write sophisticated scientific papers at the age of eleven. He earned his doctorate in science when he was twenty-two and became interested in what was then the new science of psychology. Piaget was the first to study how children's thinking developed, and his findings spawned the disciplines of child and developmental psychology. Another pioneer in child psychology, Erik Erikson, advanced the field further, studying children's emotional development.

Child guidance centers were established at universities around the world. Many women who entered psychology departments in the 1950s, '60s, and '70s were interested in children and made the formal study of child psychology take off. Today what we think about children is not based just on tradition or intuition but rooted in a large body of research. Scientists learned that children are very different from adults in how they understand the world, how they process information, and how they react emotionally. A basic axiom is that what happens at each stage of child development affects all subsequent stages. This new understanding pushed popular culture to pay more attention to how we treat children.

Explosion of Interest in Children

The growth in interest and knowledge of child psychology led to the emergence of books and magazines about parenting. In 1946, Dr. Benjamin Spock published his now classic *Baby and Child Care,* the first-ever parent-advice book, which became the bible for the parents who raised the millions of baby boomers. Now in its eighth edition, the book has become virtually the world's best-selling nonfiction publication. Dr. Spock had an enormous influence on how parents thought about child rearing with his use of the new information from child and developmental psychology. He gave parents rationales behind child-rearing decisions that allowed them to differ with what their parents had done.

Television expanded access to all sorts of information after World War II. At the same time, families were getting smaller so parents were paying more attention to the fewer children they had. Discussions about child rearing became popular TV topics beamed to millions. Dr. Joyce Brothers started her *Good Housekeeping* column on family life in 1960 and soon after that became a regular fixture on television. The result of all this was that people started to think about parenting and discipline methods.

Parenting Styles

Each parent has a unique way of interacting with a child and disciplining him, but parenting styles generally fall into one of three main categories: permissive, authoritarian, or balanced.

Before we talk about which one works best for kids, take a look at this common scenario and decide how you would handle the situation:

Greg, ten, and his younger brother, Corey, eight, have been arguing for a while about video games, which they do frequently. Greg's been playing for over an hour and Corey wants a turn. Greg has ignored Corey's whining until his little brother tried to push him out of the chair. Greg turned on Corey, punched him in the chest, and yelled at him to get lost. Corey screamed, picked up a toy lying on the floor, hurled it at Greg's head, and took off. Greg is chasing his brother from room to room threatening to tear him limb from limb as you come in the back door.

What would you do?

a. Ignore their fighting, letting them work it out.
b. Scream at the boys, grab each by the arm, drag them to their rooms, and tell them they'd better not show their faces again until you give them permission to come out.
c. Firmly intervene and send each to his room to calm down. When they have settled down, remind them of the rule against fighting and tell them that the video game console is off limits for two days.

Let's see how each style plays out with Greg and Corey and which style might eventually work the best.

Permissive	Authoritarian	Balanced
• Few rules	• Rigid rules	• Firm rules
• Few consequences	• Strict enforcement	• Firm enforcement
• Endless negotiation	• No negotiation	• Limited negotiation
• Limited or erratic leadership	• Autocratic leadership	• Stable leadership
• Emphasis on individuality	• Emphasis on conformity	• Balance
• All opinions are equal	• Only parents' opinions count	• All opinions are respected

The Permissive Style

Greg and Corey's dad, Frank, grew up in a family of five boys. His dad was a harsh disciplinarian who did not tolerate any shenanigans and often used physical punishment. Frank was determined not to be like his father so he avoided intervening. He told himself that "boys will be boys" and that fighting was just a natural part of their growing up. He preferred to let his sons fight it out. When the noise got too loud he would retreat into his office.

The permissive style has not been a particularly successful strategy of parenting.

The short definition of the permissive style of parenting is that anything goes. The permissive family has few rules. Permissive parents emphasize individuality. All opinions in a permissive family are considered equal, so kids are given a voice in decisions from small to large. There is endless negotiation, but a minimum of rules and therefore very few consequences. A permissive family's few clear ground rules tend to shift constantly. The result is chaos: Kids do not learn limits and therefore do not develop the tools necessary for adult life. They do not receive enough direction in managing their impulses and drives. Family-systems researcher David Olson and his colleagues compiled data showing that permissive parenting leads to problems. Because there are few rules, few consequences, and very little enforcement, they are essentially on their own. These kids don't develop any self-discipline and often behave in ways that bother other people, first as children and then for many years to come, because they haven't learned to treat other people with respect. They haven't learned to get things done. Their adult lives tend to be chaotic because of the chaos they lived through as part of a permissive family.

Sometimes permissiveness is an adult's excuse for not wanting to be bothered with the hard work of parenting. Parenting is demanding. Enforcing limits and consequences is difficult. It's messy. It's uncomfortable. And in the short term, the permissive approach can be the path of least resistance, the default style for parents who just don't feel like getting into a hassle with their kids. The parents fall into a permissive style because other efforts are just too much work. Some people honestly believe that permissiveness is best for their kids. Yet, they overestimate children's ability to limit themselves and forget that children need guidance and children need No.

The Authoritarian Style

As soon as she heard the boys starting to fight again, Elice, Greg and Corey's mom, intervened, grabbing each boy and screaming, "I told you to stop fighting. Now you've had it. You're in your rooms. Don't you dare let me see your face until I say so."

The opposite end of the scale from permissive parenting is the authoritarian family. A good friend of mine, Trina, grew up in an authoritarian family. Her father, an army colonel, ran his family the way a sergeant might organize a platoon. "There was never any doubt about what was expected of us," Trina recalls. "My father was never confused about rules and he didn't want us to be, either."

I asked her if there was ever any negotiation.

"Are you kidding?" Trina responded. "His answer to everything was, 'Because I said so.'"

"What was your mother's role?" I wondered.

"She handled the little stuff, but as soon as we started to get out of hand, she would tell us that she was going to tell our father. That would either shape us up or else she would follow through on her threat. If dad got a bad report when he got home, we paid for it."

"Did he ever spank or hit?"

"Oh, yeah," Trina replied. "My brothers got hit a lot more than me, but I had my share of spankings, too."

"He had a system for everything," Trina added. "We all had to be sitting on the bench near the back door every morning to have our shoes tied before going to nursery school. Then my mom or dad would walk down the line tying shoes. If you weren't there, you went to school without your shoes tied."

"So, Trina, do you raise your kids that way?" I inquired.

"No. I'm strict, but there's no way I want to raise my kids like that. My dad's been dead for quite a few years now, but none of us ever felt close to him. Even as adults we were afraid of him, although when two of my brothers were teenagers, things really got ugly. I can even remember crazy times when my brothers would actually hit my father back."

The biggest problem with the authoritarian style is that it can never work in the long run. It's based on absolute parental authority, and absolute authority can never be sustained. As kids grow up, they are headed for an inevitable power struggle with the autocratic parent, often leading to ugly confrontations such as those between Trina's brothers and their father.

Faced with an authoritarian style of parenting, Greg and Corey might stop fighting for a while, but Greg might pound Corey out of sight of their mom and threaten him with worse if he tells. Greg might grow into a husky teenager and his anger might eventually lead to defiance and violence. Studies show that violence in the home leads to children's growing into violent adults.

The authoritarian style relies on power to get an empty kind of conformity. The children are not learning to incorporate a healthy sense of self-discipline for themselves. Since their opinions are never taken into acccount, they don't get the opportunity to learn to negotiate respectfully. They don't get the opportunity to make their own decisions. Sooner or later they'll have to learn to make their own choices, and often this happens all at once, when the child at last leaves the controlling environment.

Our son Dan was surprised when he first met some of his college dormmates. He had thought Monica and I were strict parents (and if you ask him even now about not being allowed to see *Ghostbusters* when it first came out, he still sounds a little disappointed). But one of Dan's dormmates came from an authoritarian family where he had very little freedom growing up. He did not actually respond to whistle calls, but he felt forever under control, unable to explore his self-will, incapable of establishing boundaries on his own. This young man hit college with a lot of catching up to do, and Dan had a front-row seat for the whole spectacle. The dormmate had not incorporated any internal controls and soon ran into problems. He could never say no to anything. If some older guys in the hall met for a few beers, he always wanted to go. If it was late at night and everyone was tired and wanted to go to sleep and one glazed-eyed character suggested hitting one more party, he would perk up and say, "Let's do it!" He got into all sorts of trouble, and the worst part was how sadly predictable his actions were.

Counselors who work with students in college dormitories report that, typically, the kids who have the toughest time managing the freedom of college are those who come from either very authoritarian families, where all of their control came from the outside and they never incorporated it into themselves, or from very permissive families, where they were never taught to develop those internal controls.

The Balanced Style and *No*

Elice and Frank, hearing the boys fighting again, look at each other and nod in agreement. They had talked with the boys about their fighting and what the consequences would be if they chose to fight again, and now was the time to put their plan into effect. After separating the boys, Elice spoke first: "Greg, do you remember what dad and I said to you about fighting?" Next, Frank spoke to Corey; "Corey, we had the same discussion with you, do you remember?" Corey said yes, he did remember something about not fighting and what would happen, but Greg just got quiet.

Frank continued. "It's not just about what would happen, it's about what choice you are making, when you choose to fight. There're lots of ways to solve your problems with each other and we'll help you figure it out, but when you choose to fight, you're choosing the consequence for fighting. Remember the consequence is that whatever you were fighting about, you lose. You were fighting about video games, so there will be no video games or TV for the next two days. Do you understand?"

Both Greg and Corey started to protest. Elice repeated that this was their choice, since they had chosen to fight to work out their disagreement. Greg and Corey mumbled okay, then Frank and Elice sat down with them to hear about their argument and see if they could have solved it in a different manner.

The Romans had a saying, *Virtus stat in medio*, "Virtue stands in the middle." So often, the extremes get us in trouble and this is true in parenting as well. That is why the most effective parenting strategy is a balanced style that uses No.

Here are the characteristics of balanced parenting:

- Clearly establish limits with judicious use of No.
- Firmly, consistently enforce consequences.
- Be respectful and engaged with your kids and require that from them in return.
- Keep an emotional connection with your kids.
- Demand accountability and responsibility, but always combine your demands with respect and warmth.
- Negotiate, up to a point. You set the rules as the parent.
- Give and take and—only occasionally—compromise.

With a balanced approach to parenting that uses No, you will guide your kids until they need to take control of their lives as adults, by which time they will have assimilated these behaviors. In effect, these principles build up a "parenting bank account" during the early childhood and middle years so that the account is flush with credits for affection, goodwill, and good communication. As our kids get older and go through teenage rebellion, they will inevitably withdraw from that bank account, but your balance should stay pretty healthy. If you and they go into the teenage years with pretty meager credits for affection, goodwill, support, and connection in that bank account, however, the teenage years can be pretty rocky.

The way to build up that account early on is to follow a balanced approach to discipline, which has firm rules and firm enforcement but some room for negotiation. You can communicate with each other and explain—and allow your kids to explain (not make excuses for) themselves—but these exchanges don't go on forever. You, the parent, are clearly in charge in the balanced family, so there is no question about who has authority, but you have respect for your children's opinions and you allow them to assert some of their growing independence. You enforce consistent consequences, but not harsh punishment. You maintain a stable leadership.

And above all, you express warmth and connection. One of the big problems with the authoritarian approach, which might indeed produce conformity, is its lack of warmth and nurturing, which are crucial to a child's development. When we talk about the teenage years in chapter 9, we'll cover research that shows that the most protective factor for getting kids through the teenage years is a connection with caring adults. Connection begins in the first year of life and continues to build through childhood.

One of the largest youth studies ever conducted explored the importance of connection once kids enter adolescence. Michael Resnick, L. J. Harris, and Robert Blum studied more than thirty-seven thousand teens to identify the factors that protected them from falling prey to major problems like dropping out of school, crime, teen pregnancy, or alcohol and drug abuse. These teens had had their share of bumps and bruises, but they were able to steer clear of the major pitfalls. Going into the project, the researchers thought that socioeconomic status might be the best predictor of success in handling these problems, or if not that, then family makeup—single-parent family or two-parent family. Instead, they found that the factor that most protected adolescents from succumbing to these pitfalls was a secure connection with caring adults.

When I say *connection,* I'm not reaching for some greeting-card sentimentality. There is nothing quick or easy about establishing and maintaining a good connection with your kids. Real connection means that parents know what their kids are doing, who their friends are, who their teachers are and if they like them, and which subjects they're studying and how it's going with each of those subjects. Real connection means active involvement. It also means there is warmth and affection between you and a consistent attempt to keep open the lines of communication. Even when a teen says, "Get out of my life!" the parents stay connected.

So how will their parents' more balanced approach to discipline affect Greg and Corey? Greg might still have problems with his anger, but Corey will be much less of a target. When Greg becomes a teen, he will start to manage his feelings and will ask for help when he needs it. Corey will not bully at school because he was not a victim of his older brother, a pattern that is well known to psychologists. As a teen he won't be especially close to his older brother, but he will love and respect his parents even though he'd never tell them that.

It comes back to that parenting bank account. You don't want to let whole weeks or months slip by without adding to that account. A balanced parenting style and saying no will build up your credit for when you need it—because we all, as parents, need a little credit in the bank from time to time.

The Flip-Flop

Imagine this scenario: Greg and Corey are on their way to their rooms, as dictated by their mother, when they meet Dad coming out of his office. Frank asks the boys if they've stopped fighting. The boys promise they will never fight again and then start complaining about the punishment their mom gave them. They tell their dad that they were just having fun and they'd really like to go outside and play. Frank makes a quick decision without consulting Elice. "You guys go ahead. I'll talk to your mom; have fun, but no more fighting."

The flip-flop occurs in families in two ways. First, a parent can bounce back and forth between the two extreme styles of parenting. This parent might be permissive until things get out of hand and then resort to authoritarian tactics. He does that for a while until he gets tired of it and defaults back to permissive. This type of parenting often occurs in families that are under great stress or where there are problems with mental illness or chemical dependency. Often in families with a chemically dependent adult, the parent's moods are so volatile that children don't know what's going to happen next. Is dad going to be a marshmallow or a tyrant tonight? The kids are never quite sure and become hypervigilant and insecure.

The second type of inconsistent parenting involves contradictory styles between two parents. The flip-flop often occurs when parents are divorced. As Greg and Corey learned, they could play one parent off against the other, until Elice and Frank decided to present a unified front. If the parents had not agreed on a style, the boys' fighting would have continued, and Elice and Frank would also have fought with each other over how to discipline them. As the boys grew to be teenagers, each member of the family would have grown more distant emotionally.

While parents may often disagree, when two parents work at cross purposes, not communicating with each other and not working together, they exacerbate problems in the present and create more serious problems for their children in the future.

That's what happened in a family I once counseled: Gene and Susan and their three active sons. Susan tended to be very strict, while Gene was permissive. Gene thought that Susan was rigid and too hard on the boys so he constantly undercut her authority, refused to follow through on consequences, and argued with her in front of their sons. In our first counseling session Susan said, "Somebody has to discipline the boys. Gene won't do it, so I have to." Gene's response was immediate: "Susan is just so unreasonable. Somebody has to let the boys be boys."

I explained to Gene and Susan, "Flip-flopping is not good for your sons, or for your marriage either." They eventually agreed to the following:

1. Discuss and agree on a set of rules and consequences ahead of time.
2. Let the boys know what the rules and consequences are.
3. Back each other up.
4. Work out any disagreements in private.

Gene and Susan had progress to report during our next session. One of the ongoing battles was over Saturday-morning chores, so

Gene and Susan agreed ahead of time that their boys could not play with friends, or play video games, or watch TV until their chores were done. They devised a rotating schedule for the boys and called a family meeting. Gene surprised everyone by taking the lead and explaining the new system to his sons. When Saturday rolled around the boys whined and dragged their feet until Gene made it clear that he and their mother were serious. All three finished their chores before lunch.

Trisha, another parent, had a different problem. She vacillated between strict and permissive in the space of an hour. Trisha ignored her two daughters' misbehavior until she became so irritated that she would explode, lay down the law, and dish out consequences. Once Trisha calmed down, she felt guilty and worried that her daughters wouldn't like her. She wouldn't follow through on consequences and ignored violations of the rules until the cycle repeated itself. I explained to Trisha how confusing this was to the girls and how she undermined her parental authority. She took my suggestions and wrote the major family rules and consequences on a sheet of paper, taped it to the refrigerator, and did her best to follow through calmly and consistently. The more she followed through, the better the girls behaved.

Temperament

Ralph Waldo Emerson described the difference between moods and temperament using the analogy of a necklace. He compared our moods to colorful beads, each of which cast a different hue. Our temperament is like the chain that holds them all together. Although Emerson wasn't a psychologist, he had great insight—and foresight—about temperament. Recent research confirms what every parent who has more than one child already knows: Children come into the world wired with different dispositions. Some children are outgoing while their siblings are shy; some are adventurous while others are cautious; and some are easygoing while others are touchy. It is a wonder that children with such different temperaments can come out of the same gene pool.

Parenting is even more difficult when your children have different temperaments. Keeping a balanced style is more difficult because you must adapt to the unique temperament of each child. One size of parenting does not fit all children.

Gordon and Angela, who each had a daughter from a previous marriage, knew that they faced difficult blended-family challenges. The two girls, nine-year-old Robin and seven-year-old Sandra, were so different. Robin was outgoing, adventurous, and active, while Sandra was quiet, cautious, and sensitive. Gordon and Angela saw that consistency was important for both girls, but that the girls' different temperaments demanded different strategies. Whereas Robin would say everything she was thinking, Sandra was more private. The parents, careful to communicate regularly with both daughters, knew that Sandra opened up best in low-key, one-on-one conversations. Gordon also realized that he needed to adjust his discipline approach with Sandra. He could deal with Robin head-on but needed a more patient approach with Sandra. A quick "knock it off" worked fine with Robin but would devastate Sandra, who needed a more conversational approach.

Fair but Not Equal

Every parent needs to learn the lesson that fair isn't always equal. Children of different ages will have different limits and different Nos. In addition, different temperaments challenge parents to modify their approach so that the goal of learning No is not undermined by a rigid adherence to a belief that we need to treat our kids exactly the same. Our Nos need to be fair but not necessarily equal.

A friend, Michele Fallon, a child-development expert at the University of Minnesota, recently shared this story about a gifted teacher she saw handling a tricky situation. "The preschool where I was conducting training had a small gymnasium, and each morning the five-year-olds would have time to play there. Although there were a number of tricycles there was only one pink one, and that was the one all the kids wanted. Anthony was a new boy and, like all his classmates, he wanted to be the first every day to ride the pink trike. Unlike the other children, however, if Anthony didn't get the first turn on the pink trike, he wouldn't just fuss, he would have a complete meltdown. And I mean *meltdown*," added Michele for emphasis. "The teacher would be dealing with Anthony's outbursts for the rest of the morning, and I wondered how she was going to handle it. I knew that I was observing a master teacher when I saw what she did."

Michele described how the teacher explained to the other children in private conversations that Anthony didn't know how to take turns yet and she wanted them to help him learn. She asked the children to let Anthony have the first turn every day if he agreed to give them a chance to ride the pink trike later on. The children all agreed, and, not surprisingly, Anthony liked the deal too. "It worked like a charm," Michele said. "The other kids were content to wait their turn and Anthony's meltdowns were a thing of the past. Here's the best part," added Michele. "Within three weeks Anthony didn't need to have the first turn anymore."

"Somehow that doesn't seem quite fair," I said as I heard about the teacher's solution.

"That's was my reaction too," replied Michele. "So I asked the teacher about that. Her response made perfect sense. She told me that it was *fair*, but it wasn't *equal*." Michele helped me understand this important principle. "The other kids were fine with the solution because they could sense that Anthony had some special needs. They were happy to help the teacher out. In addition, they had a good lesson in empathy. What's more, Anthony learned the sharing lesson. Everybody won."

Parents know the challenge of "fair but not equal." Our Brian and Erin claimed injustice when their older brother Dan's bedtime was later than theirs. They never liked our explanation that when they were older they could stay up later, and on many occasions my final response to the protestors was, "Sorry, but that's the way it is."

DO

- Examine your parenting style to determine if it is permissive, authoritarian, or balanced.
- Use a balanced parenting style, which emphasizes clear limits and enforcement of consequences in a caring, firm, and respectful manner.
- Practice a lot of patience. Keep your sense of humor.
- Learn as much as you can about your child's stage of growth and development to gain a realistic perspective on your child's behavior. Check sources on the Internet (a good one is www.kidshealth.org). Read books (see the resource list at the end of this book). Talk to your child's teacher, check with your friends, and check out classes in your community for information.
- Adjust your strategies to fit the temperamental differences of your children. A more conversational approach will work better with a quiet, sensitive child.
- Compare notes with other parents. Sharing stories increases the enjoyment and lessens the burden.
- Decide with your partner on your parenting approach. Be consistent.
- Decide on the limits for unacceptable behavior. This is the time to talk with your child about limits and consequences.
- Respect and emotionally connect with your child. Part of the joy of parenting is taking the time to play with, read to, and enjoy each other.
- Say no to your children when it teaches an important lesson or a limit has been reached.

DON'T

- Don't flip-flop in your parenting. Be consistent.
- Don't confuse fair with equal. Age and temperament differences between children mean that we need to respond differently to each child.
- Don't give in if your child gets upset with a consequence.
- Don't turn every transgression into a battle.

- Don't ignore consistent bad behavior.
- Don't get into endless negotiations over a limit.
- Don't overreact; have the consequence fit the behavior.

What do I want to continue?

_____

_____

_____

What do I want to change?

_____

_____

_____

Six

A Baby's First Year
A Time to Connect

Being a new parent is both exciting and scary. It's easy to get frightened by stories in the media. Back in the mid-1970s, for instance, when our firstborn, Dan, was a baby, a theory covered in the media had all of us new parents in a state. New research seemed to indicate that a baby who never crawled might have a hard time learning to read. My professional training taught me not to jump to any conclusions about the development of any baby, even my own, but as a first-time father, sleep deprived and anxious, I got closer and closer to all-out panic as the months passed in Dan's first year and he showed no interest in crawling.

Dan did have a specialty back then: He liked to sit. Oh, how he liked to sit! Perched up on his diaper like a prince on a throne, he would look around the room with big, alert eyes, taking everything in. If he wanted to move, he had a way of pushing himself along, sitting the whole time. He had a real knack for sliding along in that position without a lot of fuss. It never bothered him that he had not learned to crawl.

Monica and I had no doubt that Dan was bright. He was happy and hitting all his other developmental milestones on schedule. But, as hard as I tried to ignore the research on crawling, I kept coming back to it.

"Look at him," I would say to my wife.

"Yeah, I know," Monica said, beaming. "He looks so happy."

"But he still hasn't crawled!"

"He's fine, honey."

We would sit there in silence a few minutes until Monica decided she was tired of watching my long face.

"If you're so worried about it, do something," she would say.

So I would get down on all fours next to Dan and make a big production of crawling all over the family room. Dan loved it and pumped his little fists, cheering me on. He smiled. He laughed. But he didn't crawl, even when I tried holding his little hands and pointing him in the right direction. Crawling just did not interest Dan. I tried to convince myself that I was overreacting, but my best efforts could not quiet the tiny voice in my head that said, "If Dan doesn't crawl, he'll never be able to read."

One day I was listening to a radio call-in program with a well-known pediatrician discussing his new book on early child development. I decided I had to phone in, even if there was a risk that the expert advice would only get me more worried. I reached for a pen, scribbled down the number, and then kept calling until I eventually got through, determined to do my fatherly duty and save my child from a lifetime of dyslexia and learning disabilities. My heart was pounding by the time they finally put me on the air with the pediatrician.

"Hi, it's Dave in Minneapolis. My baby boy Dan is almost ten months old, and he still has not started crawling," I blurted. "I know the research shows that an inability to crawl is sometimes linked to learning disabilities later on in life. What can I do?"

I'm sure I sounded a little desperate, and the pediatrician heard that in my voice.

"Dave, take a deep breath," he said soothingly. "Babies are individuals, and each baby has his or her own schedule for developing. It sounds like you and your wife are attentive, supportive parents, so my advice to you would be: just relax. Dan will be fine." He paused for a moment, and I thought he was finished. But his parting advice was the most important: "You know, the most important factor for your baby is to make sure you invest the time and energy establishing the connection that will last a lifetime," he concluded.

That radio pediatrician packed wise advice into those two minutes. Dan eventually did crawl and did not have any trouble learning to read. And the doctor reminded me of the importance of connection, which is the real basis for cognitive, emotional, and moral health—and the foundation for self-discipline and for No.

Baby Basics

Nothing anyone says can ever prepare you for the dramatic, life-changing event of a newborn entering your family. Amid all the excitement and with all the fatigue, parents are faced with a bewildering set of questions. Do I breast-feed or not? Do I try to establish a schedule? Why is she crying? New parents need guidance as they try to figure all these things out, and there is no end of books and magazines to fill that need.

But even as you learn all that new information, remember that a newborn's needs are fundamental and not mysterious. First and foremost, babies need you to be there, to keep them safe, to respond to their physical needs, and to comfort them when they're upset. In addition to the basics, however, they also need you to hold them, talk and sing to them, love them, and provide a warm, secure, and predictable environment as they grow.

One of the best things to do in these first months is hold them. Contact and connection rank with food and water as critically important for the survival of human infants. Human beings are wired to be social; babies' little brains need to register human contact, and lots of it, in order to work properly and keep them healthy and well adjusted.

A Terrible Experiment

Back in the thirteenth century, a debate raged in Europe about which language God spoke. While the question might seem silly

to many today, it engendered heated debates back then. Some
people assumed that God spoke Latin, because that was the language of the church. Other people said no, God must speak Ara-
maic, because Jesus was God and that was his native language.
Still others were convinced that God spoke Greek, because that
was the classical language.

Friedrich II, born in 1194, became Holy Roman Emperor in
1220 and was a most unusual leader for his time, known as a patron
of science and philosophy who studied medicine, mathematics, as-
tronomy and astrology, and mastered more than six languages. This
wide range of interests led him into the debate about God's language, which he thought he could resolve with an experiment.
Friedrich decreed that dozens of newborns be well taken care of
physically, but no one was allowed to talk to them or interact with
them beyond providing for their basic needs—food, warmth, clothing. He assumed that if the babies heard no language at all, when
they started to speak at around twelve to eighteen months, the language they spoke would have come directly from God, and God's
native tongue would finally be known.

Despite being fed, however, the babies started to fail. One by
one, they died. Friedrich II's ghastly experiment nearly eight hundred years ago indicates how important a baby's connection with a
caregiver is for his development and survival.

So, during a baby's first year, especially during the first
months, the key to helping a child's physical, psychological, and
moral development is to touch and hold, talk and sing, even dance
with your baby. This all gets easier to do as the baby starts to respond to and interact with you more in the third and fourth
month. By the sixth month, many babies are able to sit up and
reach out to be held and picked up. Holding your baby or "wearing" him in a baby sling or front pack helps form a connection,
helps you tune in to his needs and changing moods. Research
shows that babies who are held and whose needs are responded to
consistently are less fussy. You don't need to worry about spoiling
a baby in the first year.

We can track a baby's social development in his responsiveness to those around him. As early as the third month babies know the difference between a parent and a stranger, and, at times, just seeing a parent or hearing Mom's or Dad's voice helps a baby settle down. By the sixth month it's normal for a baby to be distressed when Mom or Dad goes away. They usually begin to respond to their name between six and nine months and they burst with pride when praised. They like to be held and talked to even when they're crying.

Babies Need to Explore the World

A baby's play is actually serious business, because in that play she is learning about the world and how it works. The brain triples in size during its first year, making babies nonstop learning machines. Everything they do forms new neural connections in their brains. When they crawl over to where the pots and pans are, pull them out, and start to bang on them, they are immersed in a learning experience: They are wiring their sense of hearing, learning to listen for different sounds, and learning their first lessons in physics when they hold a pot up, let it go, and watch it drop to the floor. They laugh as they learn about the laws of gravity, and that feels good. This is a natural, age-appropriate kind of learning.

Unfortunately, the growth of an aggressive media culture with sophisticated, skillfully marketed products complicates this task for parents. New parents come home from hospitals across America every day with Baby Einstein videos in their bag of free samples. In my opinion, the smartest thing about Baby Einstein videos is the title, because it implies that brilliance awaits any baby who is lucky enough to watch them. The dark implication, although it's never spoken, is that if your baby is denied these wonderful videos, she will be condemned to a life of stupidity. It's clever marketing but not based on scientific evidence.

My main problem with Baby Einstein–like media, including Teletubbies and the Baby First cable TV channel, is not the content, which seems fine—music, colors, and imaginative characters doing all sorts of things—but the fact that they are marketed to parents of babies as young as five months old. So, children start to gravitate to electronic screens even before they can crawl or talk. Bob Garfield, host of National Public Radio's *On the Media,* reacted to the claims of Baby First cofounder, Sharon Rechter, in a recent program about babies and TV by sharing that the only effect he saw from his daughter's Baby Einstein tapes was her wanting to watch as much TV as they would let her.

It's a little scary to realize that, in the United States, 25 percent of babies under two now have televisions or video players in their bedrooms. Videos and TV shows for babies are clever, but they are no substitute for concrete experiences in the real world during this intense period of brain development. Moreover, no video can ever replace the bond that builds between baby and caregiver as they roll around on the floor talking, giggling, tickling, and hugging. Electronic media will mesmerize our kids soon enough. If we start them on that path at such a young age, we are setting them on a road where their "default setting" for stimulation and entertainment will be to turn on the screen rather than explore something or learn something or even read something. Recent research shows that children who spend a lot of hours in front of screens before they're three are at greater risk for attention problems when they reach school age. Focus and attention are prerequisites for learning, but early watching of media conditions the brain to expect constant action and movement.

Products such as Baby Einstein are successful because they play on parents' natural anxieties about not providing essential experiences for their babies. Another example of manufacturers and marketers taking advantage of parental anxiety is the selling of the so-called Mozart Effect products. Intriguing research reported in a 1993 paper by two academics, University of Wisconsin psychologist Frances H. Rauscher and University of California at Irvine physicist Gordon Shaw, found that a group of college students who listened to classical music just before tackling a certain type of spatial-reasoning problem did better than those who hadn't. The researchers happened to use Mozart for their experiment. Even though the advantage evaporated after about thirty minutes, the media picked up on the study and soon were humming with variations on the theme that listening to Mozart was linked to overall intelligence. In a 1994 *New York Times* column, music critic Alex Ross reported that "researchers have determined that listening to Mozart actually makes you smarter."

Eventually, the message morphed into a widespread belief that babies who listen to classical music, particularly Mozart, are smarter than babies who don't. Entrepreneurs swung into action and produced all sorts of Baby Mozart tapes packaged with promises to create gifted children. You might think I'm exaggerating, but in January 1998 the governor of Georgia, Zell Miller, introduced his annual budget with a provision for $105,000 in funding to ensure that every child born in Georgia would receive a CD or tape of classical music when they left a Georgia hospital. At the announcement, Miller played a snippet of Beethoven's "Ode to Joy" and then asked, "Now don't you feel smarter already?"

We can laugh now, but at the time, a lot of parents worried about their babies falling behind the other babies who were listening to *The Magic Flute*.

To this day, parents ask me whether it is true that babies who listen to Mozart will be more intelligent than babies who don't. I tell them: It's wonderful to play classical music for your children, especially if they and you enjoy it. But listening to Mozart's music by itself will not somehow create a genius.

Connection Influences Behavior

Babies' brains rely on connection with a parent to figure out the world. For example, a baby will instinctively search for a familiar face to make sense of things. A fascinating article in *Scientific American* described a now-classic experiment in 1960. Eleanor Gibson and Richard Walk performed what they called the visual cliff experiment, using thirty-six babies between six and fourteen months old. They created a platform, one section covered with a clearly visible checkered pattern that was comfortable for crawling, and the other an area of clear glass. The research showed that if the mothers stood at one end and called out, the babies would crawl toward them—and when they came to the glass, they would stop. They could feel with their hands that this was a solid surface, but they could see through it, which warned them of possible danger.

The babies looked first to their mothers for clues about what to do. If the mother looked calm and reassuring, the baby crawled out onto the glass and headed toward Mom. If she looked worried, the baby stopped, sat, and started to cry. The experiment provided clear evidence that babies interpret the world by reading the emotional expressions of their parents.

Babies in infancy are like scientists feverishly running a wide range of experiments all at the same time. Some of these experiments work out well. Others don't. But whatever happens, the babies are learning. Because of the hardwired drives for connection and approval, babies experiment to satisfy those drives.

The Importance of Security

The brain's most basic job is to keep us alive. That's why our brains come equipped with an early warning detection system that enables us to respond quickly when in danger. Babies have the same system. When the brain notices a potential peril, it activates a hair-trigger mechanism that sets off the fight-or-flight response. Two hormones (the body's chemical messengers), adrenaline and cortisol, are released instantaneously. Adrenaline speeds up the heart rate so that more blood is pumped to the muscles, preparing them for action. Cortisol helps the body cope. Among other things, it dampens the memory center of the brain, the hippocampus, which explains why people in terrible automobile accidents often have no recollection later of what happened. They might remember having dinner right before they got in the car and recall waking up in the hospital, but they have no memory of the accident itself.

The effect of cortisol on a baby's brain, however, is more profound. Research shows that if babies experience traumatic stress repeatedly, and the hippocampus is repeatedly bathed in cortisol, it not only shuts down, it actually shrinks. So babies who are repeatedly shocked will often go through the rest of their lives with a diminished hippocampus and an impaired ability to register new memories. That explains why, for example, abused children often have learning disabilities when they get to school. In fact, even children who witness abuse or domestic violence have the same extreme stress reaction as those people who are victimized themselves.

All this points to babies' overriding need to experience a safe, secure, and predictable environment. The feelings that babies have at this stage of development have a deep effect on their physical and mental health and shape their experiences and perceptions throughout their lives.

Mental Operating System

I often describe what is happening inside the mind of an infant as a "mental operating system" similar to a computer operating system. "Behind" the computer software we use is an operating system, like Windows, Linux, or MacOS, which enables the computer hardware to communicate and operate with the computer software. Without an operating system, a computer would be useless.

Similarly, the activity inside a baby's brain, the mental operating system, is made up of all the reactions, expectations, and biases that make us who we are. To understand how a baby's mental operating system forms, it's helpful to start with memory, which is fundamental for learning. If I can't remember, I can't learn. If I go into the kitchen and burn my hand on the stove, but don't remember, then I'm going to do it again. Besides long-term and short-term memory, we are all equipped with dozens of types of memory.

One type, called cognitive memory, is our ability to store and recall information and facts, like the capital of Georgia or the temperature at which water freezes. In addition, we have emotional memories, which are powerful and "wordless." Here's an example of an emotional memory: Not long after my father died, my sister, two brothers, and I were helping my mother sort through my father's belongings. With my mother's okay we split up my father's collection of vintage record albums. The dozen or so I took home ended up in a cabinet. I had all but forgotten about them when a couple of years later we were putting up the family Christmas tree. I was concentrating on the ornament in my hand, looking for a good spot on the tree when my daughter Erin went to pick out some Christmas music to play.

I didn't notice that Erin had chosen one of my father's old records, the classic old Bing Crosby album *White Christmas*. She lay the vinyl on a turntable we had, then lowered the needle. Within seconds after the scratchy sound of Bing's rendition of "Silent Night" started playing, I was in tears. The music brought waves of emotion washing over me and whipped me back to childhood memories of Christmases with my father, mother, and family. I was in the grip of a powerful emotional memory.

In addition to cognitive and emotional memories we have two other kinds: explicit and implicit memories. Explicit memories are loaded with specific details—the when, the where, the how. Even years later, you remember every last detail about the day your first child was born, right down to the weather. Implicit memories, on the other hand, provide us with important bits of information, but we have no idea where they come from. For instance, when you step into an office you will immediately recognize one of the objects as a chair and you'll even remember that you sit on it. Yet, you don't remember when or how you learned those facts.

We have far more implicit memories than explicit memories. You rely on implicit memories constantly, even though you take them for granted. Explicit memories don't form until somewhere between two and a half and three years of age. So, if someone tells you he has vivid memories of his first birthday party, feel free to be suspicious. The truth is that remembering your first birthday is nearly impossible. Implicit memories, on the other hand, form even before we are born. That's why a baby responds to his mother's voice differently than to any other voice within seconds after birth.

Implicit memories form during our earliest days. A four-month-old can do very few things for himself but signal his distress or need by crying. So let's say this four-month-old is having a bad day: He's hungry, has a wet diaper, and a gas bubble. So he cries. Now, imagine that, after a short period of time, his mother comes in, picks him up, and starts to rub his back, so pretty soon that gas bubble releases. Next she changes his diaper, so he's comfortable. Then she nurses him, so he's no longer hungry. While she's tending to his needs she smiles and talks to him, even breaking into a quiet lullaby from time to time. The baby feels better.

Now, imagine a second scenario, in which the four-month-old is having the same bad day, but when he cries, he seems to cry for an eternity. Suddenly, he hears a loud crashing noise as the door slams against the wall. Seconds later a huge, angry face looms inches away from his. Already confused and frightened, he's terrified by the sound of ear-shattering yelling.

Neither four-month-old baby—in either scenario—would have any explicit memories of their experiences, but events like those and thousands of others form his mental operating system. Reassuring experiences will lay the groundwork for a sense of trust and security. Frightening incidents will lead to a sense of insecurity and mistrust. Either way, his mental operating system will filter his view of other people and the world for the rest of his life. Years later he might wonder, for example, why he becomes so frightened when his wife becomes angry with him, unaware that his anxious response was wired into him very early in life.

Connection and *No*

Responding to a baby provides a sense of safety, a secure connection between parent and child. It's not easy to be clued in to all the needs of the baby perfectly all the time, but that's okay. As long as we try to be consistent she will know that she is cherished. The research is clear that babies who have a secure connection are more capable of empathy, are much better listeners, and much better at communication later in life. Babies who do not have that secure connection—or have it only sporadically—will not fare nearly as well later on.

In addition, a secure connection is the basis for the parent's ability to set limits and say no as the baby becomes a toddler, then a child, and later a teen. The more secure the connection, the easier and more successful No will be later on. The fortunate babies who have a secure connection will want to preserve it by maintaining their parents' approval. This connection and the child's need for approval gives the parent the power *to be* a parent and, among other things, to set limits, to discipline, and to say no when appropriate. If there is no connection or a poor connection, a young child might become anxious, angry, and mistrustful. He will comply out of fear but may develop more oppositional behavior during the middle years and extreme defiance when he is a teenager. A secure connection is no guarantee for a problem-free childhood and adolescence, but it provides a firm foundation to deal with later challenges.

Some parents worry that this approach might spoil a child or create dependency, but actually the opposite is the case. A connected child feels secure enough to explore and spread his wings. A connected child is also motivated to behave properly and is thereby able to accept discipline, which prepares the way for self-discipline and independence.

Expand the Circle of Connection

Christopher is a very lucky little boy. When he was an infant, not only did his parents love and respond to him, but he had grandparents who connected with him early as well. Dana and Nancy, Christopher's grandparents, were more than happy to help out. "It is such a thrill to spend time with Christopher," Dana told me during that first year. Grandma and Grandpa relished the opportunity to connect with Christopher, and Burton and Shirley were happy to have the emotional and physical support. Christopher is now four, and it is clear that his connection with both his parents and his grandparents is rock solid. He is completely comfortable in either home, is a happy, well-mannered little boy, and has clearly benefited from his expanded network of secure connections.

Every parent knows how exhausting the first year of parenting can be. Whenever possible, expand the care network to include grandparents, other relatives, or close friends who can provide support, relief, and companionship. Bringing grandparents and other family into the relationship with your baby early, even if they live far away, will reap benefits for your child later on. New parents don't need to worry that their connection will be usurped. Babies have an inborn orientation to Mom and Dad. As long as parents build a secure connection with their baby, the expanded network only adds to the benefits, just as they have done for Christopher.

Gentle But Firm *Nos*

Although babies don't begin to understand the word *no* until the ninth or tenth month, we can start to use it earlier. The mother whose baby grabs and pulls at her eyeglasses might react with a firm but gentle No, as in, "No, no, sweetheart. That's Mommy's." This, of course, is a different type of No from the one we will use when they become toddlers, children, and teens. Babies younger than eighteen months can certainly do things we don't want them to, but they're not deliberately misbehaving. During the first eighteen months their "misbehavior" is driven by curiosity, fatigue, or fussiness. So the No for little ones is more a teaching No—gentle but firm.

Here's an example of a baby's natural behavior that brings up important safety issues. Everyone knows that babies love to put things into their mouths as soon as they are able to hang on to them. They're acting on a natural instinct. Babies arrive with five senses: sight, hearing, smell, taste, and touch, but all aren't equally developed. The first to mature fully is the sense of touch, but the one part of the body where neurons are fully working is the region around their mouths. It's logical because that enables them to nurse, which in turn ensures their survival. This also explains why a baby puts everything into her mouth—that's where she can make the most sense of it.

Sometimes parents get the mistaken notion that they can break their child of this habit, so they slap the child's hands or yell, "No!" Trying to get babies not to put things into their mouths is a futile task. Babies are doing what their brains prompt them to do, and they will stop putting things into their mouths as their other senses come on line. Parents should focus on staying alert and making sure that nothing the baby puts into his mouth will hurt him. It's just one of many safety issues you need to attend to.

No and Safety Limits

When most babies reach the eighth month, they are crawling and moving around and you need to start setting limits—not out of concern that they are going to disobey but to protect them. When their increased mobility combines with an insatiable sense of curiosity, anything can happen. Babies love to explore and will be everywhere, which is why you have to baby-proof your house and keep a close eye on them, taking away the element of chance as much as possible. It's not fair to yourself to be on pins and needless all the time, wondering what your baby is going to get into next, and it is not fair to the baby to have her in an environment where she is constantly being told no even though she is just following her natural impulse to explore new things. There isn't a baby alive who can't find the one dangerous thing you missed in your childproofing. That's where you use another gentle but firm No: "No, honey, you can't pull that lamp over. That would hurt you." You follow these Nos, distracting and diverting your child. "No, Erin, you can't play with Mommy's vase. Here, let's play with this ball." You'll do this thousands of times.

Enjoying Mealtime

The natural urge to explore kicks in with food, too. As babies get older, they will want to feed themselves. For the parent this can be funny and a little bit trying because only a small percentage of the food actually makes it into the baby's mouth. The rest goes pretty near everywhere imaginable. A parent can get angry and turn his frustration into some kind of battle of wills, convinced that the child is playing with his food just to get a reaction. But a baby must explore for her brain to develop; it's a natural expression of basic impulses. Babies are eager to learn about the feel and the texture of food, so they grab it in their hands and smear it in their hair. No parent has infinite patience, but it's important to find a way to let the child explore, within reasonable limits. Children will be fairly clear about which foods they like and which they don't like. So, they spit out the things they don't like. The wise parent looks for a balance, makes mealtimes enjoyable, does not fight over food, and learns to play all sorts of little games to get babies to eat their veggies.

What about Crying?

Probably the toughest choice a new parent will face in the baby's first year will be deciding when to let her baby cry. In the first couple of months, when a baby cries, we should provide comfort, even if it means walking for long hours with a colicky baby. Most babies start to settle into a loose schedule by the third and fourth month.

At six or eight months old, the question arises of when to let a baby cry. Many a battle has been waged over this question among parents and experts. One school of thought believes that you should never let babies cry in the first year. Others insist that crying spells are the first signs of a child's self-will and that babies are starting to learn how to manipulate their parents. I am asked about this all the time and have never seen the slightest bit of research to back up the view that babies at this age are trying to control their parents. Babies cry for two basic reasons: because they are in distress from hunger, a wet diaper, a gas bubble, a frightening dream, an earache, or one of a thousand other causes, or because they are tired.

The first thing a parent should do when a baby starts crying is to respond and try to figure out what is wrong. If you have attended to safety and comfort needs and she is still crying, it's possible the crying has to do with overstimulation and being tired. At this point parents can often tell a distress cry by its quality and intensity. With a baby of six to eight months, it's okay to let her cry for ten to fifteen minutes if you know she is not in distress. She will actually learn the skill of self-soothing. Any longer and it is best to provide comfort because something is bothering the baby. You may never know what it is.

Monica and I had to figure this out with our son Brian at about eight months, after he started to cry when we put him down for the night. One of us would check to make sure he had a dry diaper and that nothing else was wrong. Night after night he cried and we would walk him back and forth until he fell asleep. Maybe it was our fatigue or some parenting advice I don't recall, but Monica and I finally decided to try an experiment. We agreed that if Brian cried that night, we would check him, but if there was nothing wrong, we would let him cry for fifteen minutes. Sure enough, no sooner had I tiptoed out of the bedroom after laying him in his crib than he started his nightly wail. Monica and I renewed our resolve to be strong, but tossed and turned looking at the digital clock every thirty seconds. Monica started to cave in: "Dave, he's not going to stop. I think we should go in and get him." I was torn but said, "Moni, it's only been ten minutes. We agreed on fifteen. Let's just see what happens." Looking at the green digital numbers in the pitch dark—eleven, twelve, thirteen, fourteen minutes—I was about to admit defeat when Brian's crying started to weaken. We held our breath. He stopped crying and fell asleep at fourteen minutes and fifty seconds.

DO

- Enlist support—e.g., family, friends, or community resources—to help you in your baby's first year.

- Learn about your baby's physical growth and development.
- Respond to your baby when he or she cries.
- Sing, talk, and read to your baby.
- Hold or "wear" your baby in a sling or pack as often as you can.
- Childproof your home.
- Play with your baby and give age-appropriate playthings.
- Make mealtime stress free.
- Say no for safety reasons.
- Make any necessary Nos gentle but firm.

DON'T

- Don't ignore your baby's cries.
- Don't put your baby in front of a TV or video screen.
- Don't ever scream at or shake your baby.
- Don't leave a mobile baby unsupervised.
- Don't feed your newborn without holding her.

What do I want to continue?

_____

_____

_____

What do I want to change?

_____

_____

_____

SEVEN

Toddlers and Preschoolers
Limits and Consequences

When I think of how hard it can be to teach your kids about limits and consequences, I always remember a summer night in Minnesota when our younger son, Brian, was just about three and a half years old. It was really hot, one of those thick, stifling midwest scorchers where the evenings feel almost as hot as the afternoons. It was perfect weather for a visit to our local Dairy Queen, just a few blocks from our house. So that afternoon Monica and the kids and I discussed it and decided that after dinner we would all walk down for ice cream cones dipped in chocolate, a Dairy Queen specialty. It sounded like a good plan, and we were all looking forward to that evening's treat.

We sat down to supper at our normal time. For some reason Brian decided he did not want to eat any of his dinner. There was nothing wrong with the food and I did my best to coax him into picking up his fork and eating something. But it was no use. Brian was having none of it. The more I tried to persuade him, the more stubborn he became.

Our back-and-forth was turning into a contest of wills, and fortunately it occurred to me that power struggles with your kids are never a good idea. I remember reminding myself: Aha, this is the time for me as a parent to apply the notion of limits and consequences.

So, I made sure Brian understood the situation clearly.

"Brian," I said. "You remember that we're going to go to Dairy Queen after dinner?"

"Yes," he said shortly.

He didn't much want to talk, either.

"And you know that Dairy Queen is dessert, and dessert only makes sense after we've had dinner, right?"

"Yes," he said.

"So if you want a treat from Dairy Queen, you need to eat some dinner."

"No," he blurted. "I don't want to go to Dairy Queen."

There wasn't much I could say after that. I had outlined the consequence for Brian and I knew he understood me. I had hoped that by reminding him of what he would be giving up by not trying his meal, I would motivate him to eat. No such luck. I repeated myself once, just to emphasize the point, and he again said no, he didn't want a Dairy Queen, and I finally let it rest.

Things stayed calm as the rest of us finished our dinner and remained calm as we cleaned up afterward, all of us doing our chores. Even on the walk down to Dairy Queen the mood was very pleasant. Everyone was in a good spirits, enjoying the summer evening.

Not until we arrived in front of Dairy Queen and Brian actually caught sight of the familiar white-on-red logo were there any signs of trouble.

"I want an ice cream cone!" Brian declared, looking up at me.

He looked awfully cute and a part of me wanted to say the heck with it, let's give the kid some ice cream. But I knew that would have been irresponsible. I would be giving Brian mixed messages, which was not going to help either of us. It was my job to follow through on what I had said.

"Brian," I said, "you *chose* not to have an ice cream cone."

"But, Daddy, I want an ice cream cone," he said again.

We were standing on the sidewalk in front of Dairy Queen by

then, and on a hot summer night there were a lot of people gathered there to get ice cream treats.

"Remember, Brian, you chose," I said. "You didn't eat any dinner, so you don't get dessert."

That was when Brian sank into a full-blown meltdown.

"I want ice cream!" Brian started screaming. "You won't let me have ice cream!" The decibels went off the chart with, *"You're mean!"*

I'll admit, I felt more than a little awkward. Here was this little guy having a fit in the middle of all these people. But I kept reminding myself that I had to follow through and be consistent about enforcing the consequences, all the more so since Brian was screaming. The potential learning experience meant much more for him than an ice cream cone, and more for me than some temporary embarrassment.

"You're mean!" he yelled again.

At this point, a woman ahead of us in line turned around and glared at me. She had been twisting back to sneak quick looks down at Brian and up at me, and she did not hide her indignation.

"Do you really expect a child that young to understand what you're trying to do?" she hissed indignantly.

"Yes," I said, trying to stay calm. "I do."

Brian understood perfectly well what was going on. He was trying to undo the consequence of not having that ice cream cone. It was my job as the parent to make sure he didn't succeed, because through this lesson and thousands of others he would come to understand limits and consequences. My own ice cream cone didn't taste quite as good that evening, because, sure, I felt bad. But the most important decisions we face as parents are often the most difficult . . . and they sure aren't fun.

The First Eighteen Months

If Brian had still been a baby, the woman glaring at me in line in front of Dairy Queen would have had a point. Parents spend the first nine months saying yes. They spend the next nine months, or when the baby starts to crawl, distracting and redirecting. At about eighteen months, however, No takes on a different meaning and importance. Up until then, babies are not really capable of understanding limits and consequences. They naturally assume that their wants and desires are just the same as those of people around them, and it only confuses babies when they are confronted with the fact that you, the parent, do not have the same feelings as they do or that you don't want them to do what they want to do. Usually, in their confusion, they will cry. This is where distracting and redirecting come into play.

Many years ago, I was babysitting my goddaughter Kathleen, then just over a year old and newly able to walk. I wasn't distracted for more than thirty seconds when she disappeared. My quick search ended in the bathroom, where Kathleen was happily playing and splashing in the toilet. She looked at me with a huge smile, and everything in her demeanor showed how proud she was of her discovery. I quickly intervened by redirecting her interest in a healthier way. "Kathleen, I have an even better place to play in water," I said excitedly. After washing her hands the two of us went to the kitchen, where I filled the sink with warm water. She stood on a chair next to me and helped me squeeze the bottle of dish detergent into the running water. We both marveled at the billowing suds and spent the next ten minutes splashing and having a great time.

Kathleen is now in her late twenties and her inquisitive mind has already earned her a degree in physics, a position in subatomic-particle research, and a job at the Stanford Linear Accelerator in Palo Alto, which she recently left to pursue her interests in health care.

Babies keep it simple. That's a big part of their charm. They sleep, they eat, they cry, they turn clean diapers into dirty ones, and they grin and gurgle to the enjoyment of their parents. They don't ask themselves why they are doing what they are doing or why they want something. Babies' behavior is driven almost entirely by basic drives like hunger, the need for comfort, the need for attention. Their wants are usually straightforward. The intense curiosity babies feel is based on their brains' need to create new connections, to wire their brains with more complex neural networks. They are little explorers because this is what comes naturally to them. Some of their behavior might be a little scary and a little exasperating, but it's being driven by curiosity.

Keep in mind that babies are finely attuned to their parents' emotions and sensitive to disapproval or emotional turmoil around them. Practically speaking, this hardwired sensitivity is one more reason to use distraction and diversion and limit your use of No in the first eighteen months.

The main reason to say no to a child in the first year and a half is to warn against potential danger. If a toddler is playing with a sharp knife, the first thing you do is take it away, tell her no, and divert her with a toy or other activity. The second thing is to find out who was foolish enough to leave a sharp knife where a child could get to it.

While a No can be firm and emphatic, a toddler's language comprehension is still developing. Young children find it harder to comprehend the negative. A parent says, "No, don't stand on the chair." The child hears, "Stand on the chair." Telling the child what *to do*, for example, "Feet on the floor," will produce the behavior you want in language she can understand. Get in the habit of shifting the focus to something new, which plays to the toddler's strength of always being curious and avoids pointlessly upsetting the child and confusing him with a No that he doesn't yet fully understand. A good slogan for parents dealing with an inquisitive, energetic toddler is: Distract and Divert! The delightful picture book *No, David!* by David Shannon (Scholastic, 1998) will have you and your toddler laughing about all the trouble David gets into.

Big Changes

A major developmental transition occurs when babies reach eighteen months and begin to understand that there are differences between themselves and other people and also differences between their desires. This fundamental shift in perspective leads to major changes in behavior, including the onset of what are often called the terrible twos. It's important to understand that this change springs from the toddler's realization that he's a separate person from his parent with different feelings and thoughts. This has not occurred to the child until now.

A fascinating experiment helped map this change. A group of toddlers at fourteen months and then eighteen months were presented with raw broccoli and Goldfish crackers and then asked to share. As the author Malcolm Gladwell explained in a January 10, 2000, article in *The New Yorker*:

> Some years ago, the Berkeley psychology professor Alison Gopnik and one of her students, Betty Repacholi, conducted an experiment with fourteen-month-old toddlers. Repacholi showed the babies two bowls of food, one filled with Goldfish crackers and one filled with raw broccoli. All the babies, naturally, preferred the crackers. Repacholi then tasted the two foods, saying "yuck" and making a disgusted face at one and saying "yum" and making a delighted face at the other. Then she pushed both bowls toward the babies, stretched out her hand, and said, "Could you give me some?"
>
> When she liked the crackers, the babies gave her crackers. No surprise there. But when Repacholi liked the broccoli and hated the crackers, the babies were presented with a difficult philosophical issue—that different people may have different, even conflicting, desires. The fourteen-month-olds couldn't grasp that. They thought that if they liked crackers everyone liked crackers, and so they gave Repacholi the crackers, despite her expressed preferences. Four months later, the babies had, by and large, figured this principle out, and when Repacholi made a face at the crackers they knew enough to give her the broccoli.

Toddlers are not doing things parents don't want them to do just to be contrary. They are exploring this newly discovered difference between themselves and others. Alison Gopnik, the broccoli-experiment designer, examines this in an interesting book, *The*

Scientist in the Crib, which she wrote in 2000 with Patricia Kuhl and Andrew Meltzoff, both at the University of Washington.

"What makes the terrible twos so terrible is not that the babies do things you don't want them to do—one-year-olds are plenty good at that—but that they do things *because* you don't want them to," the authors note. "Toddlers are systematically testing the dimensions on which their desires and the desires of others may be in conflict . . . the child is the budding psychologist; we parents are the laboratory rats."

Kids are like little scientists, constantly running experiments to learn more about their world, and after the eighteen-month point, these experiments become much more numerous and attention-getting. They will do things just to test how far they can go. Kids will do something that they know they aren't supposed to do, all the while keeping a close eye on their parents to see their reaction. Some kids will even say no to themselves while they are misbehaving because they *know* what they are doing is wrong, but they do it anyway. Remember that the executive function, the prefrontal cortex, in a toddler's brain is still under construction and isn't fully working until after the teen years. Once a toddler is in motion she often lacks the ability to stop. A toddler may "know better than to bite someone." The toddler may even say, "No biting." But once she is in the motion of biting, she cannot stop. In fact, the biter often is as shocked by her action as the bitee.

Developmental psychology explains that our kids are not doing these things to try to drive us crazy, as much as it might seem that way at times. They are testing their limits, mapping the boundaries of their independence. But they understand that there are risks that come with this kind of testing, and their hardwired drive to stay connected with other people gives them a fear of disapproval. That is why—and this might surprise some people—a toddler's favorite word to use is *no.*

Offer a Choice

Many a contest of Nos with a toddler can be avoided and the child's self-confidence nurtured by offering the two-year-old a choice between two options.

Randy was frustrated. Every morning he battled with his two-year-old, Douglas, to get him dressed and ready to leave the house on time for day care, while he went to work.

"Douglas has a drawer full of clothes," Randy related. "But I end up getting tense, angry, and yelling at him. I'm a single dad and I can't be late for work."

"Two-year-olds can love battles and it's the parent's job to avoid them. What Douglas really wants is some control. You need to give it to him, but in a way that keeps you in charge," I said. "Try giving him a choice. Instead of opening the drawer and picking out his clothes for the day, have two outfits in mind. Then ask Douglas, 'Do you want to wear the green shirt or the blue shirt?' This way Douglas is short-circuited from the usual two-year-old No response and feels good about making a choice." Using two choices regularly with a two-year-old is a good strategy.

Learning to Care

At two, children are trying to figure out other people and how to get along with them. It's a bumpy road, of course, which is how they learn. They are also developing a new level of empathy. While the ability to share another person's emotional state is hardwired at birth, at about eighteen months empathy takes on the added dimension of caring. In other words, once a child understands that your feelings are different from his, he has a new motivation to help. So, while a small baby may become upset and anxious when his parent is sad, the eighteen-month-old develops an urge to try to comfort and soothe. Toddlers don't just feel your pain, they also want to help.

This is an important step forward in a child's moral development. You can help toddlers learn about empathy by teaching them emotional cues. When opportunities present themselves, explain what's happening emotionally for your child, for instance by saying, "Look, she's crying, she must be sad," or, "Your face is red, you must be angry."

Parent Tool Kit: Using *No* with Toddlers and Preschoolers

Toddlers and preschoolers pose new challenges for parents. Use the questions in this kit to determine how prepared you are.

			PARENT TOOL KIT Using *No* with Toddlers and Preschoolers
Yes	No		
☐	☐	1.	I know the big developmental change that is behind the "terrible twos."
☐	☐	2.	I childproof my home so that my toddler has a safe environment.
☐	☐	3.	I expect some resistance from my toddler.
☐	☐	4.	I set age-appropriate limits and enforce them.
☐	☐	5.	I can avoid power struggles and win/lose battles with my child.
☐	☐	6.	I expect my child to do some very simple chores like picking up toys.
☐	☐	7.	I am able to remain firm and calm in the face of a two-year-old's resistance.
☐	☐	8.	I offer my toddler appropriate choices from a menu of options.
☐	☐	9.	I give my toddler plenty of attention but do not overdo it.

If you found yourself agreeing with the statements in the tool kit, you already have a foundation to build on. If you found yourself answering no to some items, you may want to do things differently by the time you finish this chapter. The following pages will explain how No changes for toddlers and preschoolers.

A New Importance for *No*

By age two it comes time to really put No to work for you and your child. This development of self-will in toddlers changes the meaning of No into a way to help children learn the limits of their demands. They cannot learn those limits without consistent and firm use of No from their parents and other important adults in their lives.

How we handle the challenge of introducing toddlers to No really lays the groundwork for a big part of our parenting job. As Monica likes to say, "If you can't say no to a two-year-old, then you're in big trouble." She's right. If you can't say no to a two-year-old and follow through, then how in the world are you going to say no to a snarling, hormonally challenged fourteen-year-old?

Your goal is not to break the budding will or independence of your two-year-old or preschooler. The goal is to help the child begin to balance his will ("what I want to do") with the needs and desires of others ("what I should do"). At this age, he needs to harness his will so that it is not an out-of-control drive. We parents begin to try to strike a balance between helping our children become independent and helping them learn limits.

Jerry and Claire came to me for marriage counseling several years ago, but I realized that a lot of their stress came from their struggles to cope with their twenty-two-month-old twins, Joey and Adam. "We're exhausted," Claire explained during one of our sessions. "I love the twins but they're driving me crazy. I tell them not to do something and they do it anyway. When I yell at them they just scream louder. Then Jerry gets mad at me and tells me I'm worse than the kids. By the end of the evening I don't know who I'm more disgusted with, the kids, Jerry, or myself. Sometimes I wish we'd never had kids."

I asked Jerry how he dealt with the twins. "They're just little kids," he replied. "They don't know right from wrong yet. We just have to stop all the yelling."

"Well, I agree with you that all the yelling is not doing any good," I said. "But you didn't answer my question. I asked you how you dealt with Joey and Adam."

"I spend a lot of time playing with them. We get along great."

"What about discipline though, Jerry?" I asked.

"That's pretty much Claire's department," he said. "She's the one who gets all uptight. If she just let them alone, things would be a lot better."

I waited for a minute and then said, "Now let me see if I have this right." I turned to Claire. "You're the only one trying to rein in their behavior, and you always end up yelling and screaming." Then I looked at Jerry. "And then you criticize her because she's doing it wrong even though you haven't even tried to do it yourself." I paused for a second. "Do I have this right?"

Claire responded immediately. "That's exactly right."

Jerry didn't take long to defend himself. "They're not even two years old, for Pete's sake. You can't discipline kids at that age."

This was probably our third or fourth session, so I knew I had made a pretty good connection with them, and I was confident that they trusted me. So here's what I said next. "You guys love Joey and Adam and want to be good parents, right?" They both nodded yes. "Well, I think that you're at the perfect spot to straighten this out. If you'll work with me, I'll try to help you quit the yelling, Claire, and I'll show you, Jerry, that this is the perfect time to begin to teach your boys discipline. You need to get on board and be a partner with Claire on this. No more Monday-morning quarterbacking for you, Jerry." I waited a moment before asking, "Are you willing to do things differently?"

They both agreed to hear me out. In the sessions that followed, I taught Jerry and Claire about limits and consequences.

Limits and Consequences

The way to avoid power struggles is to let children know in advance what the limits are, let them know what the consequences will be if they don't observe those limits, and follow through as calmly and clearly as possible. Your interaction with a preschooler is different from that with a teen, of course, but the basic framework is the same.

A judicious but firm use of No is your friend and ally in establishing limits. Negative behaviors can start to become ingrained because, in the brain, "the neurons that fire together wire together." Clear limits and consequences that you start in the preschool years and continue will pay off for you and your child throughout his growing years.

Which behaviors in the preschool years should parents be concerned about and use No? It always helps to be organized in our thinking, so let's start by breaking down the three categories of behaviors.

- *Behaviors to leave alone.* Children are not miniature adults. Many immature behaviors are developmentally normal. It's quite normal for a twelve-month-old to take a bowl of spaghetti and put it on her head. If your ten-year-old does that, you should be worried. Thus, behaviors like thumb sucking or whining (especially when your toddler is tired) are developmentally normal and can be left alone.
- *Behaviors to correct.* Here's where limits come in. We should correct behaviors that might be understandable for a given developmental stage but are still unacceptable. Examples include throwing food (once they're past babyhood), teasing pets, aggression toward parents or siblings, and doing forbidden or dangerous things. Normal does not mean acceptable. It may be normal for siblings to fight but there has to be a limit to how far it goes. Likewise, it is normal for toddlers to have temper tantrums, but it is a mistake to give in to them.

- *Behaviors to reinforce.* If you want to see good behavior repeated, say to your preschooler, "I like it when you . . . [put
  your toys away; say 'please' when you ask for something]."
  Reinforcement of positive behaviors—for example, polite-
  ness, respect, caring, sharing, thoughtfulness, and independence—will ensure their development. We'll talk more
  about reinforcing positive behaviors in chapter 8, "Catching Kids Being Good: The Middle Years."

It's not always easy to know what "normal" is for different ages,
but a growing number of resources can help you figure that out.
Many communities offer parenting classes that almost always in-
clude information on developmental stages. There are also some ex-
cellent books on what to expect, including *Touchpoints: The Essential
Reference—Your Child's Emotional and Behavioral Development,
Birth–3,* by T. Berry Brazelton (Da Capo Lifelong Books, 1992), and
*What's Going On in There: How the Brain and Mind Develop in the
First Five Years of Life,* by Lise Eliot (Bantam, 2000).

We want our kids to have a sense of independence and initiative
balanced with an ability to observe limits so that they can eventually
harness their urges for themselves as they get older. We might think
of it as "outsourcing" followed by "insourcing." Babies and
preschoolers "outsource" limit setting to their parents and caregivers
so that they can eventually do more of it for themselves.

Parenting children, from the toddler years through adolescence,
means helping them develop different ways of mastering their hardwired drive for pleasure—self-will. Saying no helps them understand
that there are limits, and there are consequences, and it's their
choice. They learn that they can make choices and sort through
competing drives, like the desire to have what they want instantly
and the need to have others' approval and connection with them.

The child learns the limits by always testing them. Once you set
the limits and let the child know the consequences for transgressing
them, then if they push against those limits and go beyond them,
you must carry through on the consequences. Children have to experience the consequences of their choices.

Tips on Getting Started

I know that setting limits and following through can be difficult. By thinking about them ahead of time instead of just reacting to situations as they come up, you can better stay in control.

- *Plan ahead.* Know your child's ups and downs and how she acts when she gets tired. Try to head off problems before they happen. For example, try to avoid a trip to the supermarket when the child is tired and ready for a nap. Or steer your child to a quiet activity before bedtime so he doesn't get all wound up as you try to get him to go to bed. Preventing the need to say no is worth a pound of enforced Nos.

- *Schedule.* Try to have a regular, predictable schedule so that the child knows what to expect. When children don't know what's going to happen next, their anxiety sometimes causes them to act out.

- *Stay involved.* Toddlers and preschoolers need activities to keep them occupied. Have a special toy or activity box you can pull out when you are in a tight spot and need your kids to be safely occupied. Rotate their toys, if possible, putting some away, so that when you pull them out they are like new.

- *"No" sweat.* A toddler saying no is not a child being defiant. It is developmentally appropriate. Don't take it personally.

- *No media.* Children under two should not watch TV or other media. Limit media to under two hours for an older preschooler. Too much media can wire your child's brain to crave stimulation and put him at risk for attention and concentration problems. Media also exposes children to all the commercials that drive the "gimmes."

Steps to Stay Calm

Above all, always keep this in mind: remain calm. No parent is a robot, so don't expect to be perfect in your responses. You will have days when you can't stay as calm as you wish you could. But the more you keep your cool, the better chance you'll have of being consistent with your kids.

Henry was a good father, but he had a short temper. At the first sign of resistance from his four-year-old daughter, Henry would lose his cool and start yelling. He knew this wasn't helpful to his daughter and wanted to change. Henry was a "hot reactor," someone who has quick and strong emotional reactions, but he could learn to stay calm. I recommended he try these strategies, which can work for most parents:

1. To build up your ability to act calmly, think of a potential conflict situation with your child. Imagine yourself handling it calmly. Repeat this scene in your mind until it is familiar, until you know automatically what you will say. Now think of this scene as a video recording that you have labeled "Cool, Calm Mom/Dad" and place it on a shelf in your mind for future use.

2. When in a conflict with your child and you feel your anger escalating, picture a huge Stop sign right in front of your face. This will interrupt the cycle.

3. Then, breathe deeply three times, slow down, and remain calm.

4. After three deep breaths, go to your mental video shelf and retrieve the tape labeled "Cool, Calm Mom/Dad." Play it over in your head as you talk with your child.

5. If you start to lose your calm again, take a time-out, see the Stop sign and feel your anger stop in its tracks, breathe deeply three times; slow down, calm down; replay the calming tape.

Henry needed to have realistic goals. "You're not built to be cool, calm, and collected," I said. "Imagine a calm-scale of one to ten. You're at ten, and the goal is to lower your score to seven, then six, and then lower." After several months, Henry still struggled to stay calm, but he was making progress.

Setting Limits and Consequences

Sometimes, in their anxiety over dealing with the messiness of setting limits, parents talk too much. This is a mistake. Don't get into an argument or overexplain. That just distracts from the basic task of saying no. For instance, with an older child, say, "I'm going to say this just once: You need to put away your toys or I will put them away for the next two days."

Establish clear, simple limits and firm consequences:

- Set the limits or rules ahead of time to the extent possible.

  Of course, you cannot foresee every behavior that a creative two- or four-year-old can get into. When you see the behavior developing, however, let the child know that she has crossed a line or is about to. Letting her know what you want her *to* do is as important as telling her what not to do. So, if a child wants to climb up on a table, for example, you can say, "Play on the floor, Jennie."

- When you make a rule, enforce it consistently.

  Kayla has been told to hang up her coat and put her boots or shoes away when she gets home from preschool. Sometimes this rule is enforced and sometimes not. After a while Kayla just starts throwing her jacket into the corner and refuses to hang it up.

- Let children know what the consequence will be if they cross the limit or break the rule.

  Jason was told that the next activity (a snack after getting home), couldn't happen until he washed his hands and face.

- Select consequences that are appropriate. Whenever possible, make the consequence connect to the behavior. There are three kinds of consequences: natural, logical, and privilege.

    - Natural consequences are those that flow directly from the act. The natural consequence of not eating dinner is that the child is hungry. That means that the consequence of not eating dinner is that you don't get anything more to eat until breakfast—no dessert, no snack before bed.
    - Sometimes the natural consequence does not make sense. For example, the natural consequence of running into the street is to get hit by a car. We do not want that consequence so we look for one that has some logical connection, such as: "If you don't stay in the yard, then that shows me you aren't ready to be in the yard and you'll have to stay in the house." This consequence is reasonably connected and matches the behavior. We don't want to overreact or underreact.
    - Sometimes it's hard to come up with a logical consequence that fits well. The third alternative, but one to use only as a last resort, is to restrict a privilege, like playing with a friend, watching a favorite TV program, or playing with a favorite toy. Children more quickly see the connection between their actions and logical or natural consequences. However, as children get older, restricting a privilege is sometimes the only alternative for a parent to use.

- Remind them of the rule and the consequence if needed but don't nag or lecture. Actions speak louder than words. Do not overexplain. For example, say, "If you hit your sister, you will need to sit in time-out for three minutes." You don't need to explain that it hurts.

- Young children need you to get into their space to redirect their actions. Don't practice "remote parenting"—yelling at them from another room.
- Make sure children know that the consequence is their choice. If they *choose* to break the rule, then they are choosing the consequence.

This keeps you out of the power struggle. Children will be upset, nonetheless, because they want what they want, so you'll hear that you're mean and terrible. "I don't like you!" they will tell you, and no one wants to hear that. But as a parent you need to remain calm and not rise to the debate. Calmly remind your child, as I did with Brian in front of Dairy Queen, "No, Brian, it was your choice. You chose not to eat any dinner." Take yourself out of the debate.

- Most important, if children break the rule or limit, it is your job to enforce the consequence.
- Three-year-old Jason kept getting up from his chair and running around during lunch. Karen, his mom, asked him to stay in his chair until he was finished. Within two minutes he was running around again. Karen called for him to sit down. "You must not be hungry if you won't sit down. If you don't sit down and finish your lunch, I'm going to take your plate away and you won't have anything to eat until dinner." He looked at her for a second and then continued to play. Karen calmly removed his plate and made sure he didn't have any snacks till dinner.

You want to be firm and supportive without being domineering. Domineering involves put-downs, name-calling, threats, and tests of will or power struggles. If you are calm, clear, and firm, you teach your child that he can make choices and is responsible for his behavior. You also make it clear that you are in charge. Power struggles lead to emotional escalations that make things worse. You are not in charge in a power struggle.

It's not realistic to expect the child to accept the logic of this. That's not her job. Her job is to push against the limits. It's your job to set the limits and remind her that she has a choice. We can't expect children to like the consequences, but we need to remind them that they did choose.

Eventually, children start to accept responsibility. But if they don't have consequences, they don't learn accountability. The stakes get much higher as a child gets older. Although the everyday issues for the terrible twos and preschoolers can seem like small potatoes, that's exactly when you have to start: to make sure that they know the limits and consequences ahead of time, to make the consequences reasonably fit the behavior, and to reinforce that it's their choice. Stay consistent. These lessons are very important to learn.

Attention-getters

Sometimes children will misbehave in order to get attention. Parents have to be alert to whether they are giving their kids enough attention and to make sure that their attention does not reinforce bad behavior. All children need love and closeness from their parents—give this in abundance. But sometimes a parent does not have a good sense of how much attention is enough and in frustration adopts the rule: When in doubt, give more attention. This creates little attention addicts. Do not reward behavior that seeks to get attention through misbehavior. If a child starts to whine and nag, you explain, rather than cave in.

You say, "If you would like me to read you a story then let Mommy finish this phone call and then we'll pick a book."

Don't cut the phone call short and immediately reward the whining. It is important that children do not get everything they want immediately.

You Can't Always Get What You Want

Historically, the role of children in the family has gone through a dramatic change in the last one hundred years. For centuries, children were economically productive in the family, working as soon as they were old enough, expected to help on the farm or in the shop. A lot of children never made it to adulthood, so having more children was an advantage in a family business.

In modern society, children don't contribute to the family enterprise but become an investment. As families have fewer of them, children's welfare and happiness become more of a goal than it used to be. That's not a bad thing, but if we are not careful, we become so focused on our children's happiness, so intent on making sure all their needs are taken care of and that they are never disappointed, that they don't develop the resilience they will need to take care of themselves.

The developmental importance of a child's ability to delay gratification became clear in a famous 1960s experiment. Four-year-olds came into a room where the experimenter gave each child a choice.

"Okay, here's a marshmallow," he said. "You can eat this marshmallow now, or you can *not* eat this marshmallow now and when I come back, I will give you another marshmallow. If you eat the first one now, I'm not going to give you another one."

This presented a difficult choice for the average four-year-old: "Do I delay gratification and get two marshmallows, or do I eat the one in front of me right now?"

Some of the children were unable to resist the temptation. They ate their marshmallows within seconds or minutes after the experimenter left the room. The psychologist-scientist was, of course, watching on closed-circuit TV. Other kids did everything they could to resist that temptation. They sang songs and did not even look at the marshmallow. They did everything they could to avoid eating that marshmallow. They were able to delay gratification in order to get the reward of the second marshmallow.

The scientists kept track of these children from age four all the way up to age eighteen. At the age of twelve, the kids who as four-year-olds showed restraint and did not eat the first marshmallow were still able to delay gratification. They were happier. They were more successful in school. The kids who ate the first marshmallow and were not able to delay gratification tended at age twelve to have more behavioral problems. They were still unable to set limits for themselves. At the age of eighteen, the kids who delayed gratification as four-year-olds were predictably more successful in school and more competent than the other kids in many areas.

Randy graduated from high school at the top of his class even after taking advanced-placement classes. He played on the baseball team, was an officer in the National Honor Society, participated in his church, and found time to volunteer in service projects every summer. I'd bet that if Randy had been part of the marshmallow experiment, he would have waited for that second marshmallow.

Tim, on the other hand, probably would have gobbled up the first marshmallow before the experimenter was out of the room. Throughout elementary and high school he received low grades in spite of his above-average intelligence, and he could never resist the temptation to join friends in escapades that became more serious as he got older. Three months before high school graduation, he and two friends were arrested for vandalizing a neighbor's house after the neighbor complained to the police about their loud late-night music.

The skills of self-discipline and limits that we teach our kids early in life help them become competent to pursue a happy and productive future.

DO
- Know what's normal behavior for your toddler and pre-schooler.
- Use limits and consequences to teach your child good behavior and to help her or him develop self-discipline.
- Remain calm to avoid power struggles. Actions speak louder than words.
- Follow through consistently on consequences. Children quickly figure out if we mean what we say.

- Give your child choices within the parameters you set.
- Acknowledge your child's desire, so he feels heard even if he can't have something. "I know you really want this, but . . ."
- Learn other ways of saying no, like, "Stop, enough, later."
- Tell a child what *to* do, instead of what not to do.
- Turn Nos into positives. "You can't play with Mommy's good purse, but you can play with my old one."

DON'T
- Don't panic when your toddler becomes infatuated with the word *no*. It's an important developmental milestone.
- Don't take misbehavior personally.
- Don't ignore misbehavior. Patterns can develop quickly.
- Don't practice "remote parenting."
- Don't give in to temper tantrums or whining.
- Don't scream, yell, or humiliate your child when you become frustrated with her.
- Don't always give in to your child's demands for attention.

What do I want to continue?

_____
_____
_____

What do I want to change?

_____
_____
_____

EIGHT

Catching Kids Being Good
The Middle Years

M onica realized that we needed a "parenting adjustment" in the middle of a long, gray Minnesota winter many years ago when Brian was in fourth grade.

One Saturday morning when the kids were at various activities, Monica tracked me down as I was putting laundry into the washing machine.

"Dave," she said. "We need to talk."

"What about?" I asked.

"How we're dealing with Brian."

Since I had just fallen into another power struggle with our second son that morning, I was eager to reassess what I was doing. "Okay," I said. "Let's go."

We walked down the block to our neighborhood coffee shop and, over a cup, got down to business.

Monica started. "I'm really concerned about what we're doing with him."

Brian was bright, clever, and increasingly adept at pushing all our buttons. He seemed intent on testing the limits at every turn. Life had become filled with small and large daily battles with Brian to get him to finish his chores, pick up after himself, converse with us, control his temper, and be polite to the rest of the human race.

We had always heard that ages six through eleven, the so-called middle years, were quiet, but this wasn't true with Brian. We now laugh with him about this stage, but at the time, Monica and I had no idea that he would grow up to be a warm, sensitive, capable adult.

For a long while our exchanges with Brian had taken on a decidedly unpleasant tone. "It's getting so that all our interactions with Brian are negative," Monica said. "And that worries me."

"Yeah, you're right. I'm constantly exasperated and angry with him," I added. "He's testing every rule and limit we have."

The more we talked, the more Monica and I realized that we had slipped into a pattern of constantly focusing on the negative with Brian—on catching him being bad. We were really good at spotting all the things Brian was doing that needed correction, but a lot of his positive acts were escaping us.

"How do you think we would feel if we only heard from each other or from co-workers when we did something wrong? We can't let all our interactions with Brian be negative. He'll take that on as his identity, and these battles will get worse."

We both sat there for a minute without talking, then agreed it was time for us to check our own behavior. We decided that from that morning on, we were going to make a concerted effort not to react only to what Brian was doing wrong, so that we were not constantly using limits and consequences and No with him.

We resolved to catch Brian being good and give him a pat on the back. We would look for times to acknowledge and appreciate him in ways big and small. Since he certainly wasn't going to find anything positive about us, we were going to search for the positive in him.

I am not saying that Monica and I became softies. We did not praise Brian when he didn't deserve it and we didn't heap positives all over him. But we heightened our attention to small moments when we could say thank you, or smile, or offer encouragement. We needed to strike a balance between encouraging him and setting limits and consequences.

This was a turning point for us with Brian. I am still thankful to Monica for having the sense to insist that we sit down together to take stock of what we were doing. Our positive interactions with Brian grew little by little, which helped us both during his teen years.

I should have caught our negative pattern with Brian because my experiences in the classroom had taught me the power of "catching kids being good." One of my students, Angus, had a reputation for being surly and argumentative. From the first day of class I sought to engage him, chatting with him and others before and after class, making small jokes and taking an interest in his cross-country running. Maybe my focus on the positive helped because Angus never had behavioral problems during the two years I taught him.

How We Can Get into a Rut

It's just human nature to develop views and opinions about our kids. These views start to reinforce themselves and eventually become more set, influencing how we react to our kids. The psychological explanation for this is called "attribution theory." Our brains handle the ocean of information constantly streaming in through our five senses by sorting the data into circuits where similar data is stored. We physiologically set up that collection of files. We start to build the file about our children immediately after birth—sometimes even before, depending on how the pregnancy progressed. Once we've set up a file, two powerful psychological processes kick into action: cognitive consistency and, the flip side of the same coin, cognitive dissonance.

Cognitive consistency describes our natural tendency to have incoming information fit neatly with the data that is already there. Cognitive dissonance explains our propensity to filter out data that doesn't match up. That's the psychological reason behind the common saying, "Don't confuse me with facts. My mind is already made up."

Attribution theory describes three ways the brain keeps the files consistent. First, we pay attention only to evidence that supports our expectations and ignore evidence at variance with our expectations. Second, we interpret ambiguous data in such a way that it is consistent with what we already think. Third, we expect people to act a certain way, and that very expectation increases the chances that they will indeed behave the way we expect. This phenomenon is called the "Pygmalion effect" or the "self-fulfilling prophecy."

Psychologist Robert Rosenthal's classic experiment dramatically illustrates the Pygmalion effect. He arranged for a group of elementary-school students to take a standardized intelligence test, but told their teachers before they administered the test that it was a new measure of how fast their students were likely to advance that year. He randomly assigned scores to the students and shared the scores with the teachers. The teachers' higher expectations of certain students were shaped by scores completely unrelated to the students' actual test performance. At the end of the year, those students whom the teachers had expected to blossom made dramatic gains, while the students whom the teachers expected to lag behind did not show similar improvement.

Joan was a ninth grader with a bad reputation among her teachers. After several months of counseling her, I became convinced that the Pygmalion effect was at work. Even as she attempted to improve her behavior, teachers corrected her for small infractions that they ignored with other students. She would complain, "It doesn't make any difference what I do. My teachers have it in for me." I stopped doubting Joan when I saw it happen. I was monitoring the student cafeteria along with another teacher and saw a student, sitting at Joan's table, throw food at another girl. Before I could get there, however, my colleague immediately accused Joan. It was clear that some teachers expected Joan to be a troublemaker. Over time, and true to the Pygmalion effect, she complied.

Attribution Theory at Work in the Family

Attribution theory can explain the dynamics of family life, as well, and certainly describes what had happened between Brian and me. The file in my brain labeled "Brian" was filling with data that read, "Brian is difficult and always pushes the limits." Once that file was set up, I began to pay more attention to the information that fit my view of Brian as a limit pusher and disregard information that didn't fit. I was only filing the bad stuff and had started to interpret unclear data in a way that was consistent with my view of Brian as difficult. For example, if I called out the back door for him to take out the garbage and he didn't respond, I immediately got irritated because I thought he was ignoring me, even though there could have been several other explanations for his lack of response, including that he hadn't even heard me.

If Monica and I kept expecting Brian to misbehave, then he would. Since then, I've counseled hundreds, if not thousands, of parents over the years to make sure they don't develop a similar case of "hardening of the categories."

Parent Tool Kit: Catch Your Kids Being Good

It's easy to get caught in a negative rut with our kids. Use the questions in this section to see if you're able to catch your kids being good.

PARENT TOOL KIT
Catch Your Kids Being Good

Yes	No		
☐	☐	1.	I know many ways to say no without using the word itself.
☐	☐	2.	I set limits using positive statements like, "Thanks for keeping the volume down on the TV," instead of, "Don't have the TV loud."
☐	☐	3.	I make sure to thank my children and teens for helping out.
☐	☐	4.	I try to have more compliments than criticisms for my children.

Yes	No		
☐	☐	5.	I can avoid power struggles and win/lose battles with my child.
☐	☐	6.	I try to smile and laugh with my kids every day.
☐	☐	7.	I let my children and teens know the things I appreciate about them.

If you found yourself answering yes to most items, keep it up. If you answered no a lot, you might want to do the kind of reevaluation that I had to do with Brian.

Balancing No with Encouragement

In the last chapter I emphasized the importance of establishing limits and consequences for our kids, which are essential for saying no. However, everything can be overdone, including No. It's all about balance. Your kids need a combination of limits and consequences on the one hand and healthy encouragement and support on the other. One without the other will make it difficult for a child to grow into a mature adult.

Every psychology 101 class explains that positive reinforcement is more effective than negative. Through encouragement we help our children develop the self-confidence and knowledge they need to meet their potential. According to folk wisdom, honey works better than vinegar: In other words, positive motivation works better than negative corrections.

Encouragement is so effective because our brains are hardwired for attachment and we become anxious when that need for attachment is threatened. Disapproval creates anxiety. Encouragement and approval feel good.

Encouragement works, so let's talk about what encouragement is—and what it is not. As we discussed in chapter 4, to create positive self-esteem, encouragement cannot be empty praise. Encouragement is not constantly saying good things that have no meaning.

Kids will quickly figure out that you don't really mean what you say when you give hollow praise.

For example, if your daughter tells you about some small accomplishment at school and you walk around the house making a big deal out of it or call up her grandmother to tell her about it, she'll probably hate it. Most kids would. They are smart enough to see through the exaggeration and conclude that you do not really mean what you say. Also, they know that they did not deserve that reaction and may conclude that they cannot trust you in general. After all, you took this small thing and blew it completely out of proportion. Encouragement should match the behavior. In this kind of situation, a smile and a "that's nice" would suffice. The last thing you want is for your child not to trust what you say.

Learning Responsibility

Here's an example of how to use limits, consequences, and encouragement together. I feel it's very important for children to have ordinary household chores and take some responsibility for the upkeep of the house. Yet, in more and more households these days, the parents do much of the cleaning and chores. The kids are busy in sports, school, and a host of other activities and aren't asked to learn these lessons in responsibility. Chores help kids understand limits and consequences. For example, if your daughter has not mowed the lawn but wants to go play with her friends anyway, you need to remind her that she has a responsibility first.

Household chores help kids to feel competent and feel like part of the family. As our kids were growing up, Monica and I divided up the cleaning and cooking responsibilities so that each of us had his own job. Sometimes it was not easy to be encouraging. One Saturday morning, when Erin was only eight and it was her turn to clean the bathroom, I went to check on her and she was already in there hard at work.

She wasn't doing a bad job—not for an eight-year-old, anyway—

but her work did not meet my standards. I watched for a minute, trying to hold back, but then I couldn't help myself and started helping Erin—at least that was what I told myself. Actually, I started cleaning the bathroom myself, telling Erin, "This is the way you should do it," and left her with little to do but watch me. It didn't take long before she started to withdraw. She waited for a couple of minutes and then wandered away.

Pretty soon I heard Monica call from the next room, "Dave?" She had been watching the scene from the kitchen and wanted to talk to me out of earshot of Erin.

"Do you know what you just did?" she asked me when I went over to her.

"I'm cleaning the bathroom," I said.

She gave me a look. "That was Erin's job."

"Yes," I said, "but she can't do it very well."

"So?" Monica responded. She was right.

I had taken the path of least resistance. It was easier for me to clean the bathroom myself, because I knew I would be satisfied with the results, and quicker than having Erin do it. But when I had seen the disappointed look on Erin's face, I should have realized that I was discouraging her.

Monica's point was: "What's more important, a sparkling clean bathroom to your standards or a daughter who feels competent about being able to do things?"

That was an important lesson for me. I had to give up some of my "do things right" standards. Erin grew to become a very competent adult. She had practice, she had responsibility, and she had the leeway not to be perfect every time, but to learn.

3 Steps to Encouragement

To encourage positive behavior, follow these three steps:

- Step 1. Identify positive behavior.
- Step 2. Label it as responsible.
- Step 3. Express appreciation.

So for example, say to your seventh grader, "I saw the way that you helped your grandmother decide where to plant the flowers we gave her for Mother's Day. I know it's not always easy when she keeps changing her mind. Thanks for being so patient." Or say to your teenager, "I noticed that you returned the car with a full tank of gas. That was considerate of you. Thanks."

What to Avoid

As our kids get older, decisions about what to encourage and what not to encourage are not always easy. We don't want encouragement to lead to overpressuring our kids. If we support real effort, our kids won't always have to pull off an exceptional accomplishment in order to hear the sweet sound of encouragement. They don't have to be the most accomplished students or the most decorated athletes. We want to send this message: "I care about the effort that you're making, not what color your ribbons are."

Sometimes we surprise ourselves and let critical words slip out. We don't mean to discourage our kids, it just kind of happens. That was the trap I fell into with Erin when I did not let her finish cleaning the bathroom.

I had a similar lapse early in my career as a teacher. I cringe when I remember an incident with Jeremy, an intelligent student who was easily frustrated. My students were correcting mistakes they had made on a test. While I helped one student, Jeremy tried to get my attention to let me know he was confused. The distressed and unhappy look on his face irritated me, so I called across the room loudly enough for his peers to hear, "Jeremy, don't act like such a baby." I certainly learned not to do that again as I became alert to the major enemies of encouragement. My remark to Jeremy was an example of the first enemy: put-downs.

Enemies of Encouragement

Put-downs

Mark's father, John, was a successful, high-powered businessman. He pushed hard in everything he did, and he pushed his kids hard, too. Nothing Mark did was ever quite good enough. As Mark's soccer coach, I witnessed John's put-downs firsthand and saw the harm it did to Mark.

I met Mark for the first time when he was assigned to my youth league soccer team. I thought he was doing well in the preseason practices. I liked his hustle, cooperation, teamwork, and the fact that he took directions well. My pleasure at seeing Mark's father show up at the first game of the season didn't last long. Mark was a bit overweight and not the fastest player on the team. Within minutes John was yelling for Mark to hurry up, hustle, and asking why he didn't do this or that. At the halftime break I calmly walked over to John and introduced myself. "Thanks for coming, John," I began. "I really like Mark's attitude and I'm glad he's on our team. I think it might work a little better if you shouted some encouragement to Mark instead of getting on his back."

I was startled by what John said in response: "The problem with Mark is that he's lazy. I know my son, coach. The only way I get him to do anything is push him. He's just plain lazy."

This wasn't the time or place for me to talk with John about this so I turned and walked back to the team. Mark was looking down at the ground, trying to hold back his tears. He along with every other kid on the team had heard what John had said.

Nothing good comes from put-downs and name-calling. They eat away at a child's confidence in his own ability. Even when you need to correct your child, correct the *behavior*, never humiliate the child. Holding someone accountable is not the same as criticism, put-downs, or humiliation.

Negative Comparisons

When Taesha came out of the locker room she could see the disappointment on her father's face. She had stood at the foul line, with her team behind by one point with one second remaining. The crowed cheered as Taesha's knees trembled. She had never before had a chance to win the game for her ninth grade basketball team. The first shot bounced off the back of the rim. The second shot missed everything. It was a crushing defeat and Taesha felt totally responsible and ashamed. It didn't matter to her that the twelve points she had made had kept her team in the game. She had missed the shots when they counted the most. Her father had only one comment before he turned to leave the arena: "I told you to practice your free throws more. Do you know why your sister would never have missed that shot? Because she works harder than you."

Whether in sports, grades, or behavior, negative comparisons send the absolute wrong message. Statements like, "Why can't you do well in school, like your older brother?" or, "Why can't you be nice, like your cousin?" have never produced improvement. They create resentment between siblings and other family members and send the message that we think our son or daughter is incapable.

Doing for Kids What They Can Do for Themselves

Emily was a smart, energetic twelve-year-old, an only child. Her mom, Stacy, a single parent, took great pride in everything Emily did and gave her plenty of praise. She seemed to give Emily all the encouragement she needed. Emily's problem, however, was that her mother was overinvolved. Stacy helped Emily with everything, even when she didn't need or even want the help. Stacy practically did Emily's homework for her, put hours into her science projects, and organized play dates with friends so completely that the kids never had to think up any activities for themselves.

There are a lot of ways to do too much for our kids. We get so rushed that we end up dressing our kids instead of letting them dress themselves, tying their shoes for them even after they've already learned how. Or else we do their chores or set the table for them because we don't want to risk a broken plate. We may do this in an effort to help our kids or, all too often, just because it is easier and quicker for us to do things ourselves. The result, however, is children who not only get the idea that they are not capable but are denied the ability to test themselves and gain skills.

Casey, the youngest of five children, had overinvolved parents: They coddled her, showered her with expensive clothes and toys, intervened at every turn with teachers, and badgered coaches to give her special consideration. In tenth grade, the biology teacher assigned a major team-research project. The students on Casey's team quickly complained that Casey wasn't doing her share. "We have to do everything for her and if we ask her to do something she complains and pouts."

Overprotection

Hayley, eleven, burst through the door with exciting news: "Mom, guess what! Our phys-ed teacher is starting a running club. She talked to our class today, and it's really going to be fun. All the other kids are joining, too. The first meeting is tomorrow after school. I can't wait."

"Are you sure you want to do that, honey?" her mother responded. "You know how you get wheezy when you catch a cold."

"Mom," Hayley shot back with obvious frustration, "Amelia's joining and Mrs. Hokenstrom told her that running is a great way to build up your lungs."

Her mother furrowed her eyebrows and waited a few seconds before responding. "Hayley, honey, why don't you wait awhile before joining. That way you can see how the other girls like it and it will give us a chance to talk with Dr. Merton and see what she thinks."

"But, Mom, all the other kids are going tomorrow. I really want to do it. *Pleeease.*"

"I don't think so. You know I'm the one who has to pay the doctor's bills when you get bronchitis."

"Aw, Mom, come on. You never let me do anything."

"Now, Hayley, that's not true. You know I'm just trying to take good care of you. I love you, sweetie."

An important part of encouragement is not always what we say, it's what we do. Even if you say nice things, if you overprotect your children, you shortchange them on life experiences. Overprotecting implies that we don't think they are capable. Character, perseverance, and willpower all grow stronger with use. Letting children gain competence through trial and error is an important part of encouragement.

The Middle Years

It's not easy to find information on kids in their middle years— the stage from six to eight, although some experts consider it to be from seven to nine or nine to eleven. The middle years are often neglected. In fact, Sigmund Freud called the years from six to twelve the "latency period." I wouldn't have used *dormant* as an adjective to describe my three kids at this age, but Freud may have been more interested in the younger kids and teenagers and may have brushed over this important developmental stage.

I find it most helpful to think of this stage as the elementary school years, six to eleven. Every parent knows that there are differences between a six- and an eleven-year-old, but they also have a lot in common. Even if the preschooler has spent a lot of time in day care or nursery school, the entrance into "real school" is a big deal and brings big changes. The child's world gets a lot bigger in elementary school as she becomes more sensitive to the opinions of other kids, so fitting in becomes more important. Peer pressure intensifies at adolescence, but second, third, and fourth graders feel it too.

Performance and competence emerge as big issues in the middle (or elementary school) years. Learning to follow directions, read, calculate, memorize facts, reason things out, and behave properly are expected, measured, and reported. For the first time, the child has a wide variety of activities and responsibilities to deal with: academics, peer relationships, hobbies, clubs, and projects. The big question for boys and girls at this stage is, "Can I do this? Am I competent?" Of course, a child asks the questions in more concrete terms:

"Do the other kids like me?"

"Does my teacher like me?"

"Am I smart enough?"

"Can I learn to read?"

"Will the others want me on their team?"

"Can I stay out of trouble?"

"What are my grades?"

"How did I do on the school tests?"

It is at this stage that children's ability to manage themselves is crucial to their success. Children who have learned No will prosper and those who haven't will run into trouble. For example, children who can persevere are more likely to complete their projects and invent creative solutions. Children who can keep their mouths shut and their hands to themselves are more likely to get approval. Children who can balance their wants with those of others will be more popular.

The two overriding strategies we have discussed so far are the recipe for success during the middle years:

- Discipline through limits and consequences.
- Encouragement, or what I call "catching kids being good."

DO

- Look for opportunities to encourage or praise your child.
- Practice the three steps to encouragement: identify, label, and acknowledge.
- Learn and practice the subtle ways to give positive feedback. For example, a smile and the word *thanks* can go a long way.
- Support your child but don't take over his projects or responsibilities.

- Make sure your children have household responsibilities or chores.

DON'T
- Don't overdo the praise. Kids see through false praise.
- Don't do things for your children that they can do for themselves.
- Don't overprotect your children.
- Don't ever mock, ridicule, or humiliate your children.
- Don't compare your children to siblings or peers.

What do I want to continue?

_____

_____

_____

What do I want to change?

_____

_____

_____

NINE

The Teenage Years
Loosen but Don't Let Go

K nowing how and when to say no during the teenage years is difficult. One look at your teenager tells you that these conversations will be different from how they were five years ago. That's because teens are no longer children. In addition to the physical growth associated with adolescence, teenagers' thinking and emotions change a lot. They are itching to take on new challenges and expand their horizons. At the same time, they are not yet adults.

Teenagers are a bundle of paradoxes. They are fun, idealistic, energetic, altruistic, and enthusiastic. They are excited about new things and often willing to try new activities. They are curious about the world and eager to interact with new people. *But,* they are also prone to angry outbursts, defiant acts, foolish risk taking, and inexplicable plunges into despair. One minute you're having a serious, informed, adult conversation with them and the next minute they turn into fire-breathing dragons just because you asked them to take out the garbage. They can stay out until late at night and then lie about where they have been. One moment you feel connected and comfortable with your teen, and the next you wonder who replaced your child with a demon. You find yourself wondering if the term *teenage brain* is an oxymoron.

Because teens are neither children nor adults, it can be confusing and scary to think about giving them the independence they crave. It's not easy to strike the balance between setting critical limits on their behavior and letting them spread their wings. In addition, while it's easy for us parents to forget, teenagers are often equally confused about what is appropriate and healthy. That's why the same fifteen-year-old girl who screams at you to get out of her life at 8:00 PM turns around and wants to be tucked in at 10:00.

I've always liked teenagers, which is a good thing since they've been such a big part of my personal and professional life. My wife, Monica, and I raised three, all of whom survived into adulthood. I often joke that the reason I wrote the book *Why Do They Act That Way? A Survival Guide to the Adolescent Brain for You and Your Teen* was to get revenge on Dan, Brian, and Erin. In addition, I taught and coached in high schools for ten years, was a high school counselor after that, and later specialized in developing and managing counseling programs for teens and families for Fairview Health Services in Minnesota.

While teens are lovable, they can also test our patience and sanity. Many of the parents whom I've met at my workshops for parents of teens are struggling to cope with their kids' behavior. A woman in Maryland wrote me recently thanking me for saving the lives of her two teenage daughters. "I was about ready to kill them," she wrote. She wasn't serious, but I also know she's not alone in her feelings. Adolescence is a lot like the terrible twos, when children also get volatile, impulsive, unpredictable, and frustrating to deal with. The mood swings, the temper tantrums, their defiance, and infatuation with the word *no,* the foolish risks— doesn't this sound a lot like adolescence? Of course, there are a couple of big differences. First, adolescents are bigger, stronger, and smarter than two-year-olds. This means they are harder to deal with. Second, the stakes are much higher. The trouble they get into can be a lot more serious than screaming in a restaurant or falling off the couch.

Because teens can drive a perfectly sane person to the brink of madness, many parents find it easier to retreat from the battle and let go of their kids too soon. This is not entirely surprising given that parenting a teenager can feel like a constant struggle without a clear goal. After arguing with my daughter Erin for the tenth weekend in a row about curfew, I wondered why I wasn't advocating for her to move out into her own apartment, buy her own car, and get it over with. At times, arguing just didn't feel worth the hassle. But it is—or rather, saying no and sticking to it is worth it. In this chapter I'll try to give you some ways to circumvent an argument but still say no effectively.

During adolescence, more than ever before, teenagers are going to push their parents to say yes to things from dropping curfews to car privileges to spring-break trips to overnight coed parties. In fact, teenagers' brains are actually wired to push adults to say yes to just about everything. In spite of what teens say, however, they need limits and consequences just like their younger brothers and sisters do. Recent discoveries in neuroscience explain why teenagers need No in order to grow into happy, successful adults. Letting go of rules and consequences too soon does not help your teen. In fact, it's like sending him out onto a treacherous road with bad brakes and only a learner's permit. Do not let No become a phrase of the past for your adolescent.

Parenting teenagers is all about balance. You shouldn't treat adolescents the same as their younger siblings. You need to change some rules as they grow out of their childhood. Adolescents are eager to experience the world beyond their parents' home, to try out new ideas and experiences. You don't want to hold them back from all the important learning that happens as they figure things out for themselves, but you also need to guide them along the way. They may ask for a divorce, but they still need you. They might fight many of your rules, but they still need to have them. They may test love's limits, but they certainly still need both love and limits. Parenting, teaching, or mentoring teenagers is a balancing act that requires you to loosen the reins but not let go.

Parent Tool Kit: Teenagers and *No*

Here's a set of questions to help you think about No and adolescents.

PARENT TOOL KIT
Teenagers and *No*

Yes	No		
☐	☐	1.	I have clear and consistent rules for my teenagers.
☐	☐	2.	I'm able to avoid power struggles with my teenagers.
☐	☐	3.	I can generally stay calm even when my teenager can't.
☐	☐	4.	My teen and I have a common definition of respectful behavior.
☐	☐	5.	I model respectful behavior in the way I treat my teenager.
☐	☐	6.	I do not accept foul or abusive language from my teen son or daughter.
☐	☐	7.	I talk with my kids about alcohol, drugs, and sex.
☐	☐	8.	I have a zero tolerance policy with my teen about substance use.
☐	☐	9.	I can say no to my teen about something important even if "all the other kids are doing it."
☐	☐	10.	I don't panic when my teenagers question my values because I know that's how they shape their own.

If you found yourself agreeing with these statements, you already have a good foundation to build on with your adolescent sons or daughters. If you found yourself answering no to some items, you may want to rethink some things. The following pages will explain why teenagers need No and how we can say it.

The Teen Brain: Under Construction

When we think about all of the physical changes that happen to teenagers on the outside during adolescence, it seems obvious that there would be a lot of changes happening on the inside as well. However, it wasn't always that obvious. Until recently, scientists believed that the major wiring in the brain was completed by about age ten. From then on, the thinking went, kids matured by simply using the circuits they had already established. Maturity came with experience. Today we know that view of the brain was wrong. MRIs and other new technology have enabled scientists to peer inside living, working brains and even watch specific brain cells in action. They have discovered that the adolescent brain isn't a finished product but a work in progress, a series of major construction zones. Even though the teen brain does not alter in size or shape, a truly astounding amount of growth is still under way.

Knowing that the teen brain is growing gives us a new sense of what adolescence means and crucial information to help our kids through this difficult stage. From angry outbursts to sleeping late, awakened sexuality to depression, impulsive behavior to defiance, understanding just what is going on in their heads not only helps us have compassion for what they are going through but suggests particular tactics and strategies we can use to serve them as parents and guides.

I have known Damien's family since he was a little kid. We all lived in the same neighborhood and our kids were around the same age, so we tended to see one another at baseball games, choir concerts, and other community events. I spent a lot of time on the sidelines of soccer games with his father, Tim, and we got to know each other pretty well. Damien was really a nice boy and I always looked forward to seeing him when my son Brian invited him to our house to play. The two had fun together and Damien was always polite to Monica and me when he came over.

I wasn't surprised, however, that when Brian and Damien became preteens they started to act a little differently when they got together. Seemingly overnight, "play time" turned into "just hanging out," and sooner rather than later Monica and I were the last people either of them wanted to talk to on their quick runs between the refrigerator and Brian's shut door. As a high school counselor and later a psychologist, I've known hundreds of kids who hit adolescence and start directing a distinct "leave me alone" vibe at every adult within a twenty-foot radius of them and their friends. At that time, my older son, Dan, had already entered adolescence and we knew firsthand that parenting a little boy was a lot different from parenting an indifferent, elusive teenager. Monica and I still enjoyed having Damien over and felt lucky that the two young guys wanted to spend time at our house, but we did have to readjust our expectations and find new ways to keep up with them.

Almost a year into our boys' "adolescence," Tim and I were once again standing on the sidelines watching our sons' team warm up. Tim seemed especially agitated this particular Saturday morning.

"How are you doing?" I asked.

"Not great, to tell you the truth," Tim answered. "Damien and I had a huge fight last night and I can't even tell you how it started. It seems like all we do is argue these days. Anything I say just sets him off. And it doesn't seem to stop when he leaves the house: He got into two major shouting matches with his teachers this week. I'm worried that it's only a matter of time until he gets suspended. I can't figure it out. It makes me nervous to say anything to him."

Tim poured out his worries about the changes he was seeing in his son. I asked Tim about Damien's grades, if he had changed peer groups, and whether there were any signs of alcohol or drug use. Tim's answers told me that Damien was doing okay for himself and was staying out of trouble for the most part. It seemed to me that his quickness to anger, impulsive decisions, and sharp outbursts had another explanation: adolescence. "It sounds to me like Damien's prefrontal cortex is under construction," I said.

Every teenager has a prefrontal cortex that is growing and rewiring itself. Damien wasn't special in this regard. It is just that each kid acts it out a bit differently.

The prefrontal cortex, or PFC, is right behind the forehead. It is the CEO of the brain, the part of the brain where we think ahead, consider consequences, and manage emotional impulses and urges. And it's one of the last circuits of the brain to mature. The PFC enters a major developmental period as boys and girls enter adolescence, which doesn't end until the late teens or early twenties.

But with Damien and Brian, as well as other teenagers, the prefrontal cortex is just part of the story. The hormones kicking in at puberty cause all sorts of emotional upheaval at the very time when the emotional-regulation center of the brain is out to lunch. Adolescence is a heck of a time for the impulse control-center to be under construction. Just when adolescents need it most, the PFC's ability to act rationally and think through problems and challenges is offline. Even though the teen PFC is much closer to being mature, it's no match for their roller-coaster emotions.

"Now I know what my brother Joe meant," Tim said. "I've always told him what a great kid Damien is, and Joe would always say, 'Just wait till he's a teenager.'"

"Damien *is* a great kid," I answered. "It's just that his ability to manage his emotions is short-circuiting. It's what's going on in his brain."

It would have been really easy for Tim to chalk Damien's new impulsive behavior up to a bad attitude. That is what we did for years to kids like Damien before we learned more about the teen brain. With this information, you, like Tim, can put your teen's behavior in the correct context. More important, he saw that he needed to stay connected to Damien and not let the challenge of living with a teen brain get in the way of doing what was right for his son.

Helping Teens Put On the Brakes

Clearly, teenagers aren't as ready for all the freedoms of the world as they think they are. Monica and I constantly struggled with Dan over when he should come home at night. When our kids were in high school we enforced a strict curfew. It got later as the kids got older and by senior year it was ten o'clock on school nights and midnight on weekends. Dan thought that he deserved to be free of this childhood restraint so that he could stay out later with his friends. He would present elaborate arguments for why he should be exempt from a curfew, citing how few other parents had such stringent rules and offering examples such as his report cards as evidence that he was responsible. "When are you guys going to stop treating me like a little kid?" he would ask. At the time, all Monica and I could think of in response to his constant "Why do I need a curfew?" was "Because we said so." Knowing the challenges that the teen brain faces, I would answer him differently today, and might sound something like this: "Dan, you may think you're fully mature, but based on the latest brain research, there are still some circuits that have to get wired. Until that's done, you've got a curfew."

When you think about it, a curfew is a surrogate prefrontal cortex. The role of parent, teacher, counselor, and coach is the same: to act as the surrogate brain until the young one is finished being wired. And that's why No is still important for teenagers.

Rachel certainly needed help putting on her brakes. She started getting into minor trouble during her middle school years. Those small scrapes just previewed high school, when she skipped classes, smoked cigarettes in the girls' bathroom, and shouted at her homeroom teacher, who had given her detention for being late. That blowup earned a referral to me, the school counselor.

Rachel quickly called her homeroom teacher unfair. "Can you believe he gave me detention for being thirty seconds late?" she said. I surprised her by saying, "Sure, I can believe it. That's what I did when I had a homeroom. But as I understand it, the real issue is that you ended up telling off Mr. Sazdoff."

Rachel was spunky. "Sure I told him off. You would have too."

"No, I wouldn't have." I told Rachel. "I'm smarter than that. I might have *felt* like telling him off, but I would have realized the satisfaction was not worth bigger trouble. Now, you have to see me."

I taught Rachel some basic brain science and explained that her brain's brakes weren't fully operational, so she had to be careful. "As I see it, Rachel, a lot of your high school problems stem from bad brakes. Your friends suggest skipping class, so you do it. You feel like yelling at a teacher, so you do it." She started to understand, and she talked of times when she had successfully "put on the brakes."

Derek, sixteen, needed more extensive "brake work" than Rachel. Derek's school infractions included truancy, poor grades, and writing graffiti on the school bus. His worried parents, Abby and Rollie, described a near miss: "Two of Derek's friends were arrested for stealing a car. If he hadn't been out of town with his uncle he probably would have been with them."

Abby and Rollie rarely said no to Derek when he was younger. Now, Derek—as well as his parents—was paying the price. Derek, lacking self-discipline, usually gave in to his adolescent impulsiveness. Abby and Rollie learned how important No was and why they needed to say it, but remedial work is tough; they had a lot of behavior to undo. After I told Abby and Rollie that "a sixteen-year-old without a curfew is a recipe for trouble," they started a curfew for school nights and weekends. They asked what they should do if Derek ignored them. "He's really going to be upset," Abby worried.

"Of course he will be," I agreed. "He's done pretty much what he wants. That's okay. Both you and he can deal with upset. You need to decide what the consequence will be if he doesn't obey your curfew."

Because No was new to them, they had trouble thinking of a consequence at first. "One thing I found effective," I suggested, "was to subtract however late the kids were from the next night's curfew. For example, if my son Dan came home an hour late, then the next night's curfew would be an hour earlier." They liked that idea, but I could see that they were nervous. "What are you most worried about?" I asked them.

"I'm afraid he'll just have a tantrum and start yelling," Abby said.

"That's a legitimate worry, Abby," I responded. "That's why it's important not to get into a shouting match with him. The teenage brain is built for power struggles, so it's best to avoid one with your son. But you can't cave in, either. Many parents of teens fall into the either/or trap," I explained. "They either escalate into a power struggle with their teen or they cave in and let the kid do whatever he wants. Neither of those options is good for kids."

I shared this plan with Derek's parents to help him put on the brakes:

1. "Lay out your expectations for Derek's behavior as clearly as possible."
2. "Stay calm even if he starts to get angry. If he starts to yell or use abusive language, don't try to outshout him. Say, 'We can't have this discussion if you are going to yell. We'll talk when you're ready to discuss this respectfully. You can't go out, however, until we have the discussion.'"
3. "Be clear about the consequences for noncompliance. Ask Derek to tell you his understanding of the rule and the consequence. Saying it out loud or writing it down clears up any confusion."
4. "Follow through on the consequence. This is new for all of you, so you can expect Derek to test your resolve."
5. "If this doesn't work—in other words, if Derek completely defies your authority—we'll need to put together a team of reinforcements. The team might include relatives, the school social worker, the school police liaison officer, maybe even juvenile-court personnel. That team's purpose is to reinforce your role as parents." This step is not usually necessary, but I wanted them to know that there were backup plans.

"This won't go smoothly at first," I warned them. "The goal is progress, not perfection."

Rollie and Abby did make progress. As they feared, Derek did fight them. He stomped, stormed, and threatened to do whatever he wanted. However, they learned to say no and stick with it, and Derek began to build a set of brakes.

Windows of Opportunity

The adolescent brain is shaped by experience. The experiences we have during the growth spurts in our brains have a greater impact than those at any other time in our lives. Because the adolescent brain is going through such important growth spurts, everything teens do and see has the potential to affect the adult brains they will have.

Scientists already generally understood the importance of experience in early childhood development, but they only recently realized its similar role in adolescence. As we saw in chapter 5, children who have good attachment relationships during their first year of life end up with a greater sense of happiness, trust, and security, have better self-discipline, and can delay gratification and perform better in school. What happens at one stage of development lays the foundation for later stages.

You may recall the phrase *the neurons that fire together wire together.* In other words, when adolescents engage in any activity, certain neurons in the brain receive electrical impulses. The more often those neurons are activated, the more likely they will fuse together to form an established neural pathway, and therefore the more likely the brain will remember how to engage in that activity. When a high school student is trying to memorize French vocabulary for a quiz, she would be well advised to repeat the words, write them down, and say them out loud. Eventually she won't have to think twice to remember the words because the repetition helps wire the French terms into her brain. This phenomenon is true for matters far more complex than memorizing new vocabulary. Learning to set personal limits, think long term, and appreciate delayed gratification during adolescence will set the precedent for adult patterns and abilities.

Although it's easier to learn No as a child, Rollie and Abby did Derek a tremendous favor by teaching him No as a teen. Derek's high school career was rocky, but he graduated and attended the local community college. As he matured, he incorporated the discipline he'd learned into his adult lifestyle. He eventually transferred to a four-year public university, got a degree in journalism, and became a reporter for a suburban weekly newspaper.

Derek's two car-stealing friends, however, never learned to harness their urges. Their parents never taught them No. As their out-of-control behavior continued, their crimes became more serious, and neither finished high school. Fortunately for Derek, he drifted away from them after they dropped out of school and were bouncing from job to job, drinking and using drugs.

Adolescence is an important window of opportunity for teens to learn to manage their new set of intense impulses and urges. The growth spurt in the prefrontal cortex leaves their brains very sensitive to their experiences. While this can be terrifying to parents, given what we know about the role of the PFC in decision making, long-term planning, and impulse control, this window provides an opportunity to help our children hardwire these management skills so that they can use them for the rest of their lives. Learning to deal with anger, manage sexual urges appropriately, and communicate effectively during the teen years enable the brain to wire the appropriate circuits. Not learning to be accountable and responsible as a teen will have a greater negative impact on their lives as adults. The same window, open for opportunities to wire the brain for good habits, is open for whatever happens, good or bad.

The take-home lesson of the new revelations in brain science is not to sit around and "wait it out" until adolescence is over. This issue came up directly in a counseling session I had with an angry, defiant teenage girl, Nakesha, and her parents. Among other troubling behaviors, Nakesha yelled, screamed, and swore whenever she didn't get her way. When I gave Nakesha and her parents a minilesson in teen brain development, she looked absolutely thrilled to hear that her brain was under construction. "See, Mom," she said. "It's not my fault. It's my brain. You guys have to cut me some slack."

"Nice try, Nakesha," I responded. Despite her initial hope that science might give her a bulletproof excuse for her lousy behavior, I made sure that her parents didn't fall for that one. "Since emotional outbursts and impulsiveness come with the adolescent territory," I told her parents, "saying no, setting limits and consequences, gives

Nakesha the brakes she needs until her brain installs its own set."

Then I spoke directly to Nakesha. "Even though it is not your fault that your brain isn't fully under your control, it is your responsibility to learn to *get* it under control. And it's your parents' responsibility to assist you."

I helped Nakesha and her parents put together a plan, using the balanced style described in chapter 5. I asked her parents, Alice and Roger, to tell Nakesha how they expected her to act when she was angry with them. Alice spoke first. "I want her to be respectful."

"Okay, Alice," I said, "but Nakesha needs to know what respectful looks like. Describe the behaviors that you want to see."

Alice thought for a couple of seconds. "It's easier for me to tell her what I don't want to see."

"Okay," I said. "Let's go with that. What behaviors do you want Nakesha to stop?"

"No screaming, swearing, or name-calling," was Alice's list.

"Excellent list, Alice," I replied. "I'm sure Nakesha knows what behaviors you're talking about, right, Nakesha?" I asked as I looked at her.

"So am I supposed to act like some little goody two-shoes all the time?" Nakesha asked. "I'm never allowed to get angry when they're being unreasonable?"

"I didn't say, 'Never get angry.' Anger is not the problem. How you're expressing it is what has to change. There's nothing wrong with your feelings. Your parents are just insisting that you express them without swearing, screaming, and name-calling. Do you think that's unreasonable of their part?"

Nakesha was not going to give in without more of a fight. "But their rules are so stupid."

I didn't let Nakesha off the hook. "Why did you change the topic? What do 'stupid rules' have to do with my question?"

Nakesha looked puzzled. "What do you mean 'your question'?"

"I asked you if you thought it was reasonable that your parents won't allow you to scream, swear, and call them names when you get angry. Instead of answering, you changed the topic to complain about their rules."

Roger broke in. "This is amazing. I just realized that this happens every time we try to have a conversation. We get all confused and never get anywhere."

"Okay, then lesson number one: Stick to one topic at a time," I said.

I turned back to Nakesha. "So, now, will you please answer my question? Are your parents justified in not wanting you to swear, scream, or name-call?"

Nakesha couldn't find a way out. "I guess so."

I pressed further. "By the way, Nakesha, do you scream and swear at your teachers?"

"Of course not," she responded.

"Why not?" I asked.

"I'd get suspended or expelled."

"So it's clear that you can manage your anger when you know there will be consequences, right?" I concluded.

"I guess so," she mumbled.

We finished up the session when Nakesha agreed to work on her outbursts. I reminded all three not to expect perfection. They all agreed that progress would be the goal. I looked at Nakesha and smiled. "Okay?"

"Okay," was her barely audible reply.

Nakesha didn't reform overnight. A big test came quickly. The next Saturday evening Nakesha's friends were waiting in a car when she ran down the stairs and started putting on her coat. "Can I stay out till one o'clock tonight?" she asked as she headed for the door. "There's going to be a fun party, and it's at the O'Briens' so you know there won't be any problems." The two parents exchanged glances before Roger spoke. "I don't think so. Midnight is late enough." He held his breath. Sure enough, Nakesha exploded. She screamed, swore, and called them both unprintable names. Somehow, Roger and Alice were able to stay calm and tell Nakesha that she needed to take off her coat and calm down because she wasn't going anywhere.

"What do you mean? My friends are waiting for me. Don't be so stupid," she screamed. To make a long story short, Nakesha did not go out that night. She was furious and she stormed around her room for a long time. She wouldn't talk to her parents all evening and well into the next day. But that night was the beginning of the turnaround.

There were more episodes but, little by little, things improved. Nakesha gradually realized that her parents were going to enforce the consequences. Once Nakesha started to get her angry outbursts under control, she and her parents were able to start working on some other issues. To Nakesha's pleasant surprise, once she started to behave better, she found that her parents were a bit more flexible when she tried to negotiate with them.

Chelsea, a petite, single parent, had an even bigger challenge than Nakesha's mother and father. Her defiant fifteen-year-old son, Dylan, was much bigger and stronger than she was. He had pushed her aside on two occasions when she told him he couldn't go out with his friends. After the second episode he had apologized the next day and promised not to do it again. Within a month, however, he shoved and hit her when she confronted him on stealing money from her purse. That's when I met her.

"Dr. Walsh," she said as she choked back tears, "I'm afraid of my own son. He's gotten away with pushing and shoving me three times now. I don't know what's going to happen next."

I told Chelsea that I could understand her fear. "This is a serious situation," I told her. "Parenting a teenager can be very challenging, but when he starts to make physical threats or actually starts to push and shove like Dylan has, that's a whole different story. Does he have a good relationship with any male relatives?" I asked her.

"He's always gotten along well with my brother," she answered.

"Suppose you and your brother talk with Dylan together?" I asked.

"My brother doesn't know anything about this. No one does. I've been so embarrassed that I don't want anyone to know that Dylan hit me," Chelsea said.

I interrupted her. "I thought you said Dylan pushed you. I didn't know he hit you."

"Pushed, shoved, what's the difference?" Chelsea answered.

"Chelsea, did Dylan hit you?" I asked as gently as I could.

She hesitated, then said in a barely audible voice, "Yes, he slapped me when we argued about the money."

"There's a reason I'm pressing you," I explained. "It's important to get Dylan to understand how serious this is. If you protect him, downplay what he did, and keep it hidden from people who could help, that makes it hard."

"I'm so embarrassed," Chelsea whispered.

"I know you are, but you need to get by that so we can get some other people to help you." I waited for a few seconds before continuing. "I'd like to suggest that you have a long talk with your brother, tell him what's going on, and ask for his help. Ask him to join you; make it clear to Dylan that he is never to push, shove, or hurt you physically again. Let him know that if he does, you will go to the police."

"Would they help?" she asked.

"Yes, they will. I have worked with some families who needed to involve the police and in every instance the police were very helpful." I told Chelsea about a single mom like her who called the police because her daughter physically attacked her. The police officers sat in the living room with the mother and daughter and had a very serious and frank conversation. It was the last time the girl assaulted her mother. I reassured Chelsea that resorting to the police was unlikely. "If you and Dylan's uncle let him know how serious you are and that you are willing to call the police if necessary, that will likely be enough."

That's exactly what happened. Chelsea's brother was happy to get involved and offered to be "on call" if necessary. They met with Dylan and told him that they would not tolerate any pushing, shoving, or hitting. They also told him that they would involve the police if it happened again. They never had to make that call.

It Takes a Village to Say *No*

Teenagers love to remind us that they are no longer children and don't want to be treated as if they are. They are a big step away from adulthood, even though most of them sometimes feel that they are already there. Two common reactions to this change are withdrawal from parents and emphasis on the importance of peers. My son Dan used to ask me to walk about ten feet behind him when he was with his friends shopping in the mall so that "nobody knows you're my dad." This didn't feel particularly good, knowing that he thought just being associated with a dork like me could crumble his solid reputation as a cool guy, but knowing teenagers, I gave them their space. All three of my kids tried some version of this disassociation and every time it stung a little but I tried to keep in mind what was going on for them as teenagers.

When kids are little, parents decide most things for them. Most kids don't decide where to live, what school to go to, or what to eat for dinner every night. It makes sense, then, that as kids turn into teens, they need to put some distance between themselves and their parents. In fact, it is healthy for teenagers to strike out on their own and make some of their own decisions. Pulling away from parents— —and pushing against limits—is the way they begin to exercise their own judgment. As this happens, peers become more important. What friends think about clothing, hair, activities, and behavior becomes central to teenagers' decisions. There is something ironic about teenagers' simultaneous call for independence and their obsession with fitting in with their peer group. The push and pull to be independent and different from parents while fitting in well with peers is a powerful force in the lives of most adolescents.

Peer pressure can create some real dilemmas for parents, too, especially parents who are trying to say no. I have had countless conversations with parents about why they buy violent video games for their kids.

"Do you like the games?" I asked Marsha after a seminar for parents.

"No, the ones that I have seen are horrible. Some of them are so violent it's hard to watch," she replied.

"But you buy them for your kids?" I prodded.

"Well, all of the kids play them. If they don't play them at our house they will just go to friends' houses. It's what kids do now. If we don't let them play they'll be totally left out."

"Most kids drink before they finish high school, too. Should they have the okay on that, so they're not left out?" I asked.

"That's not fair," protested Marsha.

"Maybe not, but there is a difference between knowing our kids will do something and saying it's okay. You can't monitor every video game a teenager plays, but that doesn't mean you just throw up your hands and say that he can play any game he wants. Teenagers are going to push against the limits because that's their job. It's our job to set them."

"So what would you do?" Marsha asked.

"I'd say: 'I don't want you playing games that glorify violence or degrade women. There are lots of decent games that you and your friends can play. So, M-rated games—adult games—are not allowed.'" I added that I would also share my views with my son's friends' parents. "I don't know any parents who think that ultraviolent and antisocial games are good for teenagers. We just need to start to talk to each other and get on the same page."

"Do you really think that will work?" Marsha wondered.

"It depends on what you mean by *work*," I responded. "If the goal is to be absolutely certain that my teenage kids never play an adult-rated video game, then no, it won't work. But my goal is to let them know I don't approve. They absorb more of our values than we think they do."

There seems to be a feeling of helplessness among parents fighting against a swelling tide of "but Marsha's parents let us do it" or "everyone else's parents are saying yes." Peer pressure can be just as difficult for parents to navigate as it can be for kids. There is no question that it is difficult to feel like a lone voice in the wilderness when it comes to asserting rules and limits. In addition, teens are persuasive and good at exerting pressure when they know it works. Yet, you the parent can't cave in to this pressure. You have to act in the best interest of your kids.

Last year I got a frantic call from my friend Maria, whose sixteen-year-old daughter had been invited to a post-prom party at a friend's house. Apparently, the friend's dad had a reputation for being more lenient with his kids than Maria was. The year before, his son had given a party at which the dad was okay with the kids' drinking as long as he was there to supervise and could take all the car keys away. My friend's daughter, Shana, was exerting tremendous pressure on her to go to the party. She promised she wouldn't drink and kept reminding her mom that "everyone else's parents are letting them go. I can't believe that you don't trust me!"

Right there, I could feel Maria's pain. The T word. Every parent wants to trust her child and being questioned on this cuts right to the heart of who we want to be as parents. To make it harder, setting limits with teenagers almost *always* triggers a question like Shana's "Don't you trust me?" Kids often speak as if trust should be universally applied to every situation and scenario. Trust is just not that simple in parenting. I trust my kids in many ways, but I don't necessarily trust their ability to withstand overwhelming pressure. Temptation is difficult to resist when you are equipped with a developing prefrontal cortex. Temptation occurs when the pressure to do something strains the psychological resources to resist. Since impulse resistance is a function of the reasoning PFC, adolescents are often unable to resist impulses in situations where they are overwhelmed.

I asked Maria if she felt comfortable with letting Shana go to the party. "Absolutely not" was her immediate reply. "I do trust her . . . but this party sounds like a recipe for disaster. I am just about at the end of my rope. I have never seen Shana so set on something, or so mad at me for getting in her way."

My friend was clearly feeling isolated from other parents and was worried that her relationship with Shana wouldn't recover from this fight. In addition, Shana had succeeded in convincing her that *every* other parent in the universe was cooler than she was. I had a hunch that Shana's depiction of other parents' positions was not accurate. "Here's a suggestion: Call some of the other parents. I can almost guarantee you that they are not as comfortable with this as Shana says they are. See if you can get some other parents to hold the line with you. Then tell Shana right away that you have made a final decision, and stick to it. She might be mad at first but will get over it quickly if her friends aren't going either."

Later that night I got a call from Maria, who sounded like she had just won the lottery. "It turns out that a couple of other parents are feeling the same way that I am. We agreed to talk to our kids and are going to help them figure out something else to do."

I was glad that the other parents were so quick to agree with my friend. The conversation with Shana still wasn't going to be a walk in the park, but at least Maria felt supported by other parents. Although you can't always find a team of parents to back up your every decision, it is helpful to remember that more often than not at least one other parent feels exactly the same way you do.

The part of this story that troubled me the most was the idea of a parent hosting a post-prom party that involved open drinking. No doubt this plan was devised under the rationale that "if they are going to drink, it might as well be in a supervised location." Because teenagers have more freedom and a reputation for trying new things, some parents sense that holding a hard line is a lost cause. This philosophy is a shaky foundation on which to make important decisions about how to talk to your teens about drugs, alcohol, sex, or tobacco. As sure as teenagers can sound sometimes, many have not made up their minds yet about sex and drugs. But to assume that adolescents will always make poor decisions sends a confusing message. As the teen brain grows, it absorbs the messages teenagers hear and the examples they see. You can set a responsible tone for them, to which they can refer as they make decisions.

Teen brains are more sensitive to the effects of chemical substances. Damage to a developing brain can be permanent. All the more reason to be clear with your teen about your expectations about drinking and smoking and to set and enforce consequences when those expectations aren't met. With a prefrontal cortex that is under construction, teenagers aren't *always* going to make rational, well-thought-out decisions. However, they are never going to learn the skills to do so if we don't help them by saying no.

Connection and Guidance

The research is clear that teens need consistent, clear limits, and consequences. Yet, while setting and enforcing limits, you also need to listen and be open to some negotiating over certain activities like curfew extensions for special occasions, being excused from some family events, or the use of the computer or family car. If you take the time to listen without judging or offering advice at every exchange, you may be able to hold a real conversation when it comes time to talk. When parents and teens can really talk and listen to one another, everything gets easier.

No parent can keep track of a teen 24/7. Driver's licenses, independent activities, and their desire for privacy make this impossible. Often, the harder parents try, the farther away our teenagers feel. Giving them a little space to breathe and make their own decisions is important if we want our kids to trust us enough to let us into their lives when they really need it. Loosening the reins but not letting go is more of an art than a science. Every child is different, every family is different, and every situation is different. Staying connected to your teen while maintaining the authority to guide her to responsible, healthy choices is a daily task that can feel like juggling eight balls at once. Staying connected means staying open to different possibilities. A good rule of thumb is to spend twice as much time, and half as much money as you can afford, with your teens. Saying no doesn't have to shut down the conversation or make things taboo for teens to talk about. Ongoing conversations about the tough topics, like tobacco, alcohol, drugs, and sex, are essential to helping them make the right choices.

Parents often ask how to talk to their teens about sex. Here are some tips:

1. Start early. A history of talking about sex makes it a more comfortable topic when they're adolescents. When you are teaching toddlers the names of body parts, include the names of sexual organs. When it comes up naturally during childhood, discuss what sex is. For instance: "The rea-

son Tyler's mom is getting bigger is that she's going to have a baby. She is carrying the baby in a special part of her body where it is growing. When the baby is ready to be born it will come out through her vagina." If your child asks how the baby got there, explain it clearly. "When girls get older their bodies make a tiny egg every month. When boys get older their bodies produce sperm. The daddy puts sperm in the mommy's body through her vagina. If a sperm meets an egg then the 'fertilized egg' (that's what it's called) begins to grow into a baby."

2. Bring up the topic yourself if your child has not asked any questions. For instance, you might say to your eight-year-old daughter, "Did you notice how your sister Carol is changing? She's getting taller, her breasts are getting bigger, and there are other changes in her body, too. You will go through those changes yourself in a couple of years. We'll talk about them so you'll know what to expect." You could say to your preteenager, "Did you ever notice that they never mention the risk of unwanted pregnancies in that TV show where the girl hooked up with the guy she liked? Do you think they were taking a big chance?" Or, you can begin a conversation with your teenager like this: "I heard on the news that a lot of kids your age are having oral sex. Are many kids in your school having oral sex at parties?"

3. Do some homework so that you feel confident. Books like Patty Stark's *Sex Is More Than a Plumbing Lesson* (Preston Hollow, 1990) will give you solid information, as well as tips for talking with kids of all ages.

4. Share your discomfort with your kids. For example, say, "This is uncomfortable for me because my parents never talked to me about sex. But it's such an important topic that I want to talk about it."

5. Be ready to listen. Let your kids know. Say, "Please come to me if you have any questions or concerns."

6. Don't overdo scare tactics, but let your teens know about the risks of pregnancy and sexually transmitted diseases.

7. Don't just talk about the facts. Discuss sex within the context of relationships, values, caring, commitment, and responsibility.

8. Be clear about your values. Your children need values as they figure out how to manage their sexuality, which is an important part of who they are.

Research shows that kids whose parents talk about substance use are less likely to take big risks. Here are some suggestions:

1. Start early. Research shows that kids will often experiment with alcohol or drugs earlier than parents think. Kids who try alcohol start at age eleven, on average; for marijuana, it's twelve.

2. Take advantage of news reports and other incidents to initiate conversations. Ask, for example, "What do the kids in your school think about drinking and drugs?" Listen carefully to understand their attitudes and the pressures they might be under.

3. Be clear about your expectations and family rules. For instance, you might say, "I don't want you drinking any alcohol or taking any drugs. They're way too dangerous for kids." Let them know what the consequences will be. For example: "If you drink, you will not be allowed to use the car for a month."

4. Let them know you welcome their questions and concerns. In addition, make it clear that you will be there to help them. For example, tell them, "If you're ever in a dangerous or uncomfortable situation, just call me, and I'll pick you up. If you ever make the mistake of drinking or taking drugs, make sure that you never drive or get in the car with someone else who's been using."

Guidance comes in many shapes and sizes. Talking with our kids about values and attitudes like respect, cooperation, honesty, service, and compassion can be as important as clear-cut rules. Even more important is that you model the behaviors that reflect those values. Adolescents hate sermons, so conversations about values should be dialogues. Although they may not always be excited to participate, consistently opening up conversations with teenagers reminds them that you value their opinions and care what they think.

As your adolescents get older, you have fewer ways to enforce consequences. Use of the car is a big one. Think long and hard before you let your teen have his own car. Even though it can be a major pain to share the family car with three or more drivers, it is a powerful privilege to use as a bargaining chip. At the same time, it is exhausting if everything becomes part of a negotiation game. It is more effective to pick and choose your battles and to use your bargaining chips carefully. Your teenagers will grapple with a lot of important decisions and issues during adolescence, and you will need to have the energy and emotional stamina to deal with the issues most important to you. How many arguments can you have about what you think are messy clothes or baggy pants? Instead of arguing about loud music, negotiate a volume compromise that you can both live with. Invest your attention and energy in the areas that really matter to you. Guidance does not mean control. It means connection. Setting clear expectations about behaviors and consequences that are important to you can avoid difficult power struggles later.

An Investment in *No*

All three of my kids tried to divorce Monica and me many times during their teenage years. I could have counted on one hand the times my son Brian seemed to appreciate our efforts to connect with him. A few times he even checked rental rates on small apartments at the university near our house. The family rituals around Christmas were particularly challenging for Brian, who was convinced that he was too grown up for old family traditions. Every year of adolescence he resisted decorating the tree with all his might, asked to play his own music instead of our classic Christmas records, and generally tried as hard as he could to make the activities as disagreeable for the rest of us as they felt to him. Monica and I agreed that we couldn't force Brian to help us decorate the Christmas tree but we did want him to be part of the family tradition. We let him know that although he didn't have to participate actively, he needed to be in the room with us instead of upstairs behind the shut door of his room, where he preferred to be. Brian would stew silently on the couch most of the evening but always ended up hanging a few of his favorite ornaments on the tree.

This past Christmas, Monica and I were blessed to have all three of our children home to celebrate. The night that Erin arrived in town from her home in California, we all gathered together to put our favorite ornaments on the tree. Brian immediately went to the stereo, queued up our Christmas family favorites, and began to uncover the ornaments. Later, in front of the fully decorated tree, Erin and Brian began sharing memories of Christmases past. During a quiet moment, Brian mentioned how lucky he felt that he didn't have any negative Christmas memories and that he always felt so close to our family during that time. Monica and I quietly exchanged glances, sharing a quick mental repertoire of Christmas conflicts and fights, astonished that Brian's memory of those same events included warm, positive feelings he had carried with him into adulthood. Erin and Brian continued telling family Christmas stories for the rest of the evening, clearly enjoying every one of them. Although Monica and I would never have been able to know it at the time, our commitment to maintaining family rituals and connections despite resistance clearly paid off.

With a long history of family vacations, our friends saved up for a spectacular trip. They expected their teenage daughters to be excited about a five-day rafting trip down the Colorado River in the Grand Canyon. The girls' response, however, was, "Do we have to go? Why don't the two of you go and let us stay home? That way we'll all be happy." Our friends remembered how uninterested their teens tried to be as they floated through one of the wonders of the world. One of the girls kept referring to the Grand Canyon as nothing but a "big ditch." The sheer adventure of the trip eventually overcame the girls' teenage "allergic reaction" and today is a treasured family memory.

No matter what teenagers tell us, they still need our guidance, connection, and love. We parents, coaches, counselors, and teachers need to serve as surrogate prefrontal cortexes. The real test of this is to continue to try to connect with our teenagers without expecting much in return. We need to be willing not only to hang in with our kids but also to help guide them through one disorienting transition to the next. Any parent of teenagers knows that this effort does not yield instant gratification. Monica and I knew that Brian would not thank us for setting limits and enforcing consequences at the time. In fact, he, like most teens, voiced his dissent every step of the way. Yet, we used our adult prefrontal cortexes to plan and manage the rules and to trust in the long-term payoff for our parenting.

The time and energy we put into connecting with our teens, listening to them, encouraging them, setting and enforcing limits for them, talking to them about tough topics, and telling them that we love them continue to yield benefits. And the value of that investment increases over time. Eventually, your parenting investment pays off when they become the adults you hoped they would be.

No matter what you do, your kids will make mistakes during adolescence. The goal of parenting is not to help them avoid all mistakes. You need to help them work through disappointment, reflect on bad decisions, and know how it feels to make a wrong choice—all important parts of growing up, even if they're not easy. Don't try to keep your kids from these real-life experiences: you can't.

DO

- Know what is normal adolescent behavior, so you know what to expect and what is not normal, so you know what to look out for.

- Set clear rules and expectations for behavior. For example, instead of saying, "I want you to help out around the house," say "I want you to have the lawn mowed by Saturday evening."
- Spell out consequences for noncompliance. Consequences for teenagers usually involve the loss of privileges. "If you cannot limit your instant messaging to one hour a night, you will not be allowed to use the computer for one week."
- Loosen but don't let go. For example, even though you can make the curfews later as teens grow older, you still need to enforce them.
- Have a zero-tolerance policy for tobacco, alcohol, and drugs.
- Make sure that teenagers have household chores so that they don't become rent-free boarders.
- Have the courage to communicate with your teens about the tough topics: sex, alcohol, and drugs. Communication does not mean lecturing. It means listening and expressing your values clearly.
- Maintain a sense of humor and go out of your way to let your teen know that you love her *and* like her.

DON'T

- Patience is essential, but don't become a doormat for disrespectful behavior.
- Don't get dragged into power struggles. Calmly state your expectations and consequences. Let your teen know that you expect him to comply, but that if he chooses not to, he will have to accept the consequences.
- Don't ever attempt to outshout your teen. Say, "We don't seem able to discuss this right now. When you're ready to talk about this without yelling, let me know. We need to talk before you go out." Then make sure to come back and finish the talk. Teens should not be allowed to go on to the next activity until the discussion has been completed.

- Don't ever put your teenager down or call her names, which damages the parent-teen connection, the lifeline through these years.

What do I want to continue?

_____

_____

_____

What do I want to change?

_____

_____

_____

TEN

Wired Differently
Special-Needs Children and *No*

Jason was a handful even before he was born. His mother, Sandy, told me that her only child had started kicking in her uterus early, hard, and often. Even in the hospital nursery Jason cried and fussed louder and longer than the other infants. "I remember standing at the nursery window listening to visitors talk about how beet red Jason was as he cried," Sandy recalled. Before Jason arrived, Sandy and her husband, Eric, had fantasized about the happy, peaceful days ahead, taking walks in the cool autumn air with their new baby in the Snugli front carrier they had received at their baby shower. But the early months at home were anything but peaceful. Jason's long spells of crying and fussing left his parents sleep deprived, exhausted, and drained. "Nothing worked," remembered Sandy. "We'd hold him, rock him, and take him for car rides. We tried every bit of advice we received from our family and friends. Our pediatrician told us that Jason was 'colicky' and not to worry because he would eventually settle down."

"Did he?" I asked.

"Never," Eric said. "As the months went by we began to worry that Jason's irritability was our fault. 'You're holding him too much,' my mother told me. So we tried letting him cry himself to sleep until that seemed to make things even worse. The only real help came from our best friends, Sue and Myles. They were great. Sue kept telling us that some babies are just fussy and that she and Myles were more worried about us than they were about Jason.

"They never tried to give us advice," added Sandy. "They just tried to encourage and support us. They would take Jason for hours at a time just so we could get a break." Sandy recalled that when Jason was about six months old, their friends surprised them with a gift certificate for a weekend at a beautiful bed-and-breakfast. "When we protested, they got really mad and ordered us to go," Sandy told me. "'We're taking Jason for the weekend,' Sue said firmly. 'No ifs, ands, or buts. You guys are exhausted. You *have to* rest and relax.'"

"I started to cry when she said that," Sandy told me. "It was like a dam bursting. I don't know how long I sobbed in Sue's arms that afternoon. I don't know how she and Myles knew that we were at a breaking point after months of being overtired and emotionally exhausted."

"You were so lucky to have such good friends," I said.

Eric continued. "It got even worse when Jason started walking. He never stopped moving. He was a one-boy wrecking crew. He broke things, threw things, and screamed whenever we tried to rein him in. Everything was a battle from morning till night—getting dressed, eating, getting into the car seat, brushing his teeth, and going to bed."

"I must have said no a thousand times a day," recalled Sandy. "I gave him consequences, I punished him, and I even spanked him. We enrolled him in a preschool program, which turned out to be a disaster. While the other kids could sit in a circle, share, and get along, Jason pushed, hit, shoved, and wreaked havoc. The director of the preschool asked us to come in for a parent conference within the first month."

"Did they give you any helpful suggestions?" I asked.

"Are you kidding?" Eric responded. "Sandy and I came away more convinced than ever that we were bad parents. The director suggested that we take some parenting classes, and she recommended a book on 'spirited children.' We tried everything the experts recommended. At the end of the school year we learned that Jason was not 'invited' back for the following year. The report we received from the preschool described Jason as 'immature, aggressive, inattentive, and disruptive.'"

"It broke my heart to see how miserable Jason was," Sandy added. "I stayed at home with him the next year. One day after a particularly rough battle, Jason cried and told me that he was sorry for being such a 'bad boy.' I realized that he had probably heard those words from me.

"He wanted to play with neighbor kids, but after a while the parents usually had excuses," Sandy continued. "I was dreading kindergarten. Late at night Eric and I wondered out loud how Jason was ever going to survive school. I cried myself to sleep a lot of nights wondering what was going to happen. I could have smacked my know-it-all brother at a family birthday party when he joked, 'Wait till he's a teenager.'"

"So what happened in kindergarten?" I asked.

"We met Mrs. Parker," said Eric.

"God bless Mrs. Parker," Sandy chimed in.

Eric explained. "Within three weeks, Mrs. Parker phoned and asked for a parent meeting. We didn't sleep the entire night before the conference. Sandy was convinced that Jason was being expelled. Anyway, the next day we walked into Mrs. Parker's classroom filled with trepidation." Eric chuckled. "I half expected the police to be there."

Sandy took over the story. "Mrs. Parker walked over, shook our hands, and gave us a big smile. 'Please come in and sit down,' she said warmly. The next thing she said was, 'I really like Jason.' I'm sure she saw the tears of relief well up in my eyes," recalled Sandy.

As Sandy and Eric told me the rest of their story I learned that Mrs. Parker had quickly figured Jason out. She knew what a challenge he was and she also understood the frustration and worry that Sandy and Eric carried around every day. She told them that she suspected that Jason had a "different brain." "Not a bad brain," she had reassured them, "just a different brain." She shared with them that her oldest son had attention deficit disorder (ADD) and that he and Jason were a lot alike. She recommended that they take Jason to a child psychology clinic that specialized in assessing "special needs" children.

A few weeks later the team of psychologists diagnosed Jason with attention deficit hyperactivity disorder (ADHD). Jason had a different brain.

Different Brains

By now you have an idea of how amazingly complex the human brain is. Every brain is unique, even more so than our fingerprints. Every child, therefore, comes into the world with a unique brain. Each has his own genetic heritage, his own temperament, and his own unique mix of the jillions of interconnecting, intercommunicating cells.

All brains share great commonalities and function in similar ways even though each has its individual traits. However, some children, like Jason and others you will meet in this chapter, are born with brains that are wired differently from those of most other children. Their brains make dealing with No very difficult, which makes their parents' job of saying no very difficult as well.

Everything in this book so far has described how most kids will react to No. Some different-brain children have problems with what professionals call "self-regulation." In other words, they *cannot* respond to No the way other kids do. Teaching them limits and how to manage their emotions, drives, and behaviors poses some special challenges and requires some special techniques. I'll explore the different brains, describe typical behaviors, and then provide specific strategies to help kids with self-regulation problems.

As Mrs. Parker told Sandy and Eric, it is important to describe these kids' brains as different and requiring special handling. They're not *bad* brains. They're *different* brains. Children with these different brains often have problems in normal settings. They have so much trouble getting along with other people that they often start to think that they are bad kids. Parents need to help these children realize that they have different brains that have some special gifts. I like to remind kids with ADHD brains, for example, that they are in pretty good company: Albert Einstein, Thomas Edison, Winston Churchill, John F. Kennedy, and Robin Williams, to name a few. The challenge that they and their parents have is to learn how to manage their different brains. They have to learn No, too.

Parent Tool Kit: Special-Needs Children and *No*

If your child has a special brain, you will need to learn and practice some different strategies to help her learn No. This kit can help you assess your attitudes about kids who are "wired differently."

PARENT TOOL KIT
Wired Differently: Special-Needs Children and *No*

Yes	No		
☐	☐	1.	Different brains are often inherited. There are problems with self-regulation in kids in my or my partner's extended family.
☐	☐	2.	I know the signs (found throughout this chapter) that mean my child may be "wired differently."
☐	☐	3.	Some children cannot learn No without special help.
☐	☐	4.	Having a different brain is not my or my child's fault.
☐	☐	5.	Many children with different brains have special gifts.
☐	☐	6.	My community has resources for assessing and helping children with self-regulation problems and I know how to find them.
☐	☐	7.	It is important to intervene early for a child who is wired differently.

If you think that your child may have a different brain, it is important to get help as soon as possible. Even if you don't have such a child, the information in the rest of this chapter will help you understand the challenges that parents and children have if their brains are different.

Challenge Number One: Understanding Your Child

When parents realize that their child may have a different brain from most other kids, the first question they have is, "Well, what kind of brain does my child have?" Answering that question is not as easy as you might think. Professionals have a handful of categories or diagnoses for different brains, as if those categories cover all the possibilities. They don't. Trying to get a fix on what's going on can be exasperating. That's what happened to Pam and Troy as they tried to get help for their six-year-old son, Tyler.

Tyler had always been a "high-maintenance" child, to use Pam's words. He had enough energy for three little boys, was very "touchy," easily frustrated, and had trouble getting along with other children because of his "volcanic temper." He was also very bright. He knew more about dinosaurs than did the curators at the science museum and could talk a blue streak from the time he was two with a vocabulary that startled adults. Troy described him as quite a "character," and he was certain that Tyler was going to become a renowned lawyer. "He could argue circles around most adults by the time he was five," Troy confided to me with a hint of pride.

Serious trouble started when Tyler entered first grade. Pam home-schooled him for kindergarten, but she and Troy decided to enroll him in the local public school the next year because they were concerned about his poor social skills. It took Tyler exactly two hours to get into an argument with his teacher when she told him he had to wait for his turn at the water fountain. She had no idea how to respond when Tyler launched into a diatribe about his rights as a U.S. citizen.

Pam's heart sank when Tyler announced at the dinner table that night that his teacher was stupid and he wasn't going back to school. Before September ended there were notes and phone calls from school about how stubborn and argumentative Tyler was and how "his behavior would have to change." The principal called in a school psychologist from the district office to observe Tyler in class. Several days later Pam and Troy were in a meeting with Tyler's teacher, the psychologist, and the principal. The psychologist reported that their son's classroom behavior clearly fit the pattern of attention deficit/hyperactivity disorder. They received a referral to a pediatrician who was an ADHD specialist. Two weeks and several appointments later the doctor diagnosed Tyler with ADHD and recommended that he begin taking the medication Ritalin.

Troy was adamantly against putting Tyler on Ritalin. "There's no way I want my six-year-old son on drugs," Troy told Pam later that evening. They decided to seek a second opinion. Pam's sister, a nurse, told her about a well-known child psychologist in town. Several weeks later they were in her office getting the news that Tyler was not ADHD but rather had Asperger syndrome. Their confusion got worse when, before Thanksgiving, a child psychiatrist, recommended by their health plan, told them that he thought their son was suffering from bipolar disorder.

Pam and Troy's experience is not as unusual as you might think. One of the most controversial, confusing areas of child psychology is trying to sort out what is going on with children whose behavior is out of control—kids who are easily frustrated, argumentative, and inflexible; have raging temper tantrums; can't pay attention; have poor social skills, communication problems, and enough energy for a small army. The diagnosis is often determined by the specialty of the professional whose door you walk through. Kids diagnosed by ADHD experts tend to be diagnosed ADHD, while others with similar symptoms might be diagnosed with sensory processing disorder, pervasive developmental disorder, or Asperger syndrome. Can you imagine the parent who learns that her son (it's usually a boy) has all of the above? I've talked to many parents whose kids have a long list of labels. To make things even harder, if these kids haven't gotten help by the time they become teenagers, they often pick up other diagnoses, like oppositional defiant disorder or conduct disorder—the mental-health versions of "bad kid."

How can this be? How can highly trained professionals be so confused? How can some of them even deny the existence of some of the disorders that their colleagues diagnose regularly? The answer, I believe, is in the complexity of the human brain. Our diagnostic categories cannot capture all the features of each child. The result is a great deal of overlap in the criteria for "self-regulation" disorders. Here's a list of common behavioral problems for these children:

- Hyperactive
- Easily distracted
- Easily frustrated
- Rigid, otherwise known as "stubborn"
- Difficulties with any change
- Frequent and intense temper tantrums
- Problems getting along with other children
- Argumentative
- Easily annoyed
- Either hyper- or hyposensitive to touch
- Interrupts others

The problem is that these symptoms show up on the behavioral checklists of *all* the following: attention deficit/hyperactivity disorder, Asperger syndrome, bipolar disorder, sensory processing disorder, oppositional defiant disorder, and conduct disorder. While each diagnosis has additional distinctive features, you can see how confusing the overlap can be. To add to the confusion, some children also have many of the distinctive features that put them in multiple categories. Still other kids' brains don't fit neatly in any one of the limited diagnostic buckets. The diagnoses can be maddening for the overwhelmed parents who get conflicting advice and for the children who end up with a string of labels.

Does this confusion mean that these underlying disorders do not exist? No. It means that there is a lot of overlap and that teasing out the differences is tricky, to say the least. So, what is a parent to do?

Steps for Parents

Here are steps that you can take if your son or daughter came into the world wired with a brain that makes self-regulation a big challenge:

1. Don't take it personally. The more we learn about explosive, out-of-control kids, the more we understand that these disorders are brain-based and not the result of parenting mistakes. It's tempting to assume that the kids are misbehaving deliberately, but they aren't. It takes a lot of patience, love, and sacrifice to help these children learn No. It doesn't help if you blame yourself. We don't choose our genes.

2. Seek the help and advice of competent professionals. The strategies that fill other chapters in this book aren't going to work the same way for children who are wired differently. They will need some special approaches and tactics. While I will describe some of them in this chapter, it is a good idea to become better informed in the specific approaches that specialists have developed. I will recommend my favorite resources a bit later. Use them as starting points and expand your knowledge and skills.

3. Find professionals who have a wide scope of experience with special-needs children. There's an old saying: If the only tool you have is a hammer, then everything looks like a nail. Ask each doctor, psychologist, social worker, or nurse if he works with a range of kids with different diagnoses. You want a professional who is flexible enough to try different approaches. A school counselor recently asked me if she should be worried if 90 percent of the children referred to a certain child psychiatrist in her town were all diagnosed with bipolar disorder. "Abso-

lutely," I answered. "That borders on professional miscon-
duct."

4. Be a patient but persistent advocate for your child. I know
a mom and dad who consulted professionals for over two
years until they finally came up with a diagnosis that
made sense and an approach that worked for their son.

5. Get support. Parenting a child with a brain that makes her
explosive, rigid, and easily frustrated is hard work. Find
out which relatives and friends will help out so you can
get a break. Get to know other parents with special-needs
kids. This will give you a chance to get more information
and tips and have support so that you are not trying
alone. Avoid know-it-alls, however. They can send you
down the wrong path and leave you questioning yourself
when their "guaranteed" techniques don't work for you.

6. Pay attention to your relationship with your partner. Sep-
aration and divorce rates are higher for the parents of
special-needs children. Take time for yourselves and avoid
taking out your frustrations on each other.

7. Don't tolerate out-of-bounds behavior. Parents of children
who can't self-regulate have to redefine "normal" and re-
calibrate expectations. Nevertheless, life will be a lot better
for these kids when they build the self-control that they
are capable of.

8. Support your other children. Special-needs children demand a lot of energy and attention, which can leave siblings feeling lost in the chaos. Do what you can to make
sure each child's needs are met even if you have to bring
in some friend and family reinforcements to give you time
alone with each child. In some instances, siblings need
protection from an aggressive or assaultive special-needs
brother or sister.

There are multiple explanations for volatile, rigid, and touchy
children. Here are some of the more common ones.

Attention Deficit Disorders

Jack was a bright second grader who drove his parents and teachers crazy. He scored at the top of his class on all the standardized tests, but was chronically late for school, frequently forgot assignments, talked out of turn, blurted out answers, repeatedly misplaced or lost his books and school supplies, and often slipped into conflicts with the other kids or his teacher. Eventually, Jack and his parents discovered that he did not have an attitude problem, nor did he need to just "settle down and pay attention." A thorough evaluation led the family's pediatrician to diagnose Jack with attention deficit/hyperactivity disorder, ADHD. That diagnosis did not solve Jack's problems, of course, but it did help him, his parents, and his teachers figure out how best to help him learn in school. Attention deficit without a pattern of agitation or hyperactivity is known as attention deficit disorder, or ADD.

ADD and ADHD are not new disorders. Educational psychologists and researchers identified the pattern of symptoms more than one hundred years ago. I'm convinced that a boy in my first-grade class, Tommy, had ADHD. He was a whirling dervish from day one. If he wasn't daydreaming he was jumping out of his seat and running around. He interrupted whoever was talking, knocked things over, and talked back to the teacher. His demise came quickly on the day that he locked Sister Mary Ruth in the cloakroom. The rest of us were secretly disappointed that Tommy was expelled that day because he had provided nonstop entertainment for the rest of us, who were too scared to move, let alone lock the teacher in the closet. Tommy wasn't labeled ADHD, however. He was called a "bad kid," the diagnosis du jour for kids like Tommy in the 1950s.

Boys are six times more likely to be diagnosed with a type of ADD than girls are. Most brains focus on one thing or activity and then shift to another at an appropriate time. We call this capacity "attention," and it directs the brain's resources to focus on an idea or perform a task. Kids with ADD or ADHD either cannot make the shift to a new thing or activity, or their attention is constantly shifting to whatever comes along. Scientists are not sure what causes some brains to have trouble measuring out appropriate attention, but recent research shows that ADHD is linked to anatomical and chemical differences in the brain. Attention deficit must have a genetic component, since parents with ADD and ADHD are five times more likely to have children with attention deficits than are parents who have normal attention spans.

Parents or teachers should consider the possibility of ADD or ADHD for a kid who displays the following pattern:

- Has trouble paying attention.
- Makes careless mistakes.
- Is easily distracted.
- Loses things frequently.
- Tends to be impatient.
- Fidgets or squirms.
- Interrupts others.
- Cannot sit quietly.

Every child (and every adult) will exhibit these tendencies from time to time, so unless a child shows these symptoms frequently, you should not suspect ADD or ADHD. If these symptoms lead to problems like frequent arguments, sloppy schoolwork, and under-performance in the classroom, then the chances are even higher that you're looking at an attention deficit.

The best research shows that 3 to 5 percent of kids have an attention disorder, but in some parts of the country as many as one in five carries one of the two diagnoses. Because there is no definitive brain test to determine which kids are just being impulsive and which have ADD or ADHD, many youngsters are labeled incorrectly as having a different brain. Sometimes a physician will prescribe a medication just to see if it helps, without a thorough evaluation, which is key for a good diagnosis. A child should never be diagnosed or put on a drug without a comprehensive evaluation that includes a complete medical and family history; a physical examination; interviews with parents, teachers, and the child; completion of specialized behavior-rating scales; and observation of the child by the medical doctor or other qualified professional.

Medications have proven to be the most effective treatment for children and teens who really have ADD or ADHD, but they are controversial. In a report issued in February 2006, a Federal Drug Administration panel urged greater caution in prescribing them due to concerns about overprescribing and possible dangerous side effects. Drugs like Ritalin, Dexedrine, and Cylert are stimulants that affect the brain's neurotransmitters. These medications help the brain regulate attention and impulsivity and can make a profoundly positive effect on the lives of kids with ADD or ADHD. In the most successful cases, however, drugs are not the only means of treatment. Most experts agree that medication should never be the only treatment. Effective treatment should always include:

- Education for the child and the entire family about attention disorders so everyone knows and understands the problem.
- Behavior management that increases the chances for success. Examples include:
  - Teens with ADD or ADHD need a great deal of structure, organization, and predictability. For example, they should always write down their homework assignments in the same notebook and work on them in the same homework spot, one that is quiet and not distracting.
  - Break down instructions or directions into steps. Rather than say, "Please clean your room," give him a list of four things to do: (1) make the bed; (2) put your laundry in the basket; (3) empty the trash can; (4) vacuum the carpet. Ask him to check things off as he completes them.
  - Write down schedules, appointments, and reminders.
  - Expectations and consequences are important for all teens but are crucial for teens with ADD or

ADHD. Writing them down will reduce confusion and disagreements.
* Collaboration between home and school. Parents and
teachers should work together to identify the specific attention skills that cause the most trouble. For example,
some kids have trouble beginning a task because the directions are too complicated. Other kids have no trouble with
directions, but have a terrible time making a transition
from one activity to another. When everyone, including
the child, knows what skills need the most work, then
progress is more likely.

Another type of treatment, called neurofeedback, is proving to
be helpful with about half of the kids with ADD or ADHD. The
children are connected to a computer with painless sensors attached
to their scalp and ears. The computer processes the brain waves and
converts them to images on a video game screen. Many youngsters
are able to learn how to change and control their attention using
this technology.

One of the best resources for parents concerned about ADD or
ADHD is the book by Drs. Ed Hallowell and John Ratey, *Driven to
Distraction: Recognizing and Coping with Attention Deficit Disorder
from Childhood through Adulthood* (Touchstone, 1995). The organization Children and Adults with Attention Deficit Disorders
(CHADD) has a Web site, www.chadd.org, which provides information on research, resources, and support groups.

Asperger Syndrome

Molly's pediatrician had diagnosed her with ADHD in the first
grade and prescribed Concerta, a common ADHD medication.
The special-education teacher at Molly's school had developed
an "individualized education plan," or IEP, that Molly's parents
and teachers all signed off on. That brought good results for the
rest of first grade, but when Molly went to second grade it
seemed like they were all back at square one. She had bouts of

screaming most mornings and seemed to go out of her way to pick fights with her younger brother. Her teacher complained that Molly was defiant. The most recent episode occurred when Molly refused to redo some math problems that she had gotten wrong.

While these traits were consistent with her ADHD diagnosis, Molly had others that didn't fit. For one thing, she took language very literally. "If I tell Molly that I'll be on the phone for a minute, she blows up as soon as the sixty seconds are up and calls me a liar," her mother explained. "She never knows when to stop. She is surprised when other kids get upset with her for being bossy and insists that things have to be the way she sees them. There's no gray with her; everything is black and white."

Molly has Asperger syndrome, a neurobiological disorder named for the Viennese physician Hans Asperger, who in 1944 described children who had autisticlike behaviors and serious problems with social and communication skills. As with the other self-regulation disorders described in this chapter, there is some controversy surrounding Asperger, or AS as it is sometimes called. Some experts include it as part of the spectrum of autistic disorders; others disagree.

Here is a list of the most common behaviors associated with an Asperger brain:

- These kids have trouble getting along with other children. They often end up playing by themselves because they can't figure out the unwritten rules.
- They are not interested in what other people think, so they stop paying attention as soon as they've had their say.
- They cannot figure out common social cues. For example, they might continue an annoying behavior until everyone around them is exasperated because they fail to detect the irritation cues.
- They assume that everyone knows what they are thinking and become very impatient when other people don't know what they want.

- They overreact emotionally.
- They are uncomfortable with eye contact.
- These children interpret language literally so they are confused by puns, jokes, and idioms like a "broken heart."
- They have "meltdowns" when there is a change in plan or routine.
- They "march to their own drummer" and are often considered odd. I know a little boy, for example, who knows all about insects and lectures everyone he meets about them.
- They often lack physical coordination.

Researchers agree that Asperger syndrome is brain-based. Even though Molly can try the patience of a saint, she is not deliberately trying to be difficult. Some brain scientists believe that the "mirror neurons" don't function in an Asperger brain, which would explain why these kids have so many problems reading social cues and having empathy. Scientists haven't figured out which brain circuits account for the communication and language problems that plague these children.

There is no medication for Asperger, but education and training interventions are proving successful. These children can learn the social skills that seem to come to other children naturally. For example, parents and teachers can teach these kids how to take turns and let other people talk. While most children don't have to learn what an angry face looks like, kids like Molly have to learn to identify facial expressions the same way they tackle other school subjects. The good news is that children with Asperger syndrome can learn the skills of friendship.

Belinda, a fourth grader, exhibited all the signs of Asperger syndrome. Once the child psychologist explained why Belinda had so many school and social problems, Philip and Anne committed themselves to teach Belinda the skills that came naturally to other children. First they taught Belinda how to read faces. Children with Asperger syndrome find it difficult to interpret emotions, so Philip and Anne, with Belinda, cut pictures out of magazines and taught her to "read" different facial emotions. "This is an angry face," Anne explained. "When you see this face, the person may be angry. It might be something you did or said, Belinda, so you should ask her if she's angry with you. If she answers yes, then you should ask why."

Once Belinda could pick out angry faces, they moved on to sad faces, and then others. They were thrilled with a voice mail message from Belinda's teacher one day: "Philip and Anne, this is Mrs. Swanson. I thought you should know that I overheard Belinda ask a boy today if he was angry with her. He said he was and Belinda said she was sorry. I don't know if she understood exactly what she had done to bother him, but this is real progress."

Seventeen-year-old Desmond was pleased to land his first summer job at the local grocery store. However, an Asperger trait quickly caused him trouble. He was stocking fruits when a customer asked him where the avocados were located. "Don't you see I'm unloading apples," he answered curtly, not even looking at the stunned woman. Within minutes she complained to the store manager about the "horrible customer service." Fortunately, Desmond's parents had explained Asperger syndrome to the manager so he knew that Desmond's rudeness was caused by his brain focusing on one thing at a time, coupled with a "social tone deafness." The manager had to maintain good customer relations, but he also appreciated Desmond's work ethic. He transferred Desmond to a job where he didn't have to deal with customers.

OASIS (Online Asperger Syndrome Information and Support) is a good resource for more information about Asperger syndrome. The *OASIS Guide to Asperger Syndrome* was updated in 2005 with the latest research, and their Web site, www.udel.edu/bkirby/asperger, is excellent.

Sensory Processing Disorder

Imagine trying to pay attention in class with a jet engine roaring in your ear, while one person rubs sandpaper on your skin and another keeps punching you in the shoulder. Pretty difficult if not impossible, don't you think? That's what it's like for a boy or girl with sensory processing disorder (SPD), sometimes known as sensory integration dysfunction. The jet engine is the noisy kindergarten classroom; the sandpaper is the shirt label rubbing against the skin; and the punching is the teacher gently tapping for attention on the child's shoulder.

The normal brain constantly receives, interprets, and connects streams of information coming in through the senses. Children with sensory processing disorder (SPD) have brains that distort the incoming data by either over- or underamplifying it. The preceding paragraph describes a child whose brain overresponds. Touch and sound overwhelm this oversensitive child. He tries to cope with the bombardment by fidgeting and squirming. He tries to pay attention to the teacher but can't.

Other children with SPD have the opposite problem: Their brains underrespond. Whereas overresponders try to escape stimulation, underresponders seek it. So they run around to get a sense of movement and crash into other kids to get a sense of touch. They crave nonstop rocking, swaying, jumping, climbing, and twirling.

Not surprisingly, many SPD kids receive an ADHD diagnosis because so many of their coping behaviors look the same. The ADHD approaches aren't effective because the underlying problem is different—unless the child has both SPD and ADHD, which some children do. If you think reading this description is confusing, imagine being the beleaguered parent trying to sort it out in real life. That's why my earlier advice to be a patient but persistent advocate is so important. It can take a while to sort out what's really going on in there.

The most helpful interventions for kids wired with this type of brain do not come from medical or mental-health professionals. Occupational therapists have developed techniques to identify the specific pattern of sensory responses for each child. That, in turn, enables them to construct an individualized treatment plan of exercises, sensory experiences, and self-regulation skill building that parents can use at home. Unless the child has additional problems beyond SPD, medication is not used in treatment.

Carol Stock Kranowitz has written a very helpful book for parents of SPD children: *The Out-of-Sync Child: Recognizing and Coping with Sensory Integration Dysfunction* (Perigee, 1998). Anyone interested in SPD can also find a lot of information at the SPD Web site, http://www.spdnetwork.org. This site also has links to resources for help in local communities. These resources outline specific techniques to help children cope with their sensory dysfunction. Since children with SPD also have self-regulation challenges, the strategies described later in this chapter will be helpful.

Bipolar Disorder

Donna was a single parent at the end of her emotional rope. "Darren doesn't have temper tantrums," she told me. "He rages! He punches, kicks, and bites me. Last summer he came after me with a knife. He's only six, for pete's sake, and I can barely control him now. What am I going to do when he's bigger than me? He's already thrown toys through windows and punched huge holes in his bedroom wall." She told me that the most frustrating thing was that the strategies she had learned in parenting classes backfired with Darrren. "He will fight to the death if I try to give him consequences for misbehavior. He can scream and trash his room for hours at a time."

I asked Donna a few more questions and wasn't surprised by her answers. She told me that Darren's sleep patterns were erratic. "Some nights he'll be raring to go at three AM and other times he can't wake up at all and is late for school." She also told me that his mood could vacillate between gregarious and furious in seconds. "This is what happened last week at lunch," she said. "While I was fixing his meal he was chatting and laughing with me. When I gave him the sandwich he took one look at it and screamed at me for giving him cheese. He yelled, 'I hate cheese,' and threw the sandwich and plate right at me." By now tears were running down Donna's cheeks as she recalled the nightmare. "I was so mad, Dr. Walsh, that I slapped him as hard as I could right across the face. I'm so ashamed." Donna sobbed. "I'm such a bad parent. I never meant to hit him. Really." I started to offer some words of comfort, but she had one more thing she wanted to get off her chest. "An hour later Darren told me that he was going to kill himself."

I had heard enough to know that Donna was not describing a "difficult child." I referred Donna and Darren to an excellent child psychiatrist I work with and got a phone call from my colleague two weeks later telling me that he was confident that Darren had bipolar disorder.

My psychiatrist colleague prescribed medication for Darren. It was going to take a lot of teamwork among Darren's doctors, teachers, counselors, and Donna to help him manage one of the most challenging mental illnesses.

Dramatic fluctuations in mood, activity, thought, and behavior are the hallmarks of bipolar disorder (also known as "bipolar illness" or "manic-depressive illness"). There is a strong genetic component and symptoms can appear at any time, even during the preschool years. The early signs often look like depression as children cry for no reason and have no interest in play. Their moods can cycle between grandiosity and rage in a matter of minutes, hours, or days. When in the manic phase they may talk a blue streak, bounce off the walls, talk loudly, and race to take on multiple projects. During this phase they also have an exaggerated opinion of their abilities, thinking, for example, that they know more than their teachers do. But there is no middle ground, because minutes, hours, or days later they abruptly sink into a deep, dark funk in which they become easily frustrated and angry. Like Darren, bipolar children have rages that know no bounds. They can become violent in seconds and their storms can last for hours. Suicide threats or attempts should be taken seriously.

Bipolar disorder is brain-based. Scans reveal that activation patterns in bipolar children are different from those in other children, involving areas that regulate memory, impulse control, speech, aggression, and emotion. Bipolar disorder is also chronic, meaning there is no cure. Enforcing No with a bipolar child is very difficult. Consultation with the treatment team, a lot of trial and error, and patience often lead to strategies uniquely geared to the child. A good plan includes medication, counseling for the child and family, support for parents like Donna, and a school plan that allows accommodations like time-outs or opportunities to move around. I would recommend the book *If Your Child Is Bipolar,* by Cindy Singer and Sheryl Gurrentz (Perspective Publishing, 2004), and the Web site Bipolar Kids, http://www.bpkids.org, for more information and tips.

Anxiety Disorders

Cameron, fifteen, had been a bright but shy child. He was reluctant to try new activities and would cling to his parents and teachers for reassurance. His parents, Paul and Dawn, described him as "touchy" and more difficult to discipline than his two brothers and two sisters. "He would usually say no before he would say yes all through his childhood," Paul told me. "We walked on eggshells a lot because his initial reaction to any change or request was often resistance. He was more demanding and fragile than our other kids and his anger was often explosive."

"How did he do in school?" I asked.

"Fine," Dawn replied. "His teachers liked him a lot because he was smart and well behaved. They were always surprised when we shared some of our concerns with them at conferences because he didn't resist them like he did us. The only question they had was why he never raised his hand or volunteered an answer. "

"He got along great with other kids too," Paul added. "He was very popular."

"The problems started in junior high," Dawn said. "He started to withdraw more and more. He was always a good soccer player, but he quit the ninth-grade team the day after his coach told him how much potential he had. He was smart enough to get decent grades, but his description for all his classes and teachers was 'stupid.' We really started to get worried when we discovered he was getting into smoking pot and drinking a lot with his friends."

Cameron had an underlying anxiety disorder that had been undetected until his drinking and pot smoking landed him in a residential treatment program when he was a high school senior. He was born with a brain that was finely tuned to detect danger. In fact, his brain was so sensitive that it perceived danger and triggered fear when there wasn't any real cause for alarm.

A neurotransmitter called GABA (gamma amino butyric acid) is the "brain's tranquilizer." Recent research shows that almost 20 percent of babies are born with low levels of GABA, leaving them in a constant state of fear. They, of course, don't know they're anxious because they have always felt that way. In other words, anxiety is normal for them. Kids like Cameron are often called shy when they are young, because they're in a constant state of anxiety, which causes them to hang back and act clingy. When they get to school, some kids with "worried brains" cope by becoming perfectionists. These kids can't sleep a wink before a big test even though they always end up with the highest grade in the class. Other kids take the path that Cameron followed. They withdraw because they can't stand the panic they feel when they have to perform.

"Is that why Cameron quit the soccer team, Dr. Walsh?" Dawn asked me while I was explaining anxiety disorder to them.

"Exactly," I replied. "The minute the coach told Cameron that he could be a star, his brain panicked at the thought of the attention and pressure that would bring. It was safer for him to call soccer 'stupid' and quit the team. It was a survival mechanism for him." I also explained to Paul and Dawn that it was Cameron's "worried brain" that set him up for problems with pot and alcohol. "When teens with 'worried brains' drink, it's the first time in their lives they have ever felt relaxed. Alcohol mimics the effects of GABA. Can you imagine how tempting it is to keep getting relief from the constant state of near-panic?" I asked. "That's why a lot of teenagers who get into trouble with drugs or alcohol have an anxiety disorder, or a 'worried brain.'"

Cameron had a fairly uncomplicated case of anxiety disorder. It explained why "he always needed to say no before he would say yes" as a child. He was constantly on edge, so any request would trigger fear and he would react out of panic. Cameron got sober and learned many coping skills like relaxation, meditation, and self-talk to help him cope with his anxiety. He was also able to get tremendous support from the Alcoholics Anonymous group to which he went after treatment.

Many children or teens with ADHD, Asperger syndrome, SPD, or bipolar disorder have an underlying anxiety disorder as well. A thorough evaluation by a child psychologist or child psychiatrist will help determine if a child is anxious. Dr. Ed Hallowell's book *Worry* (Ballantine, 1998) is a good resource for parents who suspect that their child might have an anxiety disorder.

What about Medication?

Of the five types of brains that make it difficult or impossible for children to respond to No in a constructive way, only two of them, attention deficit disorders and bipolar disorder, benefit from medication, although physicians may consider medication for a serious case of anxiety disorder. Many parents are understandably nervous about introducing powerful chemicals into a growing brain. Concerns about overprescribing, long-term damage, side effects, and dependency should be taken seriously, especially in light of a 2006 report showing that prescriptions for psychoactive drugs for children and teens had increased 500 percent from 1992 to 2003. Nevertheless, medications can play an important role in managing challenging brains. Some can be used for a period of time, allowing the child or teen to develop coping strategies that will eventually eliminate the need for medicine. Other conditions, like bipolar disorder, will require a lifetime of medication, just as a type 1 diabetic needs a lifetime of insulin.

Drugs alone, however, are never the answer. They should be used only if they are combined with counseling and other behavioral and social-skills training. Here are my suggestions for parents considering medication:

- Make sure the prescribing physician is an expert in children and adolescents.

- Make sure you get a thorough evaluation before medications are prescribed.
- Know what type of medication is being recommended and how it works.
- Ask how this drug might interact with others that your child or teen is taking.
- Don't hesitate to ask the doctor how effective this drug has been for other children.
- Ask the doctor to describe the short- and long-term side effects.
- Search out information on the drug in books and on reputable Internet sites.
- Ask the doctor how and how often he or she will monitor side effects and the drug's effectiveness.
- Be sure the doctor describes in clear language any symptoms that you should watch for that might mean trouble.
- Get clear directions about drug administration and storage. Should the drug be taken on an empty or a full stomach, first thing in the morning, etc.?
- Find a pharmacist who will answer your questions and listen to your concerns. Pharmacists usually know more about the medications than doctors do.

Special-Needs Children and *No*

Whether it's a relatively simple case like Cameron's or one compounded by one of the other self-regulation disorders that I have described in this chapter, saying no requires some special strategies and techniques.

Children who are wired differently are not deliberately undermining our efforts to say no. To quote Dr. Ed Hallowell, coauthor of *Driven to Distraction,* "telling a child whose brain is wired differently to 'pay attention' or 'settle down' is like telling a person with arterial sclerosis to 'unclog your arteries.'" These kids would manage their emotions if they could. Special-needs children do not always learn from their mistakes. We keep thinking they will but they often don't.

They don't choose to be rigid, angry, or defiant any more than a child chooses to be nearsighted. That doesn't mean, however, that they don't need to learn No. It just means that their special brains demand some special strategies.

I have developed a model for saying no to special-needs kids. It involves the image of a cliff and the universal signals of red, yellow, and green. Here's how it works:

- *The cliff.* Kids with brains that make self-regulation difficult or impossible cannot control themselves once they get past a point of no return. I call this point "the cliff." Once they go over the cliff they are incapable of managing the free fall. The goal, therefore, is to prevent them from going over the cliff in the first place. Here are the ways to help them avoid falling off the cliff:

  - Teach your child to use the image of the cliff. When you can have a rational discussion with her, help her understand that her brain gets hijacked if she gets too upset. "When you get real upset it's like your brain goes off a cliff and then it's out of control." Then add, "Wouldn't it be nice if we figured out how to stay away from the cliff?"

  - Know where the cliffs are. Each child has her predictable cliffs. For one child it might be getting ready for school, for another it might be doing homework or making a trip to the supermarket, and for a third it might be battling over video games. Take a scientific approach and list the things that seem to put your child over the cliff of self-control. Go back and star the items that pose the biggest risk.

  - Look for early warning signs. She might say, "I can't do this," or "I hate you." Or you might notice the clenched jaw or steely gaze that precedes a race for the cliff.

- When you see your child starting in the direction of a cliff, do what you can to steer her away. The distract-and-divert strategy I described in chapter 3 may work. Instead of saying, "You have to do your homework now," say, "Let's have a glass of milk or some fruit before we get out the homework."

- If diversion fails, stay calm and establish eye contact. If your child tolerates touch, hold her hands in a gentle way or gently rub her back. Try to understand your child's perspective. Let her know you understand that she is angry or scared. For example, you might say, "I know you want to play on the computer now and are frustrated with me. I get upset when I can't do something I want to do, too. Can I help you get organized for your homework so you can finish with enough time left to get back to the computer?"

- If she falls over the cliff anyway, stay calm. Don't escalate. Establish eye contact and gentle touch. Repeat reassuring words like, "It's okay, honey, we can get through this. It's okay, we can calm down together."

- *Red, yellow, and green.* Saying no to an inflexible, explosive child is very challenging. It becomes important, therefore, to pick and choose battles carefully. Special-needs children cannot respond to No normally. To expect quick compliance sets you and them up for nonstop confrontations, cliff visits, and failure. I suggest that you decide in advance which limits are worth battling for. I call these the red-light limits, and they are nonnegotiable. Limits involving safety, violence, destruction, and school attendance all belong in this category.

Next, decide which behaviors are important but not worth heading for the cliff over. Examples include a messy bedroom, incomplete homework, and mouthiness or talking back. These are the yellow-light behaviors. Address these issues when possible but look out for cliff signals so you don't make yellow-light things into red-light items.

Finally, figure out which behaviors you need to let go. Given the challenge of saying no to special-needs children, is it worth spending your energy and attention on things like an unmade bed, unwashed face, wearing gloves, or a snack before dinner?

You may be worried about this advice. "How will he ever learn self-discipline if I let him get away with things?" you might wonder. I understand the question, but let's be realistic. Just as a nearsighted child will never have twenty-twenty vision, a special-needs child will never have textbook-perfect behavior. The goal is to help him develop as much self-regulation as possible. Furthermore, as you start to distinguish which behaviors are the most important, you may find that you build some success with your child and can start to move some of the yellow items up to red and that some of the greens will become yellow.

Here are some suggestions to help with the challenges involved in saying no to a child with self-regulation problems:

DO

- Establish eye contact with your child when you want to get his attention or cooperation.
- Provide frequent and immediate rewards for good behavior. "Thanks for clearing your dishes," for example.
- Try to have positive statements outnumber the negative.
- Identify your child's strengths and play to them.
- Break directions into small steps. For example, say, "We're going to clean up the family room for company. First of all, could you please put away the LEGOs." When the LEGOs are away, say, "Good. Now let's collect the books."
- Use humor and touch to get your child's attention.

- Identify which behaviors you want in the red, yellow, and green categories so that you know in advance where you want to put your energy.
- Learn which triggers send your child or teen over the cliff of uncontrollable behavior.
- Have diversions lined up in case your child starts to head for the cliff.
- Teach your child relaxation techniques. Say, "Let's both take five deep breaths and then we'll talk."
- Give choices rather than commands. Say, "What do you want to do first, wash your face or brush your teeth?"
- Provide predictability and structure. These reduce anxiety.

DON'T

- Don't set up battles. For example, if you want to have dinner in twenty minutes, don't let your child start watching a video that lasts thirty minutes.
- Don't nag. Say what you have to say and let it go.
- Don't ever spank a special-needs child. It doesn't work well with any kids, but it ignites defiance in explosive children.
- Don't spring sudden changes. Let them know in advance when change is going to happen. Say, "It will be time to come in and get ready for dinner in ten minutes," instead of, "Time for dinner."
- Don't assign chores that you know he can't do. Pick jobs that you know he can do so that you can give him some legitimate praise.
- Don't punish hyperactivity with "time-outs." Instead, insist that your child take some "quiet time." It's the same thing but the message to the child is different.
- Don't say, "Shut up." Instead, try, "Excuse me; I'm still talking. Please wait your turn."

What do I want to continue?

_____

_____

_____

What do I want to change?

_____

_____

_____

ELEVEN

Practical Questions about *No*

Raising kids involves hundreds of questions and decisions every day. Many are so routine we don't even think about them—sweater or coat? snack or no snack? Other questions are more serious and perplexing. Parents frequently ask me the following questions, which are not only perplexing but have consequences for how we say no to our children and teens.

1. Should I always use the word *no*?
2. If I want to change my pattern and need to get things on track, what steps should I take to start using No?
3. How should I handle tantrums?
4. How should I handle tantrums that happen in public?
5. What about spanking?
6. When should I use time-outs?
7. How can I handle defiance?
8. What's a behavior contract and how do I use one?
9. What about mouthiness, cursing, and swearing?
10. How can I handle my own anger?
11. When is it okay to negotiate with my kids?
12. What should I do if my kids lie?

13. Do parents have a role in backing up teachers?
14. Should I ever apologize to my kids?

1. Should I always use the word *no*?

The answer to this question is, in a word, no. The concept of No is what's important, not the word itself. In fact, overusing the word is counterproductive. Use No as your mental behavior boundary, not your only response. Well-placed nos will be more effective if they're not overused. Reserve it for the times when you want to get your child's attention or make a serious point.

An effective alternative is to give your child a choice that keeps her behavior within the boundaries you set. For instance, when three-year-old Sarah wants to wear a T-shirt to preschool even though it is winter, say, "Sarah, you need to wear a long-sleeve shirt because it's cold. Do you want to wear your T-shirt over your long-sleeve shirt or underneath?" When Jake asks if he can play video games right after school, say, "You need to finish your homework and chores before you play your half hour of video games. Do you want to do that before dinner or afterward?" When fifteen-year-old Anise wants to get a tattoo, say, "I know tattoos are very popular and it's hard not to have one, but right now you're in high school and it's too soon to make a permanent decision. You can use a washable tattoo now or wait until you're eighteen, when you can decide whether to get a permanent one."

Try to say what you want the child *to do* in positive language. Younger children in particular, because of their limited language development, often get confused by negatives. So, for example, say, "Use your inside voice, please," rather than, "No yelling." Rather than say, "Don't throw your food," say, "Food in the mouth, please."

There are lots of ways to communicate No without using the word. Body language, tone of voice, and "looks" can all be effective.

I used two inflections for Erin's name when she was little. "I usually heard my name with the accent on the first syllable," she told me. "But when I heard my name with the accent of the second syllable, I knew you meant 'no' or 'stop.'"

My friend Bob mastered nonverbal cues: He spoke slowly, over-pronounced his words, and looked straight at his daughters. They knew he meant business.

DO
- Find ways to give your child choices.
- Make a list of your most frequent No messages and think of creative alternatives that convey the message without using the word.
- Acknowledge your child's feelings so that he feels heard, even if the answer is no.

DON'T
- Don't overuse the word *no*. It will lose its effectiveness.

2. If I want to change my pattern and need to get things on track, what steps should I take to start using No?

It is never too late to get started. Here are some steps you can take:

- Take stock of your parenting style. Are you authoritarian, permissive, or balanced? A lot of parents slip into authoritarian or permissive styles because they're easier. The balanced style requires more work, but it pays off in the long run.
- Prioritize the issues that are causing you the most concern. You want to work toward a set of family rules and consequences that everybody understands.
- Choose the top one or two behaviors that you want to change. Don't try to address everything at once; pick the ones that you think are the most urgent.
- Translate the behaviors you want to reinforce and those you want to stop into family rules. As the parent, you are in charge of setting the rules.
- Next, figure out which consequences make sense if your

child or teen does not comply. So, for instance, with your four-year-old the family rule might be: "No hitting Mommy, or Daddy, or baby sister." The consequence will be immediate removal to a time-out chair or space for four minutes. Try to find a consequence that has a logical connection to the misbehavior.

- Sit down and explain the rule and the consequence as clearly as possible to your children or teens. For example, here's how you might explain the no-hitting rule to your four-year-old: "Hitting hurts and in our family we do not hurt each other. If you hit me or your baby sister, you are showing me that you cannot be with us right now and you will have to sit in the time-out chair for four minutes." Ask your child to repeat the rule and consequence to make sure he understands it. Remember to emphasize the positive behavior you want to see: "Use your words when you're angry instead of hitting."

  Or, for example, if your teen visits sexually explicit Internet chat rooms, say, "Pornographic sites are not places for teens to visit on the Web—you violated our family Internet rules. As the consequence you will not be allowed to use the computer, except for schoolwork, for two weeks. Is that clear?" The conversation should not end until your teen understands the rule and the consequence. You can also install software that filters out or tracks such sites.

- Try to enforce the rule and the consequence calmly. For instance, say, "Remember the rule. In our family we do not hit each other. You hit your sister and that shows me that you need to be in time-out for ten minutes. I know you're angry, but you need to use words to tell me. We will talk after your time-out about why you're angry and try to figure out better ways to handle it."

- Always follow through. You will pay a price when you don't follow through because you undermine your own efforts. Explaining the rule and the consequence ahead of time helps you stay out of power struggles, but it doesn't mean that children and teens will not push back and lose their tempers. It's important to keep yours. You need to remain in charge and not end up breaking the family rules yourself by going ballistic. Here are some scripts as examples:

- "By fighting over the toy, you are choosing not to play with it."
- "By coming in after ten o'clock curfew, you are choosing to have a fifteen-minute-earlier curfew for the rest of the week."

- Talk with your child or teen after the consequence to keep open the communication lines. You can talk about what happened, listen to his side of the story, and even validate his feelings. But that doesn't mean that you change the rule or the consequence. The follow-up conversation can help the child figure out a better, more positive way to get what he wants. So if Jimmy wants to play with the toy that his sister is using, talk about taking turns. If it's a favorite toy, you might ask Jimmy if it would help to set up time limits for its use.

DO

- Talk with your children about family rules.
- Set limits and consequences and follow through.

DON'T

- Don't assume your children know what the rules are.
- Don't overexplain. Stay clear.

3. How should I handle tantrums?

Crying and tantrums are normal, and they don't hurt kids. Many parents are so afraid of tantrums that they'll do anything to avoid them. But children need to feel frustrated or angry sometimes if they're ever going to learn to handle these feelings. No tantrum will last forever. Weathering them, however, takes time . . . and patience. Tantrums happen when feelings of frustration over-whelm a child's ability to cope. As his capacity for language grows, he will have more tools to use. More important, if we han-dle tantrums well, we can help him handle these difficult and sometimes scary feelings, and these lessons will help him develop his internal emotion-regulation skills.

Two-year-olds are notorious for their tantrums with good rea-son. Children at this age are beginning to explore their world and their boundaries, but they don't have the language skills to express how they feel or exactly what they want. The executive center of the brain, which helps them manage their feelings, is still immature as well. Two-year-olds' tantrums are normal. Fatigue, hunger, frus-tration, and anger are a potent brew that results in a meltdown. Don't take it personally.

Detective work can help. Figuring out her tantrum triggers might help you head off some of the big meltdowns. For instance, don't plan outings or activities that push your child past the point of endurance. Always bring along a small bag of snacks, something to drink, and a book or two. Restructure her activity to reduce frustra-tion or divert her to something else. Try to verbalize for your child what you think she might be feeling: "It's hard to wait, isn't it?" or "You're angry at your brother, aren't you?" If she boils over anyway, intervene by putting a soothing hand on her and try to help her past the frustration. Give her words for what you think she is trying to say: "You're angry because Mommy won't let you have candy right now." If your child is beyond the pale, try holding her and saying, "You're really angry right now and Daddy's going to hold you until you calm down." Holding a child may give her the control that she can't muster on her own. Some children, however, do better if you give them a simple, reassuring rub on the back, while talking sooth-ingly, instead of holding them. The only way to discover whether holding helps or makes matters worse is through trial and error.

Tantrums don't automatically end with the "terrible twos." Older children might throw tantrums as well. It's important to re-spond swiftly and not let an outburst control the household. Say, "Kevin, use your words. When you calm down and use your words,

I will talk to you." Start counting down, "five, four, three, two, one." If you get to one and the child is still having a fit, then he needs to be in time-out for a set period of time, until he can regain control. Once he has calmed down, try to find out what set off the tantrum. Talk to your child, verbalizing for him if he cannot. Then solve the problem with him and come up with a better way to handle the situation. If he broke something in anger, apply the consequence. Say, "I know you are angry, but you broke the action figure and so you cannot play with it anymore."

Don't cave in to tantrums unless you want a lot more of them. If you really feel that your child is having a tantrums just to get you to change your mind, then you may choose to ignore the tantrum: You stay close by, but you ignore. Say, "I'm sorry you're choosing to have a tantrum, but that does not change my mind."

DO
- Understand that tantrums are normal.
- See if you can identify the things that trigger or aggravate tantrums. This might give you hints about what you can change. For example, you might wait to go shopping until after your child's nap if you see that shopping trips before naps always end in disaster.

DON'T
- Don't try to outshout a child who is having a tantrum.
- Don't give in to a tantrum.

4. How should I handle tantrums that happen in public?

Murphy's Law of Tantrums states that they will happen when and where you least want them. The temptation to give in is always greater if the tantrum happens in the middle of Target, at Grandma's house, at the park, or wherever it's most difficult to handle a screaming, sobbing, angry child. But don't concede. If your child has an attack of the gimmes at the store and screams for a candy bar, don't buy it. You will only reinforce the behavior.

Keep your cool and try not to get angry yourself. If you lose it, your child's tantrum will likely intensify. Say to the child, "Justin, when you calm down and use your words, I will talk with you." Start counting down from five. If Justin is not back in control—and he probably won't be—you need to get him to a time-out area, someplace where he can have some space to regain control. This could be a quieter area of a store, in your car, or in another room if you're at Grandma's house. Don't worry about leaving your cart in the aisle if that's what you need to do in order to remove your child to a calmer place. Once you're there, tell the child, "I know you are angry [sad, hungry, tired], but you need to get control and use your words so I can talk to you." You're asking for an encore perform-ance on your next trip if you resort to bribery with a treat or some other reward from the store to get him to stop screaming. Once Justin is in control, listen to what he has to say, then repeat his feel-ing: "I know you're angry, but I said no candy at the store today. We'll have a snack when we get home. I need to go back to pay for what's in our cart. Then when we get home you can have a snack." Justin needs to know that you are in control and that you will not give in.

DO
- Remove your child to a safe time-out space.
- Validate your child's feeling after he gets control of himself.

DON'T
- Don't threaten a child who is having a tantrum.
- Don't bribe a child who is having a tantrum.

5. What about spanking?

This topic generates a tremendous amount of controversy. I think spanking kids is a poor idea for three reasons: First of all, I don't think it's effective. There are other methods to achieve the same results that work a lot better. The limits-and-consequences ap-proach is much more effective than spanking.

Second, and more important, is the great risk of resorting to spanking for the wrong reasons. People who advocate spanking always caution parents never to spank in anger. They argue that a parent should spank only in a calm, firm manner. In my years of experience counseling families I found that this advice may be good in theory, but it hardly ever works out that way in practice. Spanking and hitting almost always happen when the parent is furious and wants the child to pay for his misbehavior. It's fantasy to believe that parents who spank and hit are calm and purposeful. In addition, sooner or later, as a child grows up, spanking will become more and more problematic. Spanking or hitting preteens or teenagers is a recipe for disaster. Parents will get better behavior results if they use limits and consequences without the harmful side effects of spanking.

Third, hitting sends the wrong message to kids. It sends kids a mixed and confusing message when we tell them to resolve differences without violence and then resort to violence ourselves. As I've said, connection with kids is crucial. Spanking and hitting can weaken that connection.

DO
- Use limits and consequences.
- Stay in control.

DON'T
- Don't use physical punishment with your child.
- Don't threaten your child with physical punishment.

6. When should I use time-outs?

When using limits and consequences, the ideal consequence is a natural outgrowth of the behavior choice. So, for example, if five-year-old Anna won't sit at the table for dinner, a natural consequence would be that since she is choosing not to sit and eat dinner, she must not be hungry, so her plate is removed and she must wait until the next meal to eat.

Time-outs are useful when natural consequences don't make any sense. Time-outs are also an effective strategy to use as a consequence for disruptive behavior. If a child chooses to break a family rule and acts in a manner that is disruptive to others, then a time-out consequence is appropriate. In addition, once he's regained control, he may also lose a privilege. Parents should always be in control of the time-out, so they set the time limit and the location. Time-out for young kids is not a punishment but a time and space for them to get control of themselves. For younger children the time-out should occur near the parent. Some parents have a time-out chair for a younger child and leave the bedroom time-out for an older child.

The time limit changes with the age of the child, with a minute added for each year of the child's age. Always follow the time-out with a talk to find out what happened, why the child acted the way she did. This allows the child to be heard and feel listened to and allows the parent to restate what the child is feeling, helping her find a better way to solve the problem.

DO
- Use natural consequences when you can.
- Be in control of the duration and location of the time-out.
- Talk with your child after a time-out about what happened.

DON'T
- Don't use time-outs for everything.
- Don't let a child whine his way out of a time-out.

7. How can I handle defiance?

As children get older, especially during the preteen and teen years, you may run into outright defiance when setting limits and using No. Pushing the limits is as normal for a teen as it is for a two-year-old, but the stakes are a lot higher. First of all, there should be zero tolerance for violence in the family. It's important to nip violence in the bud when kids are young so that it doesn't become a pattern. There should always be a serious consequence for violence.

Helen and Jon never stopped their sons from hitting each other, even as preschoolers. Greg and Travis were ten and eight when I met them, and their fights were more serious. I encouraged Helen and Jon to stop the blows immediately. "It will only escalate," I told them. "Sit down and let them know you won't tolerate any more hitting, pushing, or shoving. But first, you need to agree on a consequence that will really get their attention."

"That's easy," Jon immediately replied. "They love video games. In fact, those are often the cause of the fights."

"So what would the consequence be?" I asked.

"No video games for a day for the first offense, with a day added for each additional offense," Helen suggested.

Jon agreed, so I encouraged them to make the rule and consequence clear to the boys. "Have them repeat it so there is no confusion. You could even write it down and post it in the kitchen."

Jon and Helen followed through, with limited success. "Things are better," Helen told me, "but we're up to the sixth offense, which means six days of no video games."

"That's okay," I said. "It's important, now, to stick with the consequence. If you don't see more success in the next couple of weeks, we may move to a behavior contract." (Explained later in this chapter.)

If a child or teen says that he has no intention of complying with your limit, try to remain calm and remind him of the consequence. Kids will often comply in spite of their threats to defy you. In the event that they don't follow the rules, it is crucial to enforce the consequence so that their defiance is not successful.

That's what happened to Virginia, a single parent, who struggled with her sixteen-year-old daughter, Heather. Virginia told her daughter she could not attend a party because the parents would not be home. Heather insisted that she was going anyway.

When her mom touched on this issue in our session, Heather said, "Mom, why are you bringing this up?"

"Because you told me you were going anyway," Virginia shot back.

"Well, we can talk about it later," Heather said as she glared at her mother.

I knew that Virginia needed some support so I pursued the issue. "Heather, are you clear that your mother has said no to the unsupervised party this weekend?"

Heather didn't answer, so I repeated my question. She crossed her arms, sank lower in her chair, and glowered at Virginia. She still wouldn't answer me the third time I asked, so I turned to Virginia. "You may need to be very clear about the consequence, Virginia, so Heather knows what will happen if she disobeys you."

Virginia had her answer ready. She looked at Heather and said, "You have been after me to enroll you in driving school, and we agreed that you could sign up next week. That will not happen if you go to that party."

Heather almost exploded. "What do you mean? You promised! You can't go back on your promise."

"Oh yes I can, Heather. And I will. If you disobey me about this party, you will not go to driving school. So are you going to obey me or not?"

Heather refused to talk for the rest of the session. If looks could kill, both Virginia and I would have been goners. Heather still had not answered her mother's question by the end of the session. I brought it to a close by telling Virginia, "I wouldn't argue about it anymore. Heather knows what her choices are."

The next week I asked Heather whether she had gone to the party. She pretended she didn't hear me. A couple of seconds later Virginia quietly said, "She didn't go. She's enrolling in driving school tomorrow."

DO

- Do your best to stay calm.
- Remind the potentially defiant child that he is choosing a consequence if he does not comply with the family rules.
- Follow through on consequences.
- Stop the conversation if the child screams or becomes rude or abusive.

- Give an immediate time-out to a child who becomes violent.
- If a teen becomes violent, insist that he stop immediately. If he doesn't stop, call for help from family members, friends, or the police.

DON'T
- Don't become a doormat for bad behavior.
- Don't get into a shouting match or a power struggle with your child.

8. What's a behavior contract and how do I use one?

Years ago I found a strategy for families whose kids' behavior was seriously out of line. I call it behavioral contracting. It's a written agreement that spells out in easy-to-understand language the behavior that is expected and what the consequences will be if the contract is broken. Parents and kid sign the contract and then post it in a visible location. It's important to have realistic goals. I always remind parents, "You can't turn everything around at once, and a ten-page contract won't work. Pick the most important issue and start there."

This is how it worked with a single mom and her out-of-control fifteen-year-old son, who already had a probation officer because of chronic truancy. Jesse had a violent temper, and his mom, Kelly, admitted to me privately that she was afraid Jesse would hurt her during one of these episodes. So Jesse's violence became the subject of the contract. The next task was to identify realistic consequences that she could enforce. "We will involve Jesse in negotiating the contract," I told Kelly, "but you need to decide in advance what the consequences will be." She told me that she was worried that her son would just defy any consequences. "Then we need to build that possibility into the contract," I replied. "How do we do that?" she asked. I explained to Kelly that she needed to be willing to up the ante with Jesse to a point where the contract would be enforceable and get his attention. I suggested that she communicate with his probation officer and the police to get their support and search for a relative or friend who would be willing to take Jesse in for a while. I think Kelly was shocked. "Are you serious, Dr. Walsh?"

"Yes, I am, Kelly. It doesn't make sense to start a behavior contract with consequences you don't think you can enforce. Jesse will test that right away and if there's no backup, then you reinforce his defiance. Besides, it's unlikely you will have to resort to extremes if Jesse knows you're serious."

Here is a copy of the behavior contract Kelly negotiated with her son:

BEHAVIOR CONTRACT: VIOLENCE

1. This contract is entered into between Jesse and his mother, Kelly, on _____ [date].
2. Whereas I agree that our home should be free of violence, and
3. Whereas I commit myself to resolve differences without violence,
4. Therefore I agree that I will express my anger in an appropriate way.
   a. I will refrain from screaming obscenities in the house.
   b. I will refrain from throwing items in anger.
   c. I will refrain from intentionally breaking any items.
   d. I will not strike or threaten to strike or in any other way injure or threaten to injure anyone in my family.
5. I understand and accept that any failure to uphold this contract will result in my mother immediately contacting my probation officer or immediately contacting the police at her discretion.

I have read, understand and accept the terms of this contract.

_____   _____
        Jesse   Kelly

Jesse came to the next session with his mother. I explained to him that having a behavior contract about violence was nonnegotiable. I told him that his mother and I wanted him to be involved in laying out the terms of the contract, but that the final decision on consequences for noncompliance rested with his mother. Jesse thought the whole thing was ridiculous, but Kelly was able to hold her ground with my support. Jesse eventually signed the contract. A month later he became angry and broke a window during an argument with Kelly. She called the police, who responded quickly, removed Jesse from the house, and talked with him in the squad car for fifteen minutes. They told him that if there was another complaint, they would arrest him. That was the only time Kelly needed to call the police.

DO

- Use a behavior contract for behavior that is out of control.
- Follow through on the consequences spelled out in the contract.

DON'T

- Don't include a consequence you can't follow through on.
- Don't let rude or violent behavior set the rules of the house.

9. What about mouthiness, cursing, and swearing?

When Dan was in kindergarten he arrived home with some salty language. "We don't use words like that in our family," I informed Dan at the dinner table. "They're not polite." A few days later in the car, Brian, age three, used one of the banned words and waited for our reaction. I had almost risen to the bait when I caught Monica's nonverbal "ignore it" signal out of the corner of my eye. The two mischievous brothers were giggling in the backseat, waiting to see if they could get a response. They stopped once they realized that they didn't have an audience.

Children often pick up "dirty" words from older kids and from

TV. Without even knowing the meaning, they will either try them out innocently or as an experiment in getting a rise out of adults. That's why Monica was smart not to react. While ignoring the innocent or teasing use of impolite words makes sense, it's also helpful to find the time to explain calmly, "Some words are not polite and we don't use them in our family. Mom and I don't use them and we don't want you saying them either."

A co-worker of mine has a great technique for dealing with swearing when kids are older. Gwen's family has a family rule: no swearing. And an unusual consequence: If you use a swear word, you have to put a quarter in the No Swear jar. Everybody knows the rule and the consequence. Even Mom and Dad have had to put a quarter in on occasion. At a recent family gathering, when an uncle let a swear word fly, he was immediately informed by the kids that he had to put a quarter in the jar. No arguments, but everybody is careful to watch what they say.

Angry children and teens can say hurtful things. Try not to take them personally, as hard as that is. Calmly state your expectations and consequences and let your child know that you expect him to comply, but that if he chooses not to, he will have to accept the consequences. You have to put your mind into a dispassionate mode, step back from the situation, and remain calm. Take a deep breath and count to ten. Doing this will help you stay out of a power struggle.

Never let your child get his way by yelling, threatening, or screaming. If your child starts yelling during an important discussion about rules, don't try to outshout him or argue. Say, "You don't seem to be able to have a discussion about this right now. When you're ready to discuss this without yelling, we'll talk." Then make sure to come back and finish the talk. The child should not be able to go on to the next activity until the discussion has been completed.

With an older child, a certain amount of mouthiness is to be expected. Just don't respond, or else say, "I know this is hard for you, I don't expect you to like it, but the family rule is . . ."

One of the ways to handle screaming, yelling, and general rudeness is with a respect plan. Here's an example of a plan that Chad and Shannon made up for their sons, Eric and Mark. The parents realized that they had been lax about language, and they did not like the increased yelling, put-downs, and name-calling that was going on. They developed it together and then sat down with the boys to explain it and make sure they knew the consequences. After the family meeting, the plan went up on the refrigerator.

THE RESPECT PLAN

Goals: We will treat one another with greater respect in our family.

The Behaviors:
1. No screaming.
2. No name-calling.
3. No swearing (they listed the words they wanted stopped).
4. No put-downs.

Rewards: When you accumulate five days during which you both have met the goals for respect, then you (Eric and Mark) can each choose a reasonably priced reward, e.g., movie, trip to pizza parlor, visit to batting cage, etc.

Consequences: If there is screaming, name-calling, swearing, or put-downs there will be no television or video games for the following two days.

DO
- Expect your child to be a little mouthy at times.
- Acknowledge your child's feelings.

DON'T
- Don't be a verbal doormat for your child.
- Don't continue a conversation if your child gets abusive.

10. How can I handle my own anger?

Saying no is hard, and even the most patient parent can reach the end of her rope. If you feel that you are going to lose control, you need to do something for yourself first. Step back for a second, take a deep breath, and count to ten. If that doesn't help, a "parent time-out" may be in order. Feel free to tell your kids, "Right now I'm too angry. I need a time-out to calm down. I'll talk with you in ten minutes." This not only gives you the opportunity to collect yourself, it provides good modeling for the kids.

In addition, it's important for all parents, especially single parents, to get support from family and friends. Pick out people you can trust to share your frustrations from time to time. If you feel like you're on the edge, ask trusted relatives or friends if they can serve as an emergency backup for you if you need it. Just knowing that help is a phone call away can be reassuring. Parent support groups and counseling can also help you get through the difficult days.

DO
- Get support from trusted family members or friends.
- Take a time-out to collect yourself if you feel that your anger is going to get out of control.

DON'T
- Don't wait too long to ask for help from family, friends, or professionals.

11. When is it okay to negotiate with my kids?

You can practice a balanced style of parenting and negotiate without compromising your authority. In fact, we want our kids to feel comfortable talking with us and even disagreeing with us at times. This becomes even more important as the kids get older; negotiation is an especially important tool with teenagers. It builds trust between parents and their kids and teaches them to be both respectful and assertive at the same time.

Brian, eleven, came running into the house. "Dad, Jason's father invited me to go with their family to the baseball game. They even have an extra ticket so it won't cost anything. Can I go?"

"It sounds like fun, but you promised to mow the lawn today, so why don't you hurry up and get that done before you can go," I answered.

"I can't, Dad. They're leaving in fifteen minutes. Can't I mow the lawn tomorrow?"

"Do we have a deal that you'll get it mowed tomorrow before you go playing with your friends?" I asked.

"Yes, I promise. Can I go?"

"Yeah, sure. Have a good time. Don't forget to bring your glove."

Brian enjoyed the game and mowed the lawn the next morning.

Be willing to have a give and take with your kids as long as they don't start yelling or speaking rudely; both command and give respect during discussions. You also need to remind your kids of two things: First, although you are willing to negotiate, you retain the authority to make the final decision. Second, some things are non-negotiable.

DO
- Be willing to listen to your children.
- Be willing to negotiate without compromising your authority.
- Teach your child to negotiate respectfully.

DON'T
- Don't negotiate if your child or teen is being disrespectful.
- Don't stick rigidly to a rule if there are legitimate reasons to modify it.

12. What should I do if my kids lie?

The first thing to do is avoid panic. Kids lie. In fact, we all lie. The classic French comedy *The Misanthrope,* by Molière, describes the hilarious and absurd results of an attempt to always be 100 per-

cent honest. Who among us would really tell our boss the unvar-
nished truth if she asked us how we liked her ugly new dress?

Kids lie for the same reasons we all do: to avoid hurting other
people's feelings, to be socially acceptable, to avoid punishment, to
exaggerate our accomplishments, or because it's easy or convenient.

I'm not suggesting that we condone dishonesty; I'm trying to
put it in perspective. Preschool children, for example, confuse fantasy and reality. If you hear a four-year-old, for instance, telling a
cousin about an adventure that you know never happened, don't
fret about nipping a compulsive liar in the bud. Children often fabricate tall tales for an appreciative audience. They usually stop this
kind of "lying" by the time they're seven or eight years old. Don't
confuse deliberate lying with creative storytelling. Simply let him
know that you are aware of the truth and that there is no reason to
fabricate. "Running from a grizzly bear would be exciting, wouldn't
it, Brandon? Now tell your cousin what really happened on our
camping trip."

Your response to intentional, deceptive lying depends on the
child's age and the reason for her lying. It is usually easy to tell by
her body language when a child lies—she will twist around and
avoid eye contact as you listen to her explanation. If her story is
vague or the details change, you can be pretty sure she is lying. Children will lie because of an unmet need, to avoid punishment, to
please a parent, or just out of convenience, as in "Yes, I made my
bed." They need to know that you will check and that lying won't
work. Getting angry at this age only makes the child fearful.

Kids who make up fantasies and brag to friends might have
some emotional need that is not being met. Often, when the parent
uncovers this need, the child's bragging will disappear on its own.
For example, five-year-old Kenny has been telling everyone at day
care that his daddy is going to buy him a new bike and together
they are going to ride all around the country together and buy all
kinds of things. Kenny's dad is a single parent and knows what's behind Kenny's "bragging." He says, "Kenny, I know you've been
lonely and you really want to spend more time with me. A bike ride
all around the country together would be a wonderful trip. But it's

winter right now and pretty cold outside. How about we plan something to do right now? Would you like to start with a story?"
Kenny's real need for attention is satisfied and he knows that his dad
is not angry about his "lying."

As children get older you can still rely on their body language
and the details of their stories. Sometimes, however, lying involves
a more serious issue. If your child has something new, and you
didn't buy it or agree that he could have it, or it's more expensive
than he could afford, it may in fact be stolen. Check on your
hunches; ask the child to explain. If he looks you in the eye and
calmly tells you where the item came from and how he got it, he's
probably telling you the truth. If not, keep digging.

Telling the truth, especially when it's hard, is an important lesson for children. Relationships are based on trust, and lying will
break that trust. Fifteen-year-old Alexis knew her mom would be
angry if she found out that Alexis had gone to an unchaperoned
party Friday night, so she lied about where she'd been. Her mom
had an inkling that something wasn't right when she asked her
about the movie she'd seen Friday night with her friends. She followed up on her suspicion. "Alexis, I need to know what really happened Friday night. Do you want to talk to me about the evening or
shall I call the parent who drove you and your friends?" At this point
Alexis has two options. She can confess that she lied, in which case
her mom should, without getting angry, talk about the need for trust
in their relationship. Her mom can say that she is disappointed and
follow through on the consequence. The logical consequence would
be, "You chose to go somewhere without permission. I need to trust
that you are where you say you are, so you need to stay home for
the rest of the weekend and no friends over."

Alexis's second option is to continue to lie. She could get hostile
and start yelling that she can't believe her mom doesn't trust her. In
this case, Alexis's mother could say, "Alexis, I can see you are upset,
but we are not going to talk if you shout and scream. As your
mother I am going to call Tracy's mom and check on where she
drove you Friday night. We'll talk again when you get yourself
under control. Until then, no privileges." It's important for Alexis's

mother to follow through and make the call. She doesn't need to apologize for acting like a parent. If she finds out that Alexis lied, she should let her daughter know how disappointed she is, and follow through with consequences for both the rule violation and the dishonesty.

Lying to protect someone else can have tragic consequences. From suicide threats to school shootings, from property destruction to personal threats, other kids often know who's planning mischief or dangerous exploits. Sometimes, they don't say anything because they don't realize the potential consequences or don't want to get their friends in trouble. It's important to have conversations with your children early on to help them understand that lying to protect someone only makes the situation worse and can have a tragic outcome. Discuss with your children who they can talk to if they are worried about the actions of friends.

It is even more disturbing when parents aid and abet kids' cover-ups. That's what happened when several star players on a youth hockey team groped a female cheerleader on a late-night bus ride home. When she reported the crime, all the boys denied involvement and knowledge. Team parents, instead of holding their sons accountable either to confess or to provide information, pressured the family to drop the charges. "How can you do this to the team?" they asked the girl's parents.

Exploding in anger about your child's lying can be counterproductive. The child's or teen's subsequent fear of your anger could motivate him to become more deceitful.

That happened with Brad, one of my ninth-grade students, when I met with him and his father, Charlie, at parent conferences. I told Charlie that I enjoyed having Brad in class but was worried that he was falling behind. "What do you mean?" Charlie asked. When I told him that Brad had missed the last three assignments, Charlie stared angrily at Brad. "You told me the other day that you were all caught up," Charlie began. "Did you lie to me?" Brad stared at the floor. "Look at me when I'm talking to you," Charlie said through clenched teeth. "Did you lie to me?" Charlie asked even more loudly. "I told you never to lie to me. I can't stand liars."

I had never seen this side of Charlie before and was stunned by the intensity of his anger. As Brad recoiled in fear and embarrassment, I intervened. "Brad, why don't you let your dad and me talk for a couple of minutes." After Brad left, I waited a few seconds before beginning. "Charlie, I know you really care about your kids, but it might work better if you deal with Brad more calmly."

"I don't want him lying to me," Charlie replied.

"I know you don't, and I don't blame you. But I don't think you'll encourage honesty if you frighten your son. He might become a better liar just to avoid your wrath."

"So you think I should just let him not do his work and then lie about it?" Charlie asked.

"Of course not," I responded. "But intense anger is not the most effective way to encourage responsibility and honesty. You can certainly let Brad know that you're disappointed that he lied, but you also want to keep communication channels open so he will not be afraid to tell you the truth."

"I just get so frustrated when he's not straight with me," Charlie said.

"I understand that you do, but it would be helpful to take a deep breath, count to ten, and try to talk with Brad calmly. If that's not possible, tell him you're too upset and that you'll talk with him when you're calmer."

Charlie and I talked for a few minutes longer before we invited Brad back. Charlie immediately apologized to Brad for flying off the handle. "I'm sorry I blew up earlier. I'm disappointed that you lied, but I want to you to get your assignments back on track and we'll talk about being honest with one another."

DO

- Understand how "lying" varies with each developmental stage.
- Follow your hunches if you think your child or teen is lying.
- Tell your kids about the importance of trust in your relationship.

- Follow through on consequences for any elaborate attempts to deceive.

DON'T
- Don't scream or threaten your child for lying.
- Don't ignore explanations that just don't sound right.

13. Do parents have a role in backing up teachers?

Absolutely. Adults should act as a team if kids are to learn the lessons of self-discipline and self-regulation. The traditional teamwork between parents and teachers has deteriorated in the past generation as society in general has become more adversarial. While it's appropriate for parents to advocate for their children, they should do it in a way that does not undermine the teacher. It's most helpful if you can go into these situations expecting teachers and other school professionals to be part of the team for your child. Our kids need to see a more united front.

Tim was a rude tenth grader who frequently disrupted class with wisecracks and sassy comments. After several girls complained of his lewd comments, the assistant principal called a meeting with his father. Tim and his dad arrived together, and, to my complete surprise, his father immediately went on the offensive. "What's the matter with you people? I thought you were professionals. Don't you know how to relate to young boys? You call this meeting because a couple of girls don't know how to take a joke?"

The assistant principal tried unsuccessfully to explain that the girls' complaints were serious, that teachers were concerned about Tim's attitude and classroom behavior, and that Tim needed to make a change. Tim appeared unfazed, and his faint smile told me how pleased he was that his father was taking his side.

Although Tim was suspended for three days and forbidden to have any further contact with the girls, the real lesson never got through. Subsequent parent meetings to deal with other behavior problems all ended the same way. Eventually Tim transferred to another high school.

Kathryn, an elementary-school teacher, recently told me a similar story. Her fourth-grade student Rachel yelled at her when Kathryn confiscated her iPod because she was listening to it during class. When Kathryn telephoned Rachel's mother that evening, her mother told Kathryn that she had no right to take her daughter's things. "You'd better give Rachel back her iPod tomorrow and quit picking on her. I know one of the school board members, and I'll be on the phone with her tomorrow night if Rachel doesn't come home with her iPod." She hung up before Kathryn could respond. Rachel continued to disrupt Kathryn's class, and the school's attempts to correct her were constantly undermined by her mother.

DO

- Know your child's teacher. Have an open line of communication.
- Know what's going on in your child's classrooms.
- Support your kid's teachers and back them up.
- If you have a concern, talk to the teacher privately, not in front of your child.

DON'T

- Don't assume that your child is always right.
- Don't criticize a teacher in front of your children.
- Don't react without talking to your child's teacher first.

14. Should I ever apologize to my kids?

Kids aren't the only ones who make mistakes. It's important that when we make mistakes we try to repair the relationship with an appropriate apology. It doesn't mean crawling on my hands and knees, but it does mean having the courage to say to my child, "I make mistakes too, and what I said to you, or what I did, was a mistake, and I apologize for it."

Sometimes the apologies are about little things, like the time I had promised to take Brian out to practice catching pop flies when I got home from work. An emergency came up at the end of the day and by the time I got home, it was too late for our trip to the ball field. I could see the disappointment on Brian's face. "Brian, I apologize for getting home late. I had to take care of an emergency at work. I know you were looking forward to catching pop flies, and I'm sorry I disappointed you. Can we do it tomorrow?" Brian accepted my apology and we were on the ball field the next afternoon.

At other times, apologies are about significant mistakes. Audrey had her son, Chad, when she was eighteen. Chad's father moved to the West Coast and was long out of contact when Audrey started dating Marvin, a man she had met at her church-sponsored Bible study. During a dinner date, Audrey told Marvin about a problem she had. "Chad's only seven so I don't want him home alone after school. The neighbor who has been taking care of him is moving."

"I'd be glad to help out," Marvin offered. "I work the night shift so I usually wake up about three o'clock. I could be at your house by three fifteen when Chad gets home and look after him till you get home at five."

Audrey offered a mild protest, Marvin insisted, and the plan was made. A week later, Chad asked Audrey if he could be in the after-school program at his school. "Don't you like being home with Marvin?" Audrey asked.

"It's okay, but I'd rather be with some of my friends," Chad answered.

"Let's stay with this plan till summer," Audrey said. "I want you and Marvin to get to know each other better too."

Chad looked alarmed as he asked, "How come?"

"Well, Marvin may be moving in with us this summer," Audrey replied. "Would you like that?"

"Not really," murmured Chad. "He's kind of mean."

"He is not, Chad." was Audrey's quick response. "He's a very nice man, and he told me that he really likes you."

As the weeks went by Chad became quiet and withdrawn. One night Audrey asked Chad if something was bothering him. "Mom, I don't like Marvin," Chad said. "Can't I stay at school? And please don't let him move in. Please!"

Audrey hesitated, then said, "Chad, you have to give Marvin a chance. He tells me that you guys are getting along great." Chad started to cry, but Audrey held firm. "Chad, that's enough. You and Marvin can be great pals."

Several weeks later Audrey got off work early and decided to surprise Marvin and Chad. She picked up a pizza on the way home and tiptoed in the back door with her surprise. Her stomach immediately knotted up as she listened to Marvin cursing at her son. She raced into the room and found Chad cowering in the corner with Marvin towering over him. "What's going on?" she screamed. Marvin stammered that Chad had been mouthing off. "Leave right now," Audrey ordered. Marvin protested, but Audrey screamed at him, "Get out of our house!"

By the time of our meeting Audrey had learned that Marvin had verbally abused Chad for weeks and hit him at least three times. He had threatened Chad with, "You'll be sorry if you tell your mom." Before we finished that first session, Audrey pulled Chad onto her lap and, amid sobs and tears, apologized to him. "Chad, I can't tell you how sorry I am. I'm sorry I didn't listen to you when you tried to tell me Marvin was mean. I'm sorry you had to go through this. I hope you can forgive me. I will never let anything bad happen to you again." Chad hugged his mom with all his might.

DO
- Apologize if needed.
- Give yourself a break.

DON'T
- Don't overreact.
- Don't ignore repair work you need to do on a relationship.

Twelve

Taming the Gimmes

One Sunday morning Monica and I were sharing coffee and doughnuts with a friend. His twelve-year-old, Jared, walked into the kitchen, so I asked how he was doing. Jared shrugged his shoulders and walked away, obviously in a sour mood. I turned to his father, Al, and asked, "What's with Jared? It looks like he's on the bitter bus this morning."

"I think he's *driving* the bitter bus this morning," answered Al. "He's still ticked off from yesterday. After lunch Jared asked if we could take a walk. I tried to hide my shock since walking with me is usually the last thing on his Saturday list of things to do. I said sure and asked if his sister Kelly could come. He told me he wanted to go alone because there was something he wanted to discuss with me. Kelly wasn't interested in going anyway so the two of us headed out.

"Jared began by asking me how work was going, so I knew something was up. He was chatting away and being really friendly. After a few minutes I asked him what he wanted to talk about. It didn't take long to figure out where this was going. He reminded me that his birthday was less than three weeks away and he had been doing some thinking. Now that he was getting older, he thought that it would be a good idea if he discussed his wish list well in advance so I could get him the things he really wanted and needed.

"I agreed that this was a good idea and asked him what he had in mind. I'm not sure if I was amused, shocked, or both as Jared took the next five minutes to describe the completely equipped electronic entertainment center he envisioned in his bedroom.

"'Now that I'm going to be a teenager,' he began, 'it would be really nice if I could start to have some of the things all my friends have. It would be awesome to get a TV, an Xbox 360, and a laptop computer.'"

"Can you believe it?" Al asked. "I mean, we must have been talking over a thousand dollars' worth of stuff. As soon as he saw the look on my face he went to plan B. He wanted me to know that he was being reasonable because he didn't expect it all at once. He thought that the combination of birthday and Christmas presents could get him there over time, and he would be cool with that."

"So what did you say?" I asked.

"Well, of course I said no. I tried to be pleasant, but Jared's friendly mood disappeared quickly. He practically demanded to know why he couldn't have everything that his friends had. I listened to his protests and then calmly gave him two reasons for my No. I told him that his wish list was too extravagant and expensive and, second, I wanted all the media entertainment in a family area of the house. You should have seen his reaction when I said 'extravagant.' He told me that I was so out of touch and old-fashioned."

Since Al and Ronda are divorced, Jared divides his time between his father's and mother's houses. So Monica asked, "Do you think he'll try the same thing with Ronda?"

"It won't do him any good. I called Ron right away, and she had the same reaction I had. We're on the same page on this one." Al told us that the walk had ended with Jared in a funk and that he was still pouting.

Although Al was shocked at Jared's wish list, it isn't that unusual. I know some of Jared's friends and he wasn't exaggerating when he said that they all had fully equipped bedrooms. Jared shares a case of the gimmes with millions of other kids.

New Set of Challenges

We keep hearing that modern technology makes our lives easier. In some ways, that's true. For example, chores like washing clothes, cooking, and cleaning are much easier. The job of parenting, how-ever, is a lot more difficult. One of the tougher new challenges is that the twin-headed goliath of media and advertising has com-bined to give our kids an ever more virulent case of the gimmes.

We know when an influenza virus is making the rounds, so we can be extra careful to protect our health. The virus of the gimmes is harder to notice, however, because our consumer culture is like the air we breathe—we often don't notice it. In chapter 2 I explained how the media-advertising tandem promotes the cultural messages of "more, easy, fast, and fun." In this chapter we are going to delve deeper into the impact of the message repeated to our kids over a million times a year when they demand: "Gimme more stuff."

Parent Tool Kit: Taming the Gimmes

Use these questions to assess whether you have a clear plan for how to deal with the gimmes.

PARENT TOOL KIT
Taming the Gimmes

Yes	No		
☐	☐	1.	My spouse and I agree on our rules for spending.
☐	☐	2.	We put limits on our children's exposure to commercial media.
☐	☐	3.	We avoid impulse buying for our kids.
☐	☐	4.	We distinguish between "needs" and "wants."
☐	☐	5.	We have expectations that our kids will share their money with others in need.
☐	☐	6.	We have worked out a savings plan with our children.

Yes	No		
☐	☐	7.	We resist media's pressure to buy the latest "new thing."
☐	☐	8.	We set a budget for our kids' needs and stick to it.
☐	☐	9.	We monitor our children's spending.
☐	☐	10.	We buy within our budget and do not buy everything our child wants.

Having a clear spending plan for your children helps you ward off the gimmes and will greatly help your family budget. This is a tough but important No for kids to learn. With it come financial responsibility, patience, and generosity.

Branded Kids

Nike . . . Dr. Martens . . . Abercrombie & Fitch . . . J. Crew . . . Old Navy . . .

These names are familiar across the country, conjuring up images of status and coolness for millions of American kids. How did these brands get endowed with such power? They bought it with millions of dollars of advertising. Companies spend a remarkable amount of time, energy, creativity, and money crafting the message to persuade us to buy their brand over another. As my friend Nathan Dungan, founder and president of Share Save Spend, an organization that advocates healthy financial habits, sums it up: "The predominant financial message young people receive from our consumer culture is to spend, spend, spend."

In workshops, I often ask people to complete the following sentence: "Winston tastes good like a _____."

Even though they haven't heard that message since 1971, when tobacco advertisements were banned from TV and radio, participants are stunned to see how many people are able to complete the sentence, with "cigarette should." It's even more startling to see how many people who weren't even alive in 1971 can complete the Winston jingle. The message was so well communicated and established itself so deeply in the culture that millions can instantly recall it almost four decades later.

Powerful, ubiquitous messages to buy engulf us all day long and are increasingly aimed at kids. An infamous bank robber of the 1950s was asked why he kept robbing banks. His quick and simple reply was: "Because that's where the money is." That Willie Sutton answer is the reason Madison Avenue likes kids. And advertisers didn't just discover children and teens. After all, youngsters in the 1950s wore Davy Crockett caps and Mickey Mouse ears by the millions. But the advertising industry learned an important lesson about young consumers in 1991. The recession that year hit the advertising industry especially hard and revenues plummeted. During this period there was only one bright spot: children's television programming sold out. Advertisers saw that there were two reasons for the importance of this undertapped market: the purchasing power of children and their influence on adult spending.

The Children and Teen Market

Our kids collectively have a purchasing power that is unprecedented for their age group. Last year, kids four to twelve had an estimated combined spending power of nearly $45 billion, according to the Mintel market research firm, and that figure is predicted to hit $52 billion by 2008. Teens as a group were expected to spend a combined $160 billion, based on projections by Teenage Research Unlimited. No matter how you break down the numbers, the verdict is very clear: This is big, big business.

Another important reason why advertisers target kids is to establish brand loyalty before a competitor does, so there is a race to attract younger and younger consumers. You cannot fault their logic: If they create a Pepsi drinker at the age of three, then Coke will have a hard time converting that child later on, and Pepsi will have many years to enjoy a return on its advertising investment as that child grows into adolescence and adulthood and even—this is how these companies think—into old age.

But there's a special reason companies target children—the nag factor. The real money in the kids' market resides not so much in the kids' own spending power, although that is considerable. It's found in the kids' "pester power." James McNeal, Texas A&M professor emeritus, has studied the economic impact of kids for decades. He figures that the purchasing influence of kids, the nag factor, is at least five times greater than their actual purchasing power. That means, based on the more than $200 billion in direct spending by kids detailed above, the nag factor holds sway over $1 trillion in sales per year, which corresponds to 10 percent of the annual U.S. economy. That's real money.

The marketers know that no one is better positioned to influence family spending than children. They've done the studies. They know, for example, that in 95 percent of families with children, the kids choose which brand of frozen pizza to buy. If I'm a busy parent wheeling my shopping cart around the supermarket in a big hurry, what do I care about the difference between Tony's, DiGiorno, and Freschetta, assuming the price is roughly the same? I don't, so it is much easier to take the path of least resistance and buy the one little Johnny or Isabella keeps urging me to buy.

Kids' growing influence over family purchases springs from adults' busier and busier schedules, which leave less and less time to get things done. The last thing a harried parent wants is a hassle in the supermarket. A common scenario unfolds like this: A meeting at the office went an hour longer than planned, so now you're running late. You just picked up your five-year-old from day care on your way home from work and have to make a quick stop at the supermarket. You take the crumpled list out of your pocket and begin to make your rounds. The first item on the list is paper towels, so you reach for the first brand you see—let's say Viva— but before you can even drop it into your shopping cart, your five-year-old raises a fuss.

"No, don't get Viva," he tells you. "Get Brawny. They're a lot better."

He has no idea which is better, Brawny or Viva or Bounty, but he has seen those Brawny TV commercials and they had a lasting impact. So is it worth it for you to stand there and argue with your five-year-old about which paper towels to buy? Not if you're in a hurry, already frustrated, and still have a dozen other items to track down, knowing full well that once you start arguing over paper towel brands, you will soon be arguing over orange juice brands and laundry detergent brands and who knows what else. So what do you do? You put the Viva paper towels back on the shelf, grab Brawny, and you're on your way. No big deal.

Ever More Sophisticated

This is not a big deal for you, but given the millions of shoppers buying paper towels, it is a big deal for Georgia Pacific, the maker of Brawny. Given the enormous amount of money at stake, producers of a wide array of products invest heavily in slick and sophisticated pitches to children. The average young person will endure twenty-three million advertising impressions before he reaches his twenty-first birthday, according to *American Demographics* magazine. Major ad agencies now have entire divisions dedicated to research and advertising to kids; other major agencies now specialize in the youth market. Unknown before 1990, professional conferences and conventions that are dedicated to helping professionals figure out how to market more effectively to kids crowd the calendar. The annual Kid Power conventions tout themselves as "the only conference dedicated solely to reaching the children's two-to-twelve market." Kid Power event spin-offs now take place all over the world, from the United Arab Emirates to South Africa to Australia.

Seven major advertising agencies banded together in 1998 to create the Golden Marble Awards, a type of advertising Oscars, to honor commercials specifically aimed at children and teens. The agencies, including such giants of the industry as Saatchi & Saatchi and Ogilvy & Mather, established these awards for advertising intended for children six to thirteen years old, identified as the demographic group too young for *South Park* but too old for *Teletubbies*. But, as the *New York Times* noted in an April 1998 article about the Golden Marble Awards, even then there was a "rising tide of complaints about what are perceived as overaggressive efforts by agencies and advertisers to sell products to children." The awards turned into a lightning rod for criticism of advertising targeted at children and ultimately were discontinued after only four years.

As the controversy over advertising to children has escalated, advertisers have become sneakier. In 2005, I exposed a new stealth-marketing tactic called "buzzploitation," in which paid professionals infiltrate Internet chat rooms to promote products. While many firms do this in an overt, responsible way, some use kids as the actual stealth marketers. The marketers create enticing Web sites that attract minors by offering gifts and the opportunity to meet new friends if they register as "secret agents." Once enrolled, the kids receive free products to promote to their friends, family, and peers online and offline. One firm recruits girls as young as eight years old to promote products to their unsuspecting friends at slumber parties. Kids can sign up without parental permission and they're told not to reveal their "secret agent" identity.

As if parents do not have enough to worry about already with advertisers, the trends for the future are truly alarming. James McNeal, author of *The Kids Market: Myths and Realities,* found that kids age four to twelve doubled their spending each decade from the 1960s to the 1980s—but in the 1990s their spending tripled. The top purchases for children and teens are treats, toys, apparel, entertainment, electronics, and cosmetic products.

Taken one at a time, these purchases are not worrisome. But add them all up and you have two growing problems: overspending and the gimme mentality.

Spending More and More

Kids' spending and the influence they have on the family's spending add up in a hurry and often catch families by surprise. The average family after-tax savings rate keeps dropping. In 1992 it was 9 percent, in 2002 it dropped to 3.4 percent, and in 2005 it dropped to zero. In early 2006 it dropped below zero for the first time since the Great Depression. As mentioned in chapter 2, kids today spend 500 percent more than their parents did at the same age, even adjusted for inflation. The average amount spent per child on back-to-school shopping is now five hundred dollars.

Kids are spending more and more money but understanding less and less about the basics of making good financial decisions. In 1997 a financial literacy survey was given to high school seniors— their average score was 57 percent. In 2002 the average score fell to 50 percent.

A recent National Public Radio report explained that the debt that high school students carry on credit cards drives down their FICO score, the measure widely used to determine a person's credit worthiness, which affects their future ability to get a job, car, or home. Most teens don't know they have a FICO score, let alone that that score follows them around for years, long after their SAT scores and GPAs are forgotten.

The outsized appetites created by aggressive marketing during childhood and adolescence quickly sink kids into deep financial trouble when they start living on their own. Accustomed to spending beyond their means, the average college undergraduate in the United States in 2004 owed $2,169 on credit cards. The average college senior now has four credit cards that collectively run up almost $3,000 in debt, according to Nellie Mae. The picture isn't much better for the next age group, twenty-five- to thirty-four-year-olds, who, as *BusinessWeek* reported, average nearly $5,000 in credit card debt, resulting mostly from impulse buying and overspending. In 1991, according to government reports, 60,000 young people under twenty-five filed for bankruptcy. By 2001 there were 150,000 filings by those under twenty-five. The fastest-growing segment of people filing for bankruptcy is the age group twenty-five to thirty-four, which, according to government reports, now numbers more than 175,000 a year. Education loans, another debt burden, do not disappear in bankruptcy; students' accounts are frozen, but they still need to pay back the loans.

The Gimmes

The gimmes make it very difficult for kids to learn No. Marketers and advertisers aren't just selling things; they are promoting a set of values. Although most Americans meet all our basic needs and then some, we hear every day that we need more. We are seduced into thinking that our lives will be better if only we buy one more product, receive one more service, or have one more experience.

We parents are not immune to these messages. And many messages targeting us try to get into our wallets through our love for our children. Caring, if we take the advertisers' word for it, is synonymous with giving and spending.

So many of us are lured into thinking that one of the best ways to show love is to give things—money, opportunity, and entertainment. If we go down that path, however, we'll never be good enough. There will always be something else to give our kids. Get your son a new bike—then he "needs" a car. Take your daughter to an amusement park—what she really "deserves" is a cruise.

Indulging the gimmes undercuts some of the important character assets that our kids need even more than they need things. If our kids always get everything they want, how will they learn to deal with disappointment? How can we expect them to put another person's needs ahead of their own? How will they know how to delay gratification? How will they ever be satisfied with what they have? The gimmes don't just drain the bank account. They can cripple our children's chances of becoming happy, healthy, self-sufficient, generous adults.

Diagnosing the Gimmes

So, what do we do? First, find out if your kids have a case of the gimmes. Here are two activities to try with your kids to diagnose them:

The What-if activity. When I taught high school I often did a simple exercise with my students that effectively helped them examine their values. The results may give you and your kids an idea of how the gimmes are affecting you, and can generate some important family conversations about money and values.

Here's the exercise. Ask your son or daughter to answer this question: *What would you do if someone gave you a hundred dollars?* If you're doing this with a teenager, make the amount a thousand dollars.

Ask her to write down her answer so that you can discuss it. Here are some questions to guide that conversation:

- Did you decide to use the money all for yourself or did you use any of the money for someone else?
- Did you decide to save any of the money?
- Would you spend it on things you need or on things you want?
- Was the imaginary amount enough or did you find yourself wanting more?

Toy or clothes inventory. Another way to tell whether your kids have too much is very simple. If your children are younger, spend some time with them doing a "toy inventory." For teens it might make more sense to substitute clothes for toys. Take a sheet of paper and make seven columns with these headings.

Toy	How Many?	How Often?	Last Used?	Still Need?	Still Want?	Give Away?

Then complete the inventory with your child. If he or she is too young to write, you can serve as the scribe. Older kids can do the writing themselves. Depending on the toy or clothes collection your child has, this can be a long process, so feel free to break it up into installments.

1. Write down the toys (clothes) you own.
2. How many of each do you have?
3. How often do you play with (or wear) them? This

question is important. You and your son or daughter
may discover that he or she has toys or clothing that
are never used.

4. When is the last time you played with it (or wore it)?
5. Do you still need it? Why?
6. Do you still want it? Why?
7. If you have some things that you hardly ever, or never,
   use, is it time to give it away?

The inventory not only helps kids start to distinguish needs
from wants, it helps them become aware of how much extra they
have. If they have extra, you can introduce—or suggest—that they
share with others. Agencies such as Goodwill and The Arc and
homeless shelters are always happy to accept donations.

Taming the Gimmes

I have learned a lot about taming the gimmes from Nathan Dungan, a former financial planner working for a Fortune 500 company. Fifteen years ago Nathan specialized in helping families
figure out their financial goals and in developing and implement-
ing the strategies to achieve them. As the years went by, he
began to notice that more and more families were overspending,
so, instead of future planning, he had to spend time helping them
right their leaking financial boat. He also realized that a lot of
their kids were getting into serious financial problems themselves
as soon as they were on their own. Parents asked him to help
their college-age sons and daughters, many of whom were already deep in credit card debt and some of whom were considering bankruptcy, to understand personal finance.

Although Nathan doesn't use these words, he developed an ex-
pertise in helping clients "tame the gimmes." He became so good at
it that today he travels the country giving workshops from coast to
coast on his approach to financial sanity: Share, Save, Spend. His
book *Prodigal Sons and Material Girls: How Not to Be Your Child's
ATM* (Wiley, 2003) has helped thousands. I'd like to share Nathan's

approach because it is simple, sound, and a consistent way to say no to the gimmes.

Share, Save, Spend—Share

Sharing comes first in Nathan Dungan's model for healthy financial habits because it instills an important value in children: helping others. Sharing is a potent antidote to the cultural messages that promote a "me first" attitude. When my three kids were young, our church organized volunteers every week to cook and serve a meal at a downtown soup kitchen. Monica made sure that our kids took part. We both explained that not everyone was as fortunate as they were and we all have a responsibility to help out in whatever way we can. To this day our kids have positive memories of those hours they spent talking and laughing with the people who came in from the cold Minnesota winter for a bowl of hot soup and some good company.

Ten-year-old Emily and her friends saw the powerful TV images of the devastation from Hurricane Katrina and the families left homeless. One news anchor asked the public to help, and an address for donations flashed on the screen. The next day Emily and her friends became an eight-kid relief team. They sold Kool-Aid, baked and sold cookies, and did odd jobs around the neighborhood; in two days they had more than a hundred dollars. They converted it into a money order and sent it off with a letter. Three weeks later they received a handwritten thank-you from a woman telling Emily and her friends how helpful and important their gift was. At that moment Emily learned the value of sharing.

Share, Save, Spend—Save

Saving comes next in Dungan's model because the third element, spending, is so easy, but learning to save takes work. Saving teaches discipline, patience, planning—all good values for kids to learn. It's important to teach kids how saving works, what it means to earn interest on a savings account or investment, and how this can add up in the long run. Saving is an antidote to the "gotta have it now" mentality and another way to teach kids No without ever having to use the word.

My niece Meaghan combined sharing and saving. During the tenth grade she learned of a service project in El Salvador from family friends. She was excited at the prospect of traveling to a foreign country, speaking Spanish, and helping to build a community center in a poor village. Meaghan kicked her earning, saving, and fundraising plan into high gear. The sharing experience was so positive that she started saving for the following year's trip as soon as she returned home. My nephew Philip was bitten by the sharing and saving bug, too. Inspired by his older sister, Phil found his own travel, learning, and service project. He launched a baby- and pet-sitting service through the Internet and saved enough for a trip to Guatemala.

Share, Save, Spend—Spend

Spending is the easy and fun part. We all like to buy things that we enjoy, but there are important lessons about No in the spending part of the model as well. Basically, you need to have a budget.

Decide in advance your parameters for spending. Our son Brian learned this lesson the hard way when he was twelve years old. The hot brand of jeans that back-to-school shopping season was Girbaud. Brian thought they were cool, and he was convinced that all the kids would be wearing them when classes resumed. He absolutely had to have these jeans. The problem was that Girbaud jeans were at least three times as expensive as other, generic brands. That afternoon at the mall was tough. Brian begged for Girbaud jeans and I had to come up with an imaginative solution to end the standoff.

"Brian, we have budgeted sixty dollars for back-to-school pants," I said. "You can either buy one pair of Girbaud jeans for sixty dollars or three pair of these other jeans and still have money left over for a shirt."

Brian's response was instantaneous. "I want the Girbauds."

I made sure he understood that if he blew all sixty dollars on one pair of Girbauds, when they were in the wash he would have to wear his old pants. He didn't care. So I let Brian spend sixty dollars on one pair of jeans. Within a couple of weeks he was complaining that he didn't have enough pants for school. I had to remind him of our deal.

"Christmas is still three months away," I said. "If you really need more jeans for school, you can hope you get them for a Christmas present."

Brian's Christmas list that year included some jeans. I asked him what brand he wanted. "Any brand," he said. He had learned his lesson. As an adult, Brian is now a savvy shopper. I was shopping with him a couple of months ago while he was home for a visit, and I had to smile to myself when I heard him put something back on the shelf with the words, "I'm not stupid enough to pay that much just to have their label on it."

Thank-Yous

Children with a bad case of the gimmes have a high sense of entitlement and a low sense of appreciation. One antidote for that imbalance is to make sure that children appropriately thank parents, relatives, and friends for gifts, both big and small. Jean Illsley Clarke, Connie Dawson, and David Bredehoft describe a wonderful strategy in their book *How Much Is Enough?* (Marlowe, 2004).

> Seven-year-old Joshua had a lot of relatives who overdid it on birthday and holiday presents. His parents were concerned about Joshua's case of the gimmes so they came up with a plan. They asked the relatives to send a picture of themselves with only one gift for the next birthday. Joshua got to open the first gifts the afternoon before the big day. His parents told him he could not open another gift for two hours. He whined and pleaded, but his parents held fast. They exam-

ined each gift with him and talked about how he would use it and how he would care for it. Together they looked at the picture of the givers and imagined what they had thought when they chose the gift. The remainder of the two hours was time for Joshua to play with the gift and to write a thank-you note, draw a thank-you card, or make a thank-you phone call. Joshua couldn't open the next gift until the thank you was finished. They completed the gift opening on his birthday. Instead of feeding his sense of entitlement Joshua learned something about patience and gratitude.

Allowances and *No*

I often receive questions from parents about allowances. Are they a good idea? If so, when should you start? How much makes sense? Should an allowance be tied to chores? I'm always a little puzzled by the controversies that some child development experts stir up around the topic. Since there is no research on the subject, I favor a commonsense approach that reinforces lessons that our kids need to learn.

I think allowances are a good idea because they help children and teens develop money-management skills. They can start making the Share, Save, Spend philosophy part of their lives. Allowances also eliminate the problem of kids treating their parents like cash machines. Children usually start to understand the concept of money as they start school, so that seems a good age to start allowances. There is no hard-and-fast rule on how much, but a common practice is to make the amount equal to half the child's age until they reach adolescence, when an amount equal to the age makes more sense. I favor weekly allowances because a month is too long for most children to manage.

An allowance can be a tool for saying no to the gimmes if you stick to it. Parents should cover the basics like food and clothing, but allowances should take care of treats, arcade games, and other extras. I can't for the life of me understand why some experts say that you should never tie allowances to chores. It seems to me that one of the benefits is to teach responsibility. It's a lot of work to keep a household running, and kids should do their share. If they don't, then why should they just have money handed to them?

My colleague Gwen and her husband, Jon, have a clever way to end arguments about chores and reinforce lessons of responsibility at the same time. Bobbie and Jessie receive allowances but they don't collect them until they turn in their "work cards." Gwen explained the system to me: "We have printed up cards with the list of chores that each girl is responsible for. When they finish the job, they initial that spot on the card, and then when it passes inspection, Jon or I sign off in our space. When the card is completed, they get their allowance." I asked if there was partial payment for partial completion. "Nope. It's all or nothing. It was Jon's idea and it works like a charm."

DO

- Set a good example of sharing, saving, and spending.
- Suggest that friends and relatives give more modest presents and put the extra money into a college fund.
- Talk to your child before you go to the store about what purchases are allowed.
- Set up a savings plan with your child.
- Expect and support your child in sharing with those in need. Help your child find a worthy cause to donate to or donate at your place of worship.
- Set up a budget for what to spend on your child for clothes, education, activities, etc. Stick to it.
- Listen to your child or teen when she tells you what she needs for school or a special occasion.
- Talk with your child about his needs and wants. Have your child help pay for or work toward a special purchase.
- Make sure your child sends thank-you messages for gifts.

DON'T

- Don't give in to whining. Say no.
- Don't bust your budget buying the latest advertiser's "must have" for your child.

- Don't buy your child everything he wants.
- Don't go into credit card debt.
- Don't let your teen be financially illiterate.

What do I want to continue?

_____

_____

_____

What do I want to change?

_____

_____

_____

Thirteen

Raising MediaWise Kids

Several years ago I had the opportunity to partner with the Minneapolis NBC television affiliate, KARE 11, to conduct a little experiment. What started as a project to see if TV would influence children's behavior turned into an Emmy winner, spotlighting media's powerful effect on children. We called the experiment "Barney vs. Power Rangers." Working with a local day-care center, we installed hidden cameras throughout the facility's main playroom, giving us a great view of the kids' activities and behaviors. The week before, I had met with their parents to secure permission and explain what we wanted to do. The first day we were going to play the popular kids' TV program *Barney* and record the kids' behaviors. The second day we planned to show *Power Rangers* and watch the kids' behavior again. The parents were eager to see how their children would react. The next week the KARE 11 crew installed the cameras in the playroom as planned and I sat with the parents in the next room, watching the TV monitors as they recorded their children in front of the glowing screen.

For anyone who has spent a lot of time with little kids, the results of the first day shouldn't be surprising. The moment the day-care provider slipped in the first DVD of *Barney,* all the kids immediately sat down in front of the TV, transfixed by the image of the lovable purple dinosaur bouncing around on the screen. Before long, every child was standing up, marching in time, and singing the familiar songs enthusiastically and in unison. All the kids were having a great time copying whatever Barney did.

None of the parents seemed surprised to see their children's behavior and most agreed that *Barney* had taught their children a number of good things, from dance moves to counting to colors. One mother, Susan, claimed enthusiastically, "You wouldn't believe how well my daughter remembers songs from that show, she has all of them memorized and she's only three!"

The next day, many parents also had expectations for what they thought would happen. Cheri was particularly convinced that her daughter, Hannah, would not be quite as enthusiastic about the violent *Power Rangers* show as she had been about family-friendly *Barney*. She related that her daughter gets easily scared and never watched shows like this at home.

The day-care provider started the DVD and, just as they had the day before, all the kids quickly quieted down and sat transfixed in front of the screen. A couple of them looked quite alarmed by all of the fast action and loud noises as the Power Rangers started beating the living daylights out of their adversaries. The parents sitting around me were already murmuring their approval as their kids sat looking stunned and alarmed. However, within five minutes, the previously frightened kids transformed into mini–Power Rangers, throwing punches and grabbing blocks to use as fake tasers. Before we knew it, the circle of calm kids watching TV disintegrated into chaotic child warfare and roughhousing. Hannah was a little more reluctant to get involved, just as her mother had expected. She sat on the sidelines, watching anxiously as her friends ran around the room. Her reluctance didn't last long, however. No sooner were Cheri's words, "I told you so," out of her mouth than Hannah walked over and kicked her best friend with her finest version of a Power Ranger karate kick. Cheri gasped as Hannah started wheeling around the room, delivering blows to everyone in her path. "I can't believe it! I've never seen her act like this."

The difference in mood from day one with *Barney* to day two with the *Power Rangers* was like the difference between night and day. This is predictable behavior, called "copying." I clearly remember the first time my firstborn son, Dan, smiled a genuine smile in response to my own. I was exhilarated and soon learned that Dan would copy just about everything that I did, from rooting for the same football teams to pretending to read the newspaper at three as he sat next to me on the couch.

As we learned in chapter 3, copying behavior is a natural response that stems from the "mirror cells" in our brains. These cells also help explain why television and other media have such quick effects on behavior. Numerous studies further prove that exposure to media messages directly affects how kids act. The consequences are often disturbing. A study published on September 3, 2004, in the medical journal *Pediatrics,* titled "Watching Sex on Television Predicts Adolescent Initiation of Sexual Behavior," reported that teens who watch the most programming containing sex have sexual intercourse earlier, much earlier, than their peers who don't watch as much sex on TV.

The *Pediatrics* study shows that TV does in fact teach and is doing a very effective job—even when it is teaching behavior that goes against your family's values and standards of behavior. The promiscuous, disease-free sexual escapades of so many TV characters are hard to ignore. The message that recreational sex is both normal and desirable for teens is sent and received, and the adolescents who are bombarded with this message go out into the world and act on it. Studies also prove that media promote alcohol and drug use, aggressive behavior, and many more unhealthy teen trends.

Does this mean, however, that every child who watches *Power Rangers* is immediately going to copy every action on the screen? Of course not. Despite coming equipped with mirror cells, children are not mimicking robots but real people with different personalities, judgments, experiences, and levels of self-control. Some children will be more likely to jump up and immediately copy a behavior modeled in front of them. Others will need a little more prodding. Now let's go back to Hannah, the sweet girl who astonished her mother by going over and kicking her best friend. Explaining why Hannah was compelled to join in the fight goes a long way in helping us understand the power of television and other media to create and reinforce norms.

It was only after Hannah realized that a majority of the *other children* in the room were kicking and fighting that she joined in. This is a more subtle form of copying, a version of peer pressure. Hannah didn't kick her friend because she was copying the television program. She joined in because all the other kids were doing it. When the norm in the day-care center changed from "Have a nice day" to "Make my day," Hannah felt compelled to follow suit. From the first baby years, when we mimic our caretakers by sticking out our tongues and smiling, indeed well into adulthood, the media create and nourish cultural norms that guide our behavior, thoughts, and decisions.

Parent Tool Kit: MediaWise Kids

Media have taken over the lives of many kids, who spend more time in front of screens than doing anything else except sleeping. We adults have to learn to say no and limit their exposure to media and their use of them. Use this kit to take stock of the role media play in your family.

PARENT TOOL KIT
MediaWise Kids

Yes	No		
☐	☐	1.	We have family rules limiting how much time our kids use media.
☐	☐	2.	We keep TVs, video games, and computers out of kids' bedrooms.
☐	☐	3.	We keep media off during meals.
☐	☐	4.	We pay attention to media ratings.
☐	☐	5.	We keep up with technology changes so we know what media are popular with kids.

Yes	No		
☐	☐	6.	We have clear rules about Internet use.
☐	☐	7.	Our kids, including our teens, know not to give out personal information on the Internet.
☐	☐	8.	We know what video games our kids are playing.

Answering yes to these statements shows that you understand that media are powerful forces of benefit or harm and that it's our job to decide what the effect will be.

If We Blink, Media Will Change

In chapter 2 we talked about the power of media to create a culture of Yes by sending and reinforcing messages that everything should be easy, fast, and fun. Now we're going to focus on how media have become such a prominent feature in kids' lives and discuss both the challenges and opportunities associated with growing up during the "media revolution." Finally, we are going to discuss how we can say yes to some media and when to say no so that we can set kids up for success off-screen.

Media are powerful. They are not necessarily good or bad, but powerful. Media exert their power over our kids in three ways. First, kids are born to copy, and media provide ready models for our kids to imitate. Second, media define social norms. Third, stories are powerful and the media have become the dominant storytellers in our kids' lives. What's more, media keep evolving, getting more and more powerful all the time. Fifteen years ago, the average American child spent twenty-eight hours each week in front of a screen, and most of that was television viewing. Today that same kid's screen time has risen to forty-four hours per week, and TV is just one segment of the media pie, along with video games and computer use, including Internet surfing, instant messaging, blogging, and hanging out in Internet gathering places like MySpace and Facebook.

The lines between technologies have already begun to evaporate. Sophisticated games are available on mobile phones, which also serve as text messengers, Internet devices, and cameras. I was proud a few months ago to upgrade my cell phone, something that my three grown children had been urging me to do for a couple of years. I brought the phone home, took it out of the box, and knew I was in trouble when I saw that the owner's manual was four times bigger than the phone. My old cell phone sent and received phone calls. My new one has more functions than I will ever use. It provides Internet access, text messaging, a fully equipped digital camera, music library, and a warehouse for all sorts of data, including appointment calendars, personal directories, and a photo gallery. I didn't get the model that records movies. I wouldn't be surprised if next year's version does my dishes. Whether we are "techies" or not, digital technologies are a substantial part of daily life. The industry has already set its sights on a convergence of the Internet, TV, movies, music, sports, and, of course, advertising, so that entertainment, commerce, socializing, and business can all take place on one screen in your home or in your hand.

Media, Media Everywhere

The typical eight- to eighteen-year-old American grows up in a house with an average of 3.6 CD or tape players, 3.5 TVs, 3.3 radios, 2.9 VCR/DVD players, 2.1 video game consoles, and 1.5 computers. In fact, more American households have a television set than have a functioning telephone. Many young people don't even have to leave the comfort of their own bedrooms to enjoy media. Two-thirds have TVs in their bedrooms, half have VCR/DVD players and video game consoles, and nearly one-third have computers in their rooms. The media barrage doesn't stop, of course, when young people leave home. More and more kids just take their screens and their music with them. Almost two-thirds of youth today have portable CD or MP3 players, and half have handheld video-game players. The number of kids who have portable media devices will no doubt continue to rise as more parents buy their children cell phones to keep in touch and as iPods continue to rise in popularity.

Media: A Full-Time Job Without the Benefits

This past summer my wife, Monica, and I were hiking at Gooseberry Falls State Park, on Minnesota's north shore of Lake Superior. It was a beautiful morning, with the bank of fog on the lake in a standoff with a crystal-clear morning at the shore. Monica stopped into the bathroom at the campground. A mother was in the bathroom recharging a portable DVD player. As Monica washed her hands the young mother explained that her three-year-old daughter could fall asleep only if she was watching a movie on her portable DVD player. The mother just sighed and said to Monica, "Here we are in this beautiful place and all she wants to do is watch movies." Monica didn't say what she was thinking, but what she found saddest was that the mother could not say no to her daughter.

With the number of screens in our kids' line of vision, it is no wonder that kids spend more hours with media than any other activity except sleeping. The way things are going, I won't be surprised when even sleeping falls second to media consumption as the number one activity of American kids. Children two to seventeen spend ten times more time in the company of some form of media than they do with their own mothers, and by the time they graduate from high school, kids will have spent three times as many hours sitting in front of a screen as they have spent in the classroom.

Given the incredible teaching power of media and the sheer number of hours American youth spend under their spell day in and day out, we adults should be paying closer attention to media's effect on kids. Many of today's TV programs and video games are peppered with titillating sex and grotesque violence. And though teaching isn't the primary goal of a lot of movies, shows, and games, their only lesson seems to be violence, disrespect, and crude language. It is more important now than ever before to help kids develop the ability to use media in ways that benefit their health and growth.

No Exercise=No Fitness

Most kids these days accomplish amazing things without leaving the comfort of their homes. On any old Saturday they might fly a plane, win a championship soccer game, *and* climb to the top of an ancient pyramid. And this is all before lunch! Who knows what the afternoon will hold. No doubt a fearless fight with space aliens, a harrowing car race through narrow city streets, and the chance to construct an entire city complete with parks, a police force, and energy plants. For this generation of kids, a video game controller or remote control is the only passport they need to circle the world and come back again before lunch.

Hardly a day goes by without a new report describing the growing childhood-obesity epidemic that is threatening the health and quality of life of millions of America's youth. The same kids whose Saturdays are full of virtual activities are the ones who are overweight. While kids' online personae are running up and down football fields, doing perfect backflips, and racing to escape enemies, the only real-world exercise these kids are getting is with their thumbs.

As the average American kid's weekly media diet increases, his weekly amount of physical activity plummets. In addition, the child is subject to hundreds of ads for sugary and fatty foods while surfing the Net, flipping through channels, or playing video games. Over the last couple of years, a growing body of research has confirmed: The leading cause of the dramatic increase in youth obesity is the increase in screen time. Video games and other media are so simple to use that it's easy to spend an entire weekend in front of the screen. Brain science explains how the immediate payoff of electronic media can be too seductive to turn down. The latest brain scans show that playing video games, for example, activates the pleasure center of the brain, sending dopamine, the "happy" brain chemical, cascading through brain tissue. It's not that kids don't like being outside anymore; they probably figure they'll get around to it. But once they start in on their video games, the dopamine begins to flow, and before they know it, the sun has set and it's too late to go out.

Media Violence

When it comes to teaching respect to their kids, many parents feel like they are swimming against a powerful tide. A barrage of competing messages sabotages a parent's best efforts every day. One parent told me, after a presentation on violence in video games, "It doesn't seem to matter what we tell him at home about violence and respect. It seems like every TV program he watches or video game he plays undercuts my efforts. I don't even know where he gets the language that comes out of his mouth, but I know it's not from us."

In the past, parents had to contend with peer pressure, entertainment, and the rest of society, just as they do today. But now, with the proliferation of communication technology and the increased number of screen hours, parents face more competitive influences over their children's behavior than ever before. Hundreds of youth-serving professionals with whom I have spoken across the country say the same thing: More kids are using R-rated language, adopting rude and disrespectful attitudes, and threatening others on a daily basis.

After every school shooting, I receive dozens of interview requests from journalists all over the world. In the weeks and months following the tragedies at Columbine High School in Colorado and Red Lake High School in Minnesota, I did hundreds of interviews. The conversations always returned to the fundamental question: "Are the media one of the causes of this and similar tragedies?" I don't believe that media are the sole direct cause of school shootings. I doubt that teen shooters leave their video game consoles and immediately load up their guns, but I'm sure it doesn't help that they were rehearsing murder while playing ultraviolent, first-person shooter games. Nonetheless, media play a significant role in shaping norms. And the norms, in truth, determine the extremes. I doubt anyone would disagree with the statement that events like the tragedies at Columbine and Red Lake are extreme. Unfortunately, there have always been and always will be troubled kids drawn to extreme behavior. But what qualifies as extreme depends on what's normal. If the norm is respect, then the extreme might be a verbal outburst, a kick, or a punch. But if insults and "in your face" behavior are already the norm, then the extreme behavior is going to go further and over the edge. As our culture becomes more and more violent, violent behavior will inevitably become more grotesque.

That's where media come in: Whoever tells the stories defines the culture. Today the average American child will see more than two hundred thousand violent acts on TV alone by the time high school graduation rolls around. Who knows how many simulated murders they will commit if they're "playing" video games like one of the Grand Theft Auto series? Besides TV, movies, and electronic games, many kids spend hours listening to music or visiting Web sites that reek of vulgarity, misogyny, and hatred.

The research that links violent media with attitudes and behavior is overwhelming. Recent studies show that violent media activate the aggression centers of the brain and increase aggression hormones while decreasing activity in the prefrontal cortex, the CEO or emotion-regulation center. The first studies involving mirror neurons, mentioned earlier, and video games show them activating the aggression center of the brain, which primes kids to act aggressively in real life. Few researchers would dispute that screen bloodshed affects the kids watching it. But what is the real effect of a steady diet of insulting talk shows like Jerry Springer's and video games with slogans like "Easier than killing babies with axes"? I believe the most pervasive effect is not violent behavior but rather the culture of disrespect it creates and nourishes.

Media and School Performance

Not long ago I was talking with a veteran fourth-grade teacher, Todd, after I presented a talk on media's impact on school performance. Todd thanked me for shedding some light on problems that had become too big to ignore in his classroom. "What sort of problems?" I asked.

"You name it. Attention, curiosity, reading skills. Ten years ago I could get kids to pick out a book for silent reading time. Now the kids pester me incessantly to let them play video games after they've done some work. It's harder to know how to engage them anymore."

Knowing the impact of media on literacy and reading skills doesn't change the real-life challenge of teaching media-age kids in the classroom. Todd's frustration is shared by teachers and parents across the country who are trying to improve kids' reading skills. Unfortunately, teachers like Todd and the colleges that educated him have been blamed for the decline. But the problem with our kids' reading skills isn't solely or even primarily the fault of educators. Our kids can't read because they are not reading. Instead, they are plopped in front of TVs and video games.

TV and video games offer instant rewards—no prerequisites; no effort needed. Reading, on the other hand, requires delayed gratification. It takes four to five years to master basic reading skills. The nuances of reading require hard work and persistence. Heavy TV watching or video game playing, on the other hand, reinforce the pattern of instant gratification—a dangerous situation for kids who find learning to read difficult. For them, watching TV or playing video games becomes the path of least resistance. Faced with choosing the frustration of reading or the instant kick from video games, the more enjoyable choice wins out. When these kids are pushed by teachers to work on reading, they become more frustrated because they've missed the reading practice they need and have come to expect the instant payoff of entertainment media. Not surprisingly, they are less willing to work for the rewards of reading.

The kids who work diligently at reading come to enjoy a good story. As they get that psychological reward, they want to read more. And as they read more, their skills get even better. Unfortunately, this cycle also works in reverse. Kids who have a hard time reading will continue to get more frustrated and disengaged with the process the longer they put it off and the more often they turn to TV for relief from their efforts. There's obviously a long list of factors behind our kids' reading crisis, but real progress won't happen if we continue to ignore the fact that couch potatoes can't read.

No and the Media

We don't want to raise children completely sheltered from media. Not only would that be nearly impossible to do, but it would rob kids of the opportunities that media can offer. In addition, the skills to navigate successfully through the sea of media information are essential for career success and increasingly indispensable for just getting along in life. The problem comes when things get out of balance. Some kids spend more time with media than they do developing life skills "off screen." For many, violent and disrespectful media dominate their list of favorites. The challenge is to provide guidance and limits that will lead kids to make healthy decisions for themselves.

Sometimes, however, saying an absolute no to media is exactly what children need. For example, the American Academy of Pediatrics recommends that children under two should not watch *any* television or movies at all. Media only detract from the essential brain wiring that must take place in those early years and that demand a wide range of real-world activities and relationships. Say no to your toddler who wants to watch Baby Einstein tapes.

Sometimes it's not clear right away which media deserve a yes or a no. Buying cell phones for kids presents a special problem. Often, kids and parents are in favor of cell phones. My friend Tom was eager to get his sixteen-year-old son, Jonas, a cell phone when he got his driver's license. "It makes me feel so much better to know that he can call us in case of an emergency. I also thought that it would help me keep tabs on his activities during the day."

"It isn't going as planned?" I asked him one day over breakfast.

"Well, sort of. For the most part, I am glad that Jonas has a cell phone. He called last week when his ride didn't show up after a late-night movie and I was so glad that it was easy for us to connect. The problem is that he doesn't use it just for emergencies. It has gotten totally out of control."

Tom explained that Jonas was using his cell phone to stay *too* in touch, with everyone he knew, and was averaging three hundred dollars a month in text-messaging bills. Tom figured that Jonas was sending nine messages per hour for every hour that he was awake.

"Does Jonas know that you aren't happy with his cell phone use?" I asked.

"Oh yes. We've had numerous conversations and he knows I'm serious. I've tried everything from taking away car privileges to grounding him. We have more schemes for how he can pay me back for his bills than a credit card company would. It honestly seems like he can't stop. He is addicted to keeping in touch. I don't want him to lose the 'safety net' of a cell phone, but something has got to give here."

After talking for a bit more, Tom and I agreed that it was time to say a firm no to text messaging for his son. Tom ended up calling his cell phone company and canceling the text-messaging option. He also decreased the number of minutes on the plan to a more reasonable amount that would allow him to talk to friends and family, but not for endless hours each day.

A couple of months later I called Tom to check in. "I have to admit that it was a bit rough at first. Jonas was so mad that I was saying no to his social lifeline, even though he understood that it had gotten out of hand. It blew over relatively quickly, though, and he still manages to keep in touch with his friends, without the three-hundred-dollar price tag."

Tom's experience is typical of those parents across the country who are learning when to say no and when to say yes to kids and media use. Tom was able to combine Yes and No in a way that made sense for him and his son.

There are lots of other instances where a well-placed No can make a huge difference among carefully planned Yeses. We don't have to say no to having TVs, video games, or computers in our homes, but we should say no to where some of these screens go. One of the most beneficial Nos is to keep TVs, video games, and computers out of kids' bedrooms. Sending your kid to her room isn't a punishment when she can catch up on her favorite shows or "whatever else is on." Once her door is closed, you don't know where your child goes on the Internet, what she is watching, or for how long. Keeping media out of the bedroom increases school performance and decreases the risk of obesity. Say yes to screens in a common space in the house. This may be a bit noisy, but it will help you keep track of your kids' screen time and virtual activities.

Say no to TV during mealtimes. It opens up time and space over dinner to catch up with what's going on at school and with friends. Say yes to watching high-quality movies and TV shows together, another good way to spend time with your kids.

Media ratings are not perfect, but they are one way to determine if media content is appropriate for your kids. Get to know the various ratings systems for TV, movies, and video games. Video game ratings are on the front of the game boxes as well as in most of the advertisements. The hyperrealistic violence of so-called first-person-shooter video games usually earns them M (for Mature) ratings, meaning that they are inappropriate for children and teens. Movie ratings are displayed in newspaper listings and on theater marquees. TV ratings appear in newspapers and *TV Guide*. They are also displayed on the screen for fifteen seconds at the beginning of a show. Make sure your kids understand that you take these ratings seriously and you don't want them watching shows whose ratings are inappropriate for them.

Guide to Media Ratings

Video Games	EC–Early Childhood	Games for young children
	E–Everyone	Okay for all ages
	E 10–Ten and older	Okay for ten and older
	T–Teen	Okay for thirteen and older
	M–Mature 17+	Seventeen and older
	AO–Adults Only	Eighteen and older but seldom used

Television	TVY–All Children	Geared toward children ages two to six
	TVY7–Older Children	Geared toward children seven and older
	TVG–General Audience	Appropriate for all ages
	TVPG–Parental Guidance	Not suitable for younger children
	TV14–Strong Caution	Not suitable for children under fourteen
	TVMA–Mature Only	Not suitable for teens under seventeen
Movies	G–All Ages	Appropriate for all ages
	PG–Parental Guidance	May not be suitable for younger ages
	PG13–Parental Guidance	May not be suitable for under thirteen
	R–Restricted	Under seventeen not admitted without parent
	NC-17–Not admitted	Under seventeen not admitted

The Internet poses a real challenge to parents who are concerned about inappropriate content. The Internet is a vast, unregulated world that offers amazing educational resources as well as dangerous content. Filtering software claims to block out sites deemed inappropriate for teens and children and is a good choice for younger children, but media-savvy adolescents generally have no problem getting around content-blocking software. Unfortunately, these filters sometimes block out perfectly acceptable sites. Monitoring software, which simply logs the sites visited while surfing the Net, is a great alternative. Monitoring software ensures your kids that you will check in from time to time to see where they've been online. In the end, no monitoring or blocking software is a substitute for talking to your kids about where they are going and who they are talking to in cyberspace. Help kids understand that personal information shouldn't be shared online and that meeting people from the Internet in person is permissible only under parental supervision.

This is especially important with the growth of wildly popular "social networking" sites. Rather than meet face-to-face, it's cooler for lots of kids these days to meet online to socialize, get dates, share good music, and chat. Young people have always looked for places to gather, to gossip, be seen, be cool, listen to music, and hang out. What *is* new is where these gathering places are and who else is there with them or around them.

Social networking favorites, like MySpace.com, offer great opportunities for teenagers to express themselves and to have fun connecting with friends. They can give their own MySpace profiles a new look and feel with just a few mouse clicks. It allows teenagers to do what they have always done: try out new identities and looks, express themselves in new ways, and socialize.

Unfortunately, these sites are not all fun and games. Teachers across the country are dealing with the effects of mean messages and degrading photographs aimed at other kids posted online, called "cyberbullying." Bullying other kids seems easier and free of consequences in an online, anonymous environment. In addition, lewd language and pictures are commonly posted by kids.

Kids often have numerous online identities that they create by lying about their ages, their activities, exploits, and much more. Many kids post very personal, accurate information on their site, including their school, neighborhood, age, and interests. These social networking sites are, sadly, perfect cruising grounds for online predators. This threat is real. Although kids don't take it seriously, the number of murders, rapes, and other crimes connected with online meeting places is growing. This isn't to say that teenagers can't have safe and healthy fun in the cyberworld. But it is important for adults to monitor their kids and talk with them about online safety, where they've been, and whom they're hanging out with in the virtual world. Do not take it personally and do not be put off when kids say, "Get out of MySpace!" It's your job to monitor their space.

Anyone with a video camera can now post videos on sites like YouTube.com. While most are clever and entertaining, some teens post homemade pornography or "candid camera" assaults. "Happy Slapping" involves one teen recording a friend slapping unsuspecting victims. This nasty form of assault was spread over the Internet and serious injuries have occurred. Even more disturbing, teens have paid homeless people to fight, videotaped the beatings, called "Bum Fights," and sold millions of the tapes over the Internet.

The MediaWise Family

Be MediaWise. Make sure your kids understand your family rules for which TV shows they can watch, which video games they can play, and which Internet sites they can visit when. Listen to your kids about which video games they enjoy, which new online sites they're enthusiastic about, and which new movies top their lists. Knowing what your kids are interested in can help guide your focus. Learning more about their favorites helps you evaluate whether they deserve a Yes, a No, or, perhaps more important, a "Let's talk." Know what your kids think and check in with them from time to time. This can be much more effective with teenagers than forbidding them from doing something that can be safe and fun.

The media revolution isn't going to slow down anytime soon. Every generation of parents has to keep pace with a changing world and redefine what it means to care for kids. As we hurtle deeper into the media age, caring for children needs to include becoming Media Wise. My organization's Web site, www.mediawise.org, can give you a multitude of resources, ideas, tips, and tools.

DO

- Have clear family rules about "screen time." The clearer the rules, such as, "no TV or video games before school, or until homework is done," the better. Consistency is important.
- Limit the amount of entertainment "screen time." I recom-

mend a total of ten hours per week for entertainment screens, TV, and video games. Computer time for research, homework, and e-mail is separate and not included in the ten hours.
- Practice "appointment television." Decide in advance what is worth watching and then make an appointment to watch it.
- Know what your kids are watching and what games they are playing.
- Follow the media rating systems.
- Install Internet filtering software for children and Internet monitoring software for preteens and teenagers. Let your teens know that you will be paying attention to how they are using the Internet.
- Keep up with the changing media landscape by becoming a MediaWise parent at www.mediawise.org.

DON'T
- Don't have the TV or other media on during meals.
- Don't allow TVs, video games, or computers in kids' bedrooms.
- Don't let media time crowd out all the other activities that are important for kids and adolescents.
- Don't let kids play ultraviolent "first-person shooter" video games.
- Don't let kids give out personal information over the Internet.
- Don't allow kids to meet Internet friends without adult supervision.

What do I want to continue?

_____

_____

_____

What do I want to change?

_____

_____

_____

Fourteen

No Is Not a Destination;
No Is the Road to *Yes*

In 1961 President John F. Kennedy uttered his now-famous words during his inaugural address on the wind-blown steps of the U. S. Capitol: "My fellow Americans, ask not what your country can do for you—ask what you can do for your country." Five months later he echoed the theme in his State of the Union address. "I have not asked for a single program which did not cause one or all Americans some inconvenience, or some hardship, or some sacrifice."

In 2006 I listened to a radio interview with one of the nation's most prominent political strategists. He stated unequivocally, "Any politician who uses the word *sacrifice* today is committing political suicide."

Those statements illustrate the cosmic shift in our cultural values over the past two generations. How did we get from *sacrifice* as a rallying cry to *sacrifice* as unthinkable? I will leave it to historians to explore the impact on our politics and our country. My concern is how this shift has affected our parenting and our kids.

We Lost Our Balance

We human beings struggle to maintain balance in our pursuits and attitudes, and history chronicles constant pendulum swings throughout the centuries. Loss of balance inevitably leads to problems. The early chapters of this book describe our current problem: Parents have reacted against an era during which the attitude was "children should be seen but not heard" and have gone to extremes in the other direction, the "child-centric" extreme, in which children's voices dominate family life. The imbalance shows up when parents attack teachers for disciplining their unruly children. Teachers look the other way when kids do sloppy work. Kids know the songs that hail them as special, but they shrink from tough classes that will make them feel special when they master a subject. Kids aren't learning how much is enough. Parents don't say no and then wonder why their kids are so poorly behaved.

We need to reestablish balance. It would be a mistake to overcorrect. We don't need to send our kids to boot camp, crack a whip, or become so obsessed with rules that we lose our connection with kids. It's all about balance—balancing a No with a Yes; balancing a reprimand with a hug; balancing a rule with reasonable negotiation. That's why it's called a *balanced* style of parenting.

Kids Actually Know about *No*

I've worked with some community leaders and educators in San Angelo, Texas, over the past several years. In 2005, a group of teenagers met to give adults some advice about what kids today really need. Listen to what they said:

"We don't need more friends. We have plenty of friends. We need parents."

"Sure, I want freedom, but that doesn't mean I can handle it."

"Well, yes, I push against the limits. That's my job. It's your job as adults to set them."

These teenagers had the wisdom to realize that in order to be successful they needed the connection, guidance, and accountability that would help them develop crucial character traits like competence, perseverance, sacrifice, patience, integrity, compassion, generosity, and responsibility. They were also astute enough to know that they couldn't develop those habits on their own. They realized that they needed the adults—their parents, teachers, counselors, coaches, relatives, and neighbors—to teach them. These traits won't develop in a culture enamored with "more, easy, fast, and fun" unless their adult life-coaches make a conscious, deliberate choice to override the messages of indulgence with lessons in self-discipline. That's why No is so important and why our kids need it.

The Stakes Are High

Tom Friedman is right: The world has become flat. This generation of kids will be competing with peers all over the world. Those who succeed will have to be highly educated and competent. They will need to work hard, delay gratification, make sacrifices, cooperate with others, and persevere through hardship. Those who are intellectually, emotionally, and morally flabby will be at a real disadvantage. They will need all the psychological muscles they can build, and No is a training regimen to hone those muscles.

- The latest brain research confirms what generations of parents have intuitively known: Children need a secure connection with loving adults to give them the trust and confidence to explore and reach for the stars.
- Kids need self-discipline to harness and balance their powerful emotional drives in order to be successful in school and later in their work and relationships. If dominated by the drive for pleasure, they will become lazy and self-indulgent.
- Self-discipline entails the ability to say no to oneself.
- Saying no to your kids is the key to their developing self-

discipline. The word *no* itself is not important. The concept of No is. You can say no in many positive ways.

If we want to avoid playing second, third, or fourth fiddle within a generation or two to countries whose kids are poised for achievement, we'd better restrike the balance that we have lost.

How Do We Say *No*?

We say no to our kids whenever we hold the line on a family rule when it would be much easier to give in; go out of our way to stay connected with our kids, their friends, and their teachers; deal with problems head-on rather than take the easy way out; put a note of encouragement in their lunch bags or backpacks; share a good laugh; set and enforce limits; confront disrespectful language; let them figure things out for themselves when it would be so much quicker and easier to do it ourselves; bite our tongues when we want to lash out in anger and harsh criticism; get them what they need but not everything they want; insist that they do chores around the house; respond to an infant's needs; remain constant in the face of a toddler's tantrums; hug our kids; tell our teenagers that in spite of our frustration we will never give up on them; swallow our pride and apologize when we should; teach them never to hit or strike out in violence; insist that kids take care of their possessions; encourage them to volunteer and help others; teach them how to share, save, and spend their money; are clear about no tolerance for alcohol and drugs; put limits on media use; and do the million other things we can to connect with, guide, and love our kids.

You're in charge of getting your kids from here to there; from dependency to self-reliance and self-sufficiency.

The Road to *Yes*

We say no to our kids to build character; it's a long-term investment. The reward doesn't come when we are enforcing a consequence; when we are handling a temper tantrum in the middle of the supermarket; when we tell our kids that their wish list is too expensive; when we tell our teens that they need to take the challenging courses; when we expect our kids to share their money with those less fortunate; when we refuse to tolerate swearing or disrespect; when we help our kids with homework instead of doing it for them; when we back up their teachers; when we enforce a curfew for a sullen teenager; when we confront suspicions of drug or alcohol use; when we tell a four-year-old that he can't have that candy bar before dinner; when we tell a twelve-year-old that he can play video games or watch TV only ten hours a week; or when we say the other Nos that must be said.

The reward does come, however. It happens when we realize that we have led our kids on the perilous journey from infancy, through preschool and the middle years, past adolescence, and into adulthood. It comes when our kids turn out to be the kind of adults we hoped they would be.

My kids—Dan, Brian, and Erin—are adults now. On my last birthday I was pleased to find birthday cards from each of them when I returned home from work. I had trouble reading the cards and notes inside because my eyes were clouded with tears. I never thought that I would read the things my kids wrote or hear the things that I have heard them say in recent years. Because when they were kids, there were times when they thought I was mean. When they were teenagers there were times when they thought that I was the biggest jerk in the world.

The reward for saying no comes when our kids are the adults who know when to say no and when to say yes to themselves; who can delay gratification in order to accomplish greater achievements. No is not the goal. It is the road to Yes.

Notes

CHAPTER ONE

7   *One out of three teachers told Public Agenda pollsters in 2004:* Public Agenda, "Teaching Interrupted: Do Discipline Policies in Today's Public Schools Foster the Common Good." http://www.publicagenda.org/research/research_reports_details.cfm?list=3 (accessed May 27, 2006).

8   *An Associated Press–Ipsos poll released in October 2005 found that nearly 70 percent of Americans said that children are ruder:* AP/Ipsos Poll, "The Decline of American Civilization, or at Least Its Manners," October 14, 2005. http://www.ipsosna.com/news/pressrelease.cfm?id=2827 (accessed January 15, 2006).

8   *Dr. Jean Twenge, social psychologist and author of* Generation Me: Jean Twenge and C. Im, "Changes in the Need for Social Approval, 1958–2001," *Journal of Research in Personality* (in press).

9   *An eighteen-member National Commission on Excellence in Education published a thirty-six-page report:* National Commission on Excellence in Education, *A Nation at Risk: The Imperative for Educational Reform.* http://www.ed.gov/pubs/NatAtRisk/index.html (accessed July 8, 2006).

10   *The latest international comparison was done in 2003:* M. Martin, I. Mullis, E. Gonzalez, and S. Chrostowski, *Findings from IEA's Trends in International Mathematics and Science Study at the*

Fourth and Eighth Grades (Boston: Boston College: TIMSS & PIRLS International Study Center, 2004).

10 *University of Pennsylvania psychologists Angela Duckworth and Martin Seligman:* A. L. Duckworth and M. E. Seligman, "Self-discipline Outdoes IQ in Predicting Academic Performance of Adolescents," *Psychological Science* 16: 939–944 (2005).

12 *ACT®, the company that administers the widely recognized college entrance exam, issued a report:* Report released by ACT on August 16, 2005, and reported in *USA Today* on August 17, 2005, on page 6D in article by Mary Beth Marklein.

12 *In December 2005, the National Assessment of Adult Literacy:* "Literacy Falls for Graduates from College, Testing Finds," reported in *New York Times* on December 16, 2005, on page A28 in article by Sam Dillon.

15 *There were so many corporate scandals in the past ten years:* Forbes, http://www.forbes.com/home/2002/07/25/accounting-tracker.html (accessed December 28, 2005).

15 *Ameriquest Mortgage Company asked a research firm to conduct a national poll of students:* Report for Ameriquest Mortgage Company at http://sharesavespend.com (accessed December 16, 2005).

17 *Thomas L. Friedman, in his 2005 best seller* The World Is Flat: Thomas Friedman, *The World Is Flat: A Brief History of the Twenty-First Century* (New York: Farrar, Strauss, & Giroux, 2005), 237.

CHAPTER TWO

22 *In the early 1970s, government and business leaders in Mexico:* William Ryerson, "Population Communications International: Its Role in Family Planning Soap Operas," *Population and Environment* 15: 255–264 (1994).

26 *Before the industrial revolution, the dominant form of mass media was the newspaper:* Joseph Turow, *Breaking Up America* (Chicago: University of Chicago Press, 1997).

27 *The savvy advertiser avoids the brain's thinking center:* David Walsh, "Slipping Underneath the Radar: The Neuroscience of Advertising," *Proceedings from the World Health Organization,* Geneva, Switzerland, April 2002.

28 *The average child in the United States will see more than forty thousand ads each year on TV alone:* Victor Strasburger, "Children and TV Advertising: Nowhere to Run, Nowhere to Hide," *Journal of Developmental & Behavioral Pediatrics* 22:185–187 (2001).

30   *The high school prom has ballooned from a dance into an extrava-*
      gant affair: "Proms Big Business," reported in *Star Tribune* on
      April 30, 2005, on page 1 in article by Allie Shah.

34   *Parents in Wayzata, an upper-middle-class Minneapolis suburb:*
      http://www.puttingfamilyfirst.org/about_us.php (accessed De-
      cember 20, 2005).

CHAPTER THREE

40   *The new technology helps us understand how children's and teens'*
      brains develop: Richard Restak, *The Secret Life of the Brain*
      (Washington: Joseph Henry Press, 2001).

41   *A human baby is born with about one hundred billion neurons:*
      Marian Diamond and Janet Hopson, *Magic Trees of the Mind*
      (New York: Penguin Putnam, 1999), 37.

42   *The late Francis Crick, the codiscoverer of DNA:* Francis Crick, *The*
      Astonishing Hypothesis: Scientific Search for the Soul (New York:
      Scribner, 1994), 91–105.

42   *When a baby is born, only 17 percent of the neurons are linked:* J.
      Dobbing, J. Sands, "Quantitative Growth and Development in
      the Human Brain," *Archives of Disease in Childhood* 48: 757–767
      (1973).

42   *But important recent discoveries about the brain reveal:* P. Thomp-
      son, J. Giedd, R. Woods, D. MacDonald, A. Evans, and A. Toga,
      "Growth Patterns in the Developing Brain Detected by Using
      Continuum Mechanical Tensor Maps," *Nature* 404:190–193
      (2000).

42   *The process of wiring together these neurons is driven by two power-*
      ful forces: Lise Eliot, *What's Going On in There? How the Brain*
      and Mind Develop in the First Five Years of Life (New York: Ban-
      tam, 1999), 9.

43   *Neuroscientist Marian Diamond of the University of California at*
      Berkeley found that: Marian Diamond and Janet Hopson, *Magic*
      Trees of the Mind (New York: Penguin Putnam,1999).

45   *Phonemic awareness, our ability to distinguish different sounds, is an-*
      other example: Eliot, *What's Going On in There?,* 370–385.

45   *This window of opportunity also explains why one of the strongest*
      predictors of a child's reading ability: D. Walker et al., "Predic-
      tion of School Outcomes Based on Early Language Produc-
      tion and Socioeconomic Factors," *Child Development*
      65:606–621 (1994).

47   *Adolescents' developmental windows relate to the wiring of impulse*

control and anger management: David Walsh, *Why Do They Act That Way? A Survival Guide to the Adolescent Brain for You and Your Teen* (New York: Free Press, 2004), 55–73.

48   *In addition to all the things we learn, our brains come equipped with certain powerful drives that are hardwired:* Jerome Kagan, *The Nature of the Child* (New York: Basic Books, 1984).

49   *Another innate drive is the seeking of pleasure and avoidance of pain:* Sigmund Freud, *Interpretation of Dreams* (New York: Avon, 1980; reissue edition).

50   *Other drives include those for connection, approval, empathy, and guilt:* Jerome Kagan, *Three Seductive Ideas* (Cambridge: Harvard University Press, 2000).

51   *we are hardwired to connect to other people:* Kathleen Kovner and thirty-two other authors, *Hardwired to Connect: The New Scientific Case for Authoritative Communities* (New York: Institute for American Values, 2003).

52   *The third of the moral drives is empathy:* Vittorio Gallese, "The Roots of Empathy: The Shared Manifold Hypothesis and the Neural Basis of Intersubjectivity," *Psychopathology* 36:171–180 (2003).

52   *As a* New York Times *article explained, fifteen years ago in Parma, Italy:* "Cells That Read Minds," reported in *New York Times* on January 10, 2006, on page D1 in article by Sandra Blakeslee.

53   *The University of Washington child psychologist Andrew Meltzoff has demonstrated that within one hour of birth:* Alison Gopnik, Andrew Meltzoff, and Patricia Kuhl, *The Scientist in the Crib* (New York: Harper Paperbacks, 2000), 29.

53   *Research on the moral brain indicates that we are also hardwired for guilt:* Jerome Kagan, *Three Seductive Ideas* (Cambridge: Harvard University Press, 2000), 175–176.

53   *The renowned psychologist Jerome Kagan says that our brains have evolved to have an innate sense of right and wrong:* Ibid., 175.

CHAPTER FOUR

59   *Over the past twenty-five years, self-esteem scores and academic grades have risen as SAT scores have dropped:* A. Astin, L. Oseguera, L. Sax, and W. Korn, *The American Freshmen: Thirty-five-Year Trends* (Los Angeles: Higher Education Research Institute, UCLA, 2002).

59   *Other studies involving tens of thousands of students demonstrate that self-esteem does not boost academic achievement:* Jean Twenge

and W. K. Campbell, "Age and Birth Cohort Differences in Self-Esteem: a Cross Temporal Meta-analysis," *Personality and Social Psychology Review* 5: 321–344 (2001).

59   *Researchers could not find any connection between high self-esteem scores and popularity:* Julia Bishop and Heidi M. Inderbitzen-Nolan Bishop, "Peer Acceptance and Friendship: An Investigation of Their Relation to Self-esteem," *Journal of Early Adolescence* 15: 476–489 (1995).

60   *Teens who have high self-esteem are just as much at risk for substance abuse:* Robert McGee and Sheila Williams, "Does Low Self-esteem Predict Health Compromising Behaviours Among Adolescents?," *Journal of Adolescence* 23: 569–582 (2000).

60   *There is no demonstrable link between positive self-esteem and career success:* Roy Baumeister, Jennifer Campbell, Joachim Krueger, and Kathleen Vohs, "Does High Self-esteem Cause Better Interpersonal Success, Happiness, or Healthier Lifestyles?," *Psychological Science in the Public Interest* 4: 1–44 (2003).

63   *Martin Seligman, author of* Authentic Happiness *and* Learned Optimism, *identified this trend toward learned helplessness almost twenty years ago: Authentic Happiness* (New York: Free Press, 2004) and *Learned Optimism* (New York: Free Press, 1998).

64   *The Connecticut Junior Soccer Association has a novel way:* reported in *New York Times* on May 28, 2006, on page CT6 by Fran Silverman.

65   *The great American psychologist William James wrote about it:* William James, *The Principles of Psychology* (New York: Dover Publications, 1950 reprint), 291–309.

70   *A recent article in* Psychology Today *reported that a university counseling center:* Hara Estroff Marano, "A Nation of Wimps," *Psychology Today,* November–December 2004: 59–70.

71   *Ronald Feldman and his colleagues found that close relationships in the family are the best predictors:* Ronald Feldman, Arlene Stiffman, and Kenneth Jung, eds., *Children at Risk: In the Web of Parental Mental Illness* (Piscataway, NJ: Rutgers University Press, 1987).

72   *Resilient kids have parents, teachers, and other adults who believe in their ability to succeed:* Terry Williams and William Kornblum, *Growing Up Poor* (D. C. Heath, 1985).

75   *Resilient kids set goals, work toward them, and learn from mistakes:* Michael Rutter, "Resilient Children," *Psychology Today,* March 1984, 57–65.

CHAPTER FIVE

85   *That all changed thanks to the brilliant scientist Jean Piaget:* Jean Piaget and B. Inhelder, *The Growth of Logical Thinking from Childhood to Adolescence* (New York: Basic Books, 1958) and *The Psychology of the Child* (New York: Basic Books, 1962).

85   *Another pioneer in child psychology, Erik Erikson, advanced the field further, studying children's emotional development:* Erik Erikson, *Childhood and Society* (New York: W. W. Norton, 1993 reissue).

88   *Family-systems researcher David Olson and his colleagues compiled data:* David Olson, Douglas Sprenkle, and Candace Russell, "Circumplex Model of Marital and Family Systems I: Cohesion and Adaptability Dimensions, Family Types, and Clinical Applications," *Family Process* 18:3–28 (1979).

90   *Studies show that violence in the home leads to children's growing into violent adults:* "Protecting Children from Abuse and Neglect," *The Future of Children,* Spring 1998.

93   *One of the largest youth studies ever conducted explored the importance of connection once kids enter adolescence:* Michael Resnick, L. J. Harris, and Robert Blum, "The Impact of Caring and Connectedness on Adolescent Health and Well-being," *Journal of Pediatric Child Health* 29 (supplement): S3–S9 (1993).

CHAPTER SIX

103   *Contact and connection rank with food and water as critically important:* Thomas Lewis, Fari Amini, and Richard Lannon, *General Theory of Love* (New York: Random House, 2000).

103   *Back in the thirteenth century, a debate raged in Europe:* Ibid., 69.

105   *It's clever marketing but not based on scientific evidence:* Allen D. Kanner, "The Corporatized Child," *California Psychologist* 39:1–2 (2006).

106   *Bob Garfield, host of National Public Radio's* On the Media: Bob Garfield, "Boob Tube" from May 27, 2006, broadcast of National Public Radio's *On the Media,* http://www.onthemedia.org (accessed May 28, 2006).

106   *Recent research shows that children who spend a lot of hours in front of screens:* D. Christakis, F. Zimmerman, D. DiGiuseppe, and C. McCarty, "Early Television Exposure and Subsequent Attentional Problems in Children," *Pediatrics* 113:708–713 (2004).

106   *Another example of manufacturers and marketers taking advantage of parental anxiety is the selling of so-called Mozart Effect:* F.

Rauscher, G. Shaw, and K. Ky, "Music and Spatial Task Performance," *Nature* 365: 611 (1993).

107 *You might think I'm exaggerating, but in January 1998 the governor of Georgia:* "Georgia's Governor Seeks Musical Start for Babies," reported in *New York Times* on January 15, 1998, on page A12 in article by Kevin Sack.

107 *A fascinating article in* Scientific American *described a now-classic experiment in 1960:* E. J. Gibson and R. D. Walk, "The Visual Cliff," *Scientific American*, April 1960, pp. 64–71.

109 *Research shows that if babies experience traumatic stress repeatedly:* Bruce Perry, "Neurobiological Sequelae of Childhood Trauma: Post-traumatic Stress Disorders in Children," in M. Murberg (ed.), *Catecholamines in Post-traumatic Stress Disorder: Emerging Concepts* (Arlington, VA: American Psychiatric Press, 1994), 253–276.

110 *In addition to cognitive and emotional memories we have two other kinds: explicit and implicit memories:* Daniel Schacter, *Searching for Memory* (New York: Basic Books, 1996), 161–183.

111 *The research is clear that babies who have a secure connection are more capable of empathy:* Thomas Lewis, Fari Amini, and Richard Lannon, *General Theory of Love* (New York: Random House, 2000).

113 *The first to mature fully is the sense of touch:* Lise Eliot, *What's Going On in There? How the Brain and Mind Develop in the First Five Years of Life* (Bantam, 2000), 123–143.

CHAPTER SEVEN

137 *The developmental importance of a child's ability to delay gratification became clear in a famous 1960s experiment:* Yuicki Shoda, Walter Mischel, and Philip K. Peake, "Predicting Adolescent Cognitive and Self-regulatory Competencies from Preschool Delay of Gratification," *Developmental Psychology* 26: 978–986 (1990).

CHAPTER EIGHT

143 *Psychologist Robert Rosenthal's classic experiment dramatically illustrates the Pygmalion effect:* Robert Rosenthal and Lenore Jacobson, *Pygmalion in the Classroom: Teacher Expectation and Pupils' Intellectual Development* (New York: Irvington Publishers, 1992).

Notes

CHAPTER NINE

159 *They have discovered that the adolescent brain isn't a finished product but a work in progress:* Jay Giedd, J. Blumenthal, N. Jeffries et al., "Brain Development During Childhood and Adolescence: A Longitudinal MRI Study," *Nature Neuroscience* 2: 861–863 (1999).

161 *The hormones kicking in at puberty cause all sorts of emotional upheaval:* C. Buchanan, J. Eccles, and J. Becker, "Are Adolescents the Victims of Raging Hormones: Evidence for Activational Effects of Hormones on Moods and Behavior at Adolescence," *Psychological Bulletin* III: 62–107 (1992).

165 *The experiences we have during the growth spurts in our brains:* Marian Diamond and Janet Hopson, *Magic Trees of the Mind* (New York: Penguin Putnam, 1999), 44–64.

166 *Adolescence is an important window of opportunity for teens:* David Walsh, *Why Do They Act That Way? A Survival Guide to the Adolescent Brain for You and Your Teen* (New York: Free Press, 2004).

174 *Teen brains are more sensitive to the effects of chemical substances:* H. Swartzwelder, W. Wilson, and M. Tayyeb, "Age Dependent Inhibition of Long-term Potentiation by Ethanol in Immature vs. Mature Hippocampus," *Alcohol Clinical Experimental Research* 19:1480–1485 (1995).

CHAPTER TEN

193 *Kids with ADD or ADHD either cannot make the shift to a new thing:* Daniel Amen, *Healing the Hardware of the Soul* (New York: Free Press, 2002), 54.

195 *a Federal Drug Administration panel urged greater caution:* "FDA Panel Advises Risk Warning on Stimulants Prescribed for ADHD," reported in *New York Times* on February 10, 2006, on page 1 in article by Gardiner Harris.

198 *Some brain scientists believe that the "mirror neurons" don't function in an Asperger brain:* Mirella Dapretto, Mari Davies, Jennifer Pfeifer, Ashley Scott, Marian Sigman, Susan Bookheimer, and Marco Iacoboni, "Understanding Emotions in Others: Mirror Neuron Dysfunction in Children with Autism Spectrum Disorders," *Nature Neuroscience* 9: 28–30 (2006).

202 *Bipolar disorder is brain-based:* http://www.bpkids.org/site/DocServer/edbrochure.pdf?docID=166 (accessed on January 21, 2006).

205 *especially in light of a 2006 report showing that prescriptions for psy-*

choactive drugs: Mark Olfson, Carlos Blanco, Linxu Liu, Carmen Moreno, and Gonzalo Laje, "National Trends in the Outpatient Treatment of Children and Adolescents with Antipsychotic Drugs," *Archives of General Psychiatry* 63: 679–685 (2006).

CHAPTER TWELVE

242 *As my friend Nathan Dungan, founder and president of Share Save Spend:* Nathan Dungan, *Prodigal Sons and Material Girls: How Not to Be Your Child's ATM* (New York: Wiley, 2003).

246 *The top purchases for children and teens are treats, toys, apparel, entertainment, electronics, and cosmetic products:* James U. McNeal, "Tapping the Three Kids' Markets," *American Demographics,* April 1998.

246 *In early 2006 it dropped below zero for the first time since the Great Depression:* http://www.msnbc.msn.com/id/11098797 (accessed July 9, 2006).

247 *In 1997 a financial literacy survey was given to high school seniors:* McNeal, "Tapping the Three Kids' Markets," 25.

247 *A recent National Public Radio report explained:* http://www.npr.org/templates/story/story.php?stryId= 5416319 (accessed June 3, 2006).

247 *the average college undergraduate in the United States in 2004 owed $2,169:* http://www.nelliemae.com/library/research_12.html (accessed May 30, 2006).

247 *In 1991, according to government reports, 60,000 young people:* Charles Haddad, "Congratulations Grads–You're Bankrupt," *BusinessWeek,* May 21, 2001.

CHAPTER THIRTEEN

259 *A study published on September 3, 2004, in the medical journal* Pediatrics*:* Rebecca L. Collins, Marc N. Elliott, Sandra H. Berry, David E. Kanouse, Dale Kunkel, Sarah B. Hunter, and Angela Miu, "Watching Sex on Television Predicts Adolescent Initiation of Sexual Behavior," *Pediatrics* 114: e280–e289 (2004).

261 *Today that same kid's screen time has risen to forty-four hours:* Donald Roberts, Ulla Foehr, and Vicki Rideout, *Generation M: Media in the Lives of 8–18-Year-Olds* (Menlo Park, CA: Kaiser Family Foundation, 2005).

262 *The typical eight- to eighteen-year-old American grows up in a house:* Ibid.

264 *The leading cause of the dramatic increase in youth obesity:* Thomas

Robinson, "Reducing Children's Television Viewing to Prevent Obesity," *Journal of the American Medical Association* 282: 1561–1567 (1999).

266   *Today the average American child will see more than two hundred thousand violent acts on TV alone:* Aletha Huston et al., *Big World, Small Screen: The Role of Television in American Society* (Lincoln: University of Nebraska Press, 1992).

266   *The research that links violent media with attitudes and behavior is overwhelming:* Craig Anderson and Brad Bushman, "The Effects of Media Violence on Society," *Science* 295:2377–2378 (2002).

266   *Recent studies show that violent media activate the aggression centers of the brain:* Vincent Mathews, William Kronenberger, Yang Wang, Joseph Lurito, Mark Lowe, and David Dunn, "Media Violence Exposure and Frontal Lobe Activation Measured by Functional Magnetic Resonance Imaging in Aggressive and Nonaggressive Adolescents," *Journal of Computer Assisted Tomography* 29:287–292 (2005).

267   *Knowing the impact of media on literacy and reading skills:* D. Reinking and J. Wu, "Reexamining the Research on Television and Reading," *Reading Research and Instruction* 29:30–43 (1990).

268   *For example, the American Academy of Pediatrics recommends that children:* American Academy of Pediatrics, Committee on Public Education, "Children, Adolescents, and Television," *Pediatrics* 107:423–426 (2001).

Suggested Readings

CHILD AND ADOLESCENT
DEVELOPMENT

Brazelton, T. Berry. *Touchpoints: The Essential Reference–Your Child's Emotional and Behavioral Development.* Cambridge, MA: Da Capo Lifelong Books, 1992.

Eliot, Lise. *What's Going On in There? How the Brain and Mind Develop in the First Five Years of Life.* New York: Bantam, 2000.

Kagan, Jerome. *The Nature of the Child.* New York: Basic Books, 1984.

Lewis, Thomas, Fari Amini, and Richard Lannon. *A General Theory of Love.* New York: Random House, 2000.

Murkoff, Heidi, Sandee Hathaway, and Arlene Eisenberg. *What to Expect the First Year.* New York: Workman, 2003.

Sears, William, Martha Sears, Robert Sears, and James Sears. *The Baby Book: Everything You Need to Know about Your Baby from Birth to Age Two.* New York: Little Brown, 2003.

Strauch, Barbara. *The Primal Teen: What the New Discoveries about the Teenage Brain Tell Us about Our Kids.* New York: Anchor, 2004.

Walsh, David. *Why Do They Act That Way? A Survival Guide to the Adolescent Brain for You and Your Teen.* New York: Free Press, 2004.

BRAIN SCIENCE

Damasio, Antonio. *Descartes' Error: Emotion, Reason, and the Human Brain.* New York: Putnam, 1994.

Diamond, Marian, and J. Hopson. *Magic Trees of the Mind.* New York: Penguin Putnam, 1999.

Goleman, Daniel. *Emotional Intelligence.* New York: Bantam: 1995.

Gopnik, Alison, Andrew Meltzoff, and Patricia Kuhl. *The Scientist in the Crib: Minds, Brains, and How Children Learn.* New York: Morrow, 1999.

Kagan, Jerome. *Three Seductive Ideas.* Cambridge: Harvard University Press, 2000.

Kotulak, Ronald. *Inside the Brain: Revolutionary Discoveries of How the Mind Works.* Kansas City: Andrews McMeel Publishing, 1997.

LeDoux, Joseph. *The Emotional Brain.* New York: Simon & Schuster, 1996.

———. *Synaptic Self.* New York: Viking Penguin, 2002.

Restak, Richard. *The Secret Life of the Brain.* Washington: Joseph Henry Press, 2001.

Schacter, Daniel. *Searching for Memory.* New York: Basic Books, 1996.

Children with Special Needs

Hallowell, Ed, and John Ratey. *Driven to Distraction: Recognizing and Coping with Attention Deficit Disorder from Childhood through Adulthood.* New York: Touchstone, 1995.

Hallowell, Ed. *Worry.* New York: Ballantine, 1998.

Kranowitz, Carol Stock. *The Out-of-Sync Child: Recognizing and Coping with Sensory Integration Dysfunction.* New York: Perigee, 1998.

Singer, Cindy, and Sheryl Gurrentz. *If Your Child Is Bipolar.* Glendale, CA: Perspective Publishing, 2004.

Media and Consumerism

Buddenburg, Laura, and Kathleen McGee. *Who's Raising Your Child? Battling the Marketers for Your Child's Heart and Soul.* Boys Town, NE: Boys Town Press, 2004.

Clarke, Jean Illsley, Connie Dawson, and David Bredehoft. *How Much Is Enough?: Everything You Need to Know to Steer Clear of Overindulgence and Raise Likeable, Responsible, and Respectful Children.* New York: Marlowe, 2003.

Dungan, Nathan. *Prodigal Sons and Material Girls: How Not to Be Your Child's ATM.* New York: Wiley, 2003.

Kindlon, Daniel. *Too Much of a Good Thing: Raising Children of Character in an Indulgent Age.* New York: Miramax Books, 2001.

McNeal, James. *The Kids Market: Myths and Realities.* Ithaca, NY: Paramount Market Publishing, 1999.

Walsh, David. *Dr. Dave's Cyberhood.* New York: Fireside Books, 2001.

SOCIETY

Damon, William. *Greater Expectations*. New York: Free Press, 1993.

Friedman, Thomas. *The World Is Flat: A Brief History of the Twenty-first Century*. New York: Farrar, Strauss, & Giroux, 2005.

Twenge, Jean. *Generation Me: Why Today's Young Americans Are More Confident, Assertive, Entitled–and More Miserable Than Ever Before*. New York: Free Press, 2006.

Walsh, David. *Selling Out America's Children*. Minneapolis: Fairview Press, 1995.

RESOURCES

Elkind, David. *The Hurried Child: Growing Up Too Fast Too Soon*. Reading, MA: Addison-Wesley, 1981.

Faber, Adele. *How to Talk So Kids Will Listen and Listen So Kids Will Talk*. New York: Avon, 1999.

Keeshan, Bob. *Books to Grow By*. Minneapolis: Fairview Press, 1996.

Kilpatrick, William. *Books That Build Character: A Guide to Teaching Your Child Moral Values Through Stories*. Touchstone, 1994.

Seligman, Martin. *Authentic Happiness: Using the New Positive Psychology to Realize Your Potential for Lasting Fulfillment* (paperback). New York: Free Press, 2004.

———. *Learned Optimism: How to Change Your Mind and Your Life* (paperback). New York: Free Press, 1998.

Shannon, David. *No, David!* New York: Scholastic, 1998.

Stark, Patty. *Sex Is More Than a Plumbing Lesson: A Parent's Guide to Sexuality Education for Infants Through the Teen Years*. Dallas, TX: Preston Hollow Enterprises, 1990.

Zemach, Margot (illustrator). *It Could Always Be Worse: A Yiddish Folk Tale*. New York: Farrar, Straus, and Giroux; reissue edition 1990.

Acknowledgments

The thousands of conversations and experiences I have had as a teacher and a psychologist helped shape many ideas expressed in this book. I am indebted to the children, teens, and parents I have had the privilege of teaching or counseling over the years. Many of their stories are included in this book, although identities have been sufficiently masked to respect their confidentiality. I have always learned from them, as I hope they have from me.

Of course, my thoughts also stem from my experiences as the father of Dan, Brian, and Erin. There are stories about them in these pages as well. These stories are all included with my love, respect, and appreciation.

Our family has been blessed with a large circle of close friends whom we consider extended family. They will undoubtedly recognize some of their words as well. Thanks to the following not only for their insights, but also for their support and friendship: Bob Donnelly, Dale and Karen Panton, Cathy Seward and Tom Peichel, Michael and Jane Brodie, Phil and Julie Ledermann, Thad and Melinda Ludwiczak, Tim and Pam Mc-Conville, Michele Fallon and Steve Cook. A deep hole was left in our lives when Josie Donnelly died during the course of my writing this book. It is dedicated to her memory.

As for the book itself, it has truly been a team effort. My literary agent, Marly Rusoff, was a constant source of guidance, support, and encouragement. My Free Press editor, Leslie Meredith, was her usual insightful, professional, and talented self. Her influence is found throughout the book. I also want to acknowledge the contributions Steve Kettman made to early drafts and the special help that Cathy Seward and Michele Fallon gave to a number of chapters.

My daughter Erin deserves special credit and thanks for the substantial work she did on chapters nine and thirteen.

I have been fortunate to work with wonderful colleagues at the National Institute on Media and the Family and at Fairview Health Services in Minneapolis. There are too many to name so I would just like to thank all of them.

Finally, and most important, I want to acknowledge and thank Monica, my wife of thirty-five years. This book is as much hers as mine. I learned so much about parenting by doing it with her for the past thirty years. Her ideas are on every page. In addition, she was involved in every step of the manuscript itself. "Thank you" is too weak to convey my gratitude for her help and for being my wife and parenting partner.

Index

About the Author

David Walsh, PhD, is the president and founder of the National Institute on Media and the Family, based in Minneapolis, Minnesota. Psychologist, educator, author, and parent of three, Dr. Walsh has emerged as one of the leading authorities in North America on parenting, family life, and the impact of media on children. He has written eight books, including the award-winning *Selling Out America's Children*. He also wrote the American Medical Association's *Physician Guide to Media Violence* as well as many articles for the professional and general press. His most recent book, *Why Do They Act That Way? A Survival Guide to the Adolescent Brain for You and Your Teen* (Free Press, 2004), is a national best-seller. His monthly column runs in more than thirty newspapers.

Dr. Walsh is a frequent guest on national radio and television. He has appeared on such programs as NBC's *Dateline, CBS Early Show, The News Hour with Jim Lehrer, Good Morning America,* the *Today* show, and National Public Radio's *All Things Considered.* His work has been covered in major newspapers such as the *New York Times, Wall Street Journal, Washington Post, Los Angeles Times, Time* magazine, *Reader's Digest,* and others. He has been featured in three nationally broadcast specials on PBS.

Dr. Walsh received his PhD in psychology from the University of Minnesota, where he is currently on the faculty, and he is a consultant to the World Health Organization. He has been the recipient of many awards, including the 1999 "Friend of the Family Award" presented by the Council on Family Relations, and the University of St. Thomas outstanding alumni award. He and his wife, Monica, have three grown children, Dan, Brian, and Erin.

NO

Why Kids—of All Ages—
Need to Hear It
and Ways Parents Can Say It

David Walsh, PhD

Discussion Group Guide

ABOUT THIS GUIDE

The following discussion group guide is intended to help you find interesting and rewarding approaches to your reading of *No*. We hope this enhances your enjoyment and appreciation of the book.

DISCUSSION GROUP GUIDE FOR

NO

Discussion Questions

1. Do you agree that today's parents have a more difficult time saying "no" than parents did in previous generations? Why do you agree or disagree?

2. If you agree that today's parents have a harder time saying "no," why do you think that is the case?

3. Do you see evidence of "discipline deficit disorder" in today's youth?

4. Research shows that self-discipline is twice as strong a predictor of school success as is intelligence. Does that make sense to you? Do you have any experiences of your own or of your children that support the research findings?

5. What do you think are the key ingredients of self-discipline? How can you help your children cultivate them?

6. Dr. Dave states that the word "no" is not as important as the strategy, and that there are many ways to say "no" without using the word. Can you identify some examples?

7. Do you agree that our country's economic competitiveness is in jeopardy unless we teach our children and youth the lessons of "no"?

8. Do you think that the lessons of "no" are important in building self-discipline in children?

9. *No* describes three styles of parenting: permissive, authoritarian, and balanced. How would you describe your own style of parenting?

10. In your opinion, what are the best ways that parents can build self-esteem and self-discipline in their children?

11. Discuss your views on spanking as a discipline strategy.

12. Discuss how you manage media in your home.

13. Were there any "aha" moments for you while reading *No*? If so, what were they?

14. Will you make any changes or adjustments to your parenting approaches as a result of reading *No*? If so, what are they?